Egyptian Hieroglyphs
in the Late Antique Imagination

Egyptian Hieroglyphs in the Late Antique Imagination

Jennifer Taylor Westerfeld

PENN

UNIVERSITY OF PENNSYLVANIA PRESS

PHILADELPHIA

Published by
University of Pennsylvania Press
Philadelphia, Pennsylvania 19104-4112
www.upenn.edu/pennpress

Printed in the United States of America on acid-free paper
1 3 5 7 9 10 8 6 4 2

A catalogue record for this book is available from the Library of Congress.
ISBN 978-0-8122-5157-9

For my parents

Les antiquités me sortent par les yeux. Ne m'en parlez pas. La seule vue d'un hiéroglyphe me ferait évanouir.

—Prosper Mérimée, *Le vase étrusque* (1830)

On pourrait écrire un livre, et des plus agréables, sur les légendes d'Égypte nées de la réanimation, par les hommes, des images d'un passé qu'ils ne comprenaient plus.

—Serge Sauneron, "Villes et légendes d'Égypte §XXXII" (1971)

Contents

Abbreviations

Classical and patristic sources are abbreviated throughout according to the conventions of *The Oxford Classical Dictionary*, 4th ed., edited by S. Hornblower, A. Spawforth, and E. Eidinow (Oxford: Oxford University Press, 2012), supplemented where appropriate by *A Greek-English Lexicon*, 9th ed. with revised suppl., edited by H. G. Liddell, R. Scott, and H. S. Jones (Oxford: Clarendon, 1996); *Thesaurus Linguae Latinae, Index* (Leipzig: Teubner, 1990); and *A Patristic Greek Lexicon*, edited by G. W. H. Lampe (Oxford: Press, 1961–68).

Papyri are cited according to the *Checklist of Editions of Greek, Latin, Demotic, and Coptic Papyri, Ostraca, and Tablets*, edited by Joshua D. Sosin, Rodney Ast, Roger S. Bagnall, James M. S. Cowey, Mark Depauw, Alain Delattre, Robert Maxwell, and Paul Heilporn, http://www.papyri.info/docs/checklist.

Titles of periodicals and series are abbreviated according to the conventions of *L'année philologique* and the *Lexikon der Ägyptologie*. Additional abbreviations utilized in this volume are as follows:

ANF	*The Ante-Nicene Fathers: Translations of the Writings of the Fathers Down to* A.D. *325*, edited by Alexander Roberts and James Donaldson. 10 vols. Edinburgh: T. and T. Clark, 1867–83.
ANRW	*Aufstieg und Niedergang der römischen Welt*, edited by W. Haase and H. Temporini. Berlin: De Gruyter, 1972– .
ArchJ	*Archaeological Journal*
ASP	American Studies in Papyrology
BARCE	*Bulletin of the American Research Center in Egypt*
BSFE	*Bulletin de la Société française d'égyptologie*
CBC	Cahiers de la bibliothèque copte
CIG	*Corpus Inscriptionum Graecarum*, edited by August Böckh (Berlin: G. Reimer, 1828–77).

CSCO	*Corpus scriptorum Christianorum orientalium*. Leuven: Peeters, 1903–.
Edfou I	*Le Temple d'Edfou I*. Le Marquis de Rochemonteix. Cairo: Institut Français d'Archéologie Orientale, 1897.
Esna II	*Le Temple d'Esna*. Serge Sauneron. Cairo: Institut Français d'Archéologie Orientale, 1963.
FC	*Fathers of the Church*. Washington, D.C.: Catholic University of America Press, 1947– .
FGrHist	*Die Fragmente der griechischen Historiker*, edited by Felix Jacoby. Leiden: Brill, 1923–58.
I.Philae II	*Les inscriptions grecques et latines de Philae, Tome II: Haut et Bas Empire*, edited by Étienne Bernand. Paris: Centre Nationale de la Recherche Scientifique, 1969.
I.Philae.Dem.	*Catalogue of the Demotic Graffiti of the Dodecaschoenus*, edited by F. Ll. Griffith. 2 vols. Oxford: Oxford University Press, 1935–37.
I.Syring.	*Inscriptions grecques et latines des tombeaux des rois ou syringes*, edited by Jules Baillet. Cairo: Institut Français d'Archéologie Orientale, 1926.
JCoptStud	*Journal of Coptic Studies*
JCSCS	*Journal of the Canadian Society for Coptic Studies*
JJS	*Journal of Jewish Studies*
JLA	*Journal of Late Antiquity*
LÄ	*Lexikon der Ägyptologie*, edited by Wolfgang Helck and Eberhard Otto. Wiesbaden: Harrassowitz, 1972–92.
LCL	Loeb Classical Library. Cambridge, Mass.: Harvard University Press, 1911– .
MMAJ	*Metropolitan Museum of Art Journal*
NPNF	*A Select Library of Nicene and Post-Nicene Fathers of the Christian Church*, edited by Philip Schaff and Henry Wace. 28 vols. in 2 series. Edinburgh: T. and T. Clark, 1886–89.
OBO	Orbis biblicus et orientalis
OIMP	Oriental Institute Museum Publications
OLA	Orientalia Lovaniensia Analecta
Philae II	*Das Geburtshaus des Tempels der Isis in Philä*, edited by H. Junker and E. Winter. Vienna: Hermann Bohlaus Nachf., 1965.
PLB	Papyrologica Lugduno-Batava

PO   Patrologia Orientalis
ROrChr   *Revue de l'Orient Chrétien*
SB Kopt.   *Koptisches Sammelbuch*, edited by Monika Hasitzka.
              Vienna: Verlag Brüder Hollinek, 1993– .
SC   Sources Chrétiennes
StP   *Studia Patristica*
WB   *Wörterbuch der ägyptischen Sprache*, edited by Adolph
              Erman and Hermann Grapow. 6 vols. Berlin: Akademie-
              Verlag, 1926–61.
YES   Yale Egyptological Studies

Note on Translations

In attempting to reconstruct a picture of late antique attitudes toward hieroglyphs, I have drawn on sources in several languages, including Demotic Egyptian, Coptic, Greek, Latin, Syriac, and Arabic. For the sake of accessibility, all
quotations from primary sources are presented here in English translation; the
first time that a source is quoted, the identity of the translator is indicated in
the notes. Scriptural passages, except when drawn from the Septuagint or the
various Coptic manuscript witnesses, are given in the translation of the New
Revised Standard Version.

Introduction

Confronting Pharaonic Egypt
in Late Antiquity

In his 2007 monograph *The Rosetta Stone and the Rebirth of Ancient Egypt*, John Ray discusses a late antique inscription found in the tomb of Ramesses IV in the Valley of the Kings. According to his interpretation, this text, painted in Coptic near the entrance to the tomb, reflects a particularly Christian approach to the hieroglyphic inscriptions carved and painted in the tomb's interior:

> A later Christian hermit took refuge in the tomb of Ramesses IV in the Valley of the Kings, living alone among the figures which had been painted on its walls more than a millennium and a half before his day. Just inside the entrance he left an inscription in red ink in Coptic, the descendant of the old language of the Pharaohs, which was now written in a version of the Greek alphabet. He tells us how he was driven to cover up the inscriptions he could see around him, because he was terrified of the power of the words they contained. He could not read them, but he knew that they were capable of taking over his thoughts and cutting him off from his God. An Egyptologist is the last thing this nervous monk would have wanted to be.[1]

Ray uses this inscription (Figure 1) to support his larger argument that there was a profound disjuncture between the Christian Egyptian culture represented by his nervous graffiti-writing monk and the pharaonic Egyptian culture embodied in the tomb of Ramesses IV, its relief carvings, and its hieroglyphic inscriptions. He states that although Egyptian Christians lived surrounded by "the monuments of their past" in the form of pharaonic religious architecture, "the gods and the spirits of the dead who inhabited the

Figure 1. Coptic inscription of the monk Jacob (*SB Kopt.* II 1058) from the tomb of Ramesses IV in the Valley of the Kings, Thebes. Photo courtesy of Steve Vinson.

temples and tombs were no longer theirs to revere: they had become demonic, something alien which could be feared but should not be approached. Nor could they be studied, since they were dangerous."[2] Similar arguments have been advanced for the early Islamic period, and Egypt's double conversion, to Christianity and then to Islam, has been seen as a constituting a decisive break with the memory of the pharaonic past.[3] Favorable assessment of Egypt's pharaonic monuments ended, it has been said, with the Greeks, and later Christian and Muslim communities were prevented by biblical traditions of "the land of Egypt" from seeing that land in anything but a negative light. However, just as a closer reading of Jacob's graffito casts doubt on Ray's interpretation, closer examination of the late antique literature on hieroglyphs challenges this dominant narrative. Late antique Christian authors, as this book shows, expressed a wide range of attitudes toward the hieroglyphic tradition in their works, and their responses were shaped both by the classical discourse that they inherited and by contemporary political and theological considerations.

Confronting Pharaonic Egypt

Ray's claim that late antique Christians saw the pharaonic monuments and their hieroglyphic décor as inherently problematic, even dangerous, echoes a long tradition of scholarship on the transition to Christianity in the eastern Mediterranean world and the treatment of traditional religious architecture in newly Christianized areas. Historians and archaeologists throughout much of the nineteenth and early twentieth centuries relied heavily on polemical works of Christian literature and were clearly influenced by the triumphalist tone of those sources. Consequently, their work often emphasized the demonization of the old gods under the new Christian cosmology and the concomitant fear and disgust with which early Christians were purported to have approached the sacred spaces of their ancestors. In a 1953 article on the Christian reuse of pharaonic-period tombs, for example, Alexandre Badawy argues that the monks who adapted those spaces for use as hermitages were disgusted by the visible reminders of pharaonic ritual practice that they saw in the reliefs and inscriptions carved on the walls of the tombs, and that this repugnance drove them to mutilate the reliefs.[4] According to this model, Christian Egyptians, like their counterparts throughout the Mediterranean world, existed uneasily in a demon-haunted landscape, confronted at every turn in the road by threats to their spiritual well-being. Unlike their Greco-Roman forebears, who frequently commented on the aesthetic and historical value of ancient temples and tombs, these early Christians were seen as incapable of approaching such monuments from a nonreligious standpoint.[5] This problematic assumption has had far-reaching implications for scholarship on the late antique afterlife of pharaonic architecture; destruction of pharaonic monuments has typically been attributed to Christian zealots, while the preservation of the same has been taken as reflecting a last, desperate attempt by adherents of traditional Egyptian religion to conserve their cultural patrimony in the face of militant Christianization.[6]

Scholarship on late antique Christian responses to pharaonic monuments has undergone significant changes in the past few decades, thanks to the publication of new archaeological and documentary source material, greater sensitivity to the late antique literary sources' highly rhetorical nature, and a new recognition of the fact that although the destruction of temples and other monuments did occur, this was not necessarily the only (or the primary) Christian response to those spaces.[7] Hand in hand with this tempering of the traditional view of militant Christian opposition to earlier cult places has come an appreciation of the particular local factors governing each instance where we can see late antique Christian communities engaging with the earlier monumental landscape.[8] From Byzantine art lovers amassing collections of classical mythological statuary to ambitious bishops seeking to Christianize their cityscapes by the removal of such statuary and monuments, and from Christian laypeople preserving a vestigial memory of the earlier cultic topography in their use of archaic toponyms to Christian hermits utilizing ancient (and apparently haunted) tombs for the dual purposes of housing and spiritual combat, the plurality of possible Christian responses is now understood to reflect the intersection of a host of local factors—economic, political, and pragmatic, as well as cultural and religious.[9]

At the same time that this more complex view of the fate of pharaonic monuments in late antiquity has come into focus, the reception history of pharaonic Egypt more broadly conceived has also proven to be a highly productive area of inquiry. The question of how communities remember the past—and which past(s) they choose to remember—has preoccupied scholars since the pioneering work of Maurice Halbwachs in the first decades of the twentieth century, and a growing body of scholarship is devoted to exploring the ways in which societies throughout history have constructed images of the past and employed those images in forging distinctive identities for themselves.[10] In the field of Egyptology, this burgeoning interest in what Jan Assmann terms "mnemohistory" has resulted in a proliferation of scholarly works dealing with the production and consumption of images of pharaonic Egypt.[11] Scholars addressing the memory of Egypt from the perspective of the classical sources have painted the picture of a culture that was at once rich and strange, fascinating and repulsive, familiar and deeply alien to Greco-Roman eyes.[12] From the Renaissance to the Victorian era, scholarship has shown that the reception of ancient Egypt in western European thought changed with shifting political and cultural currents, as Renaissance popes, Enlightenment clergymen, and Victorian politicians and entrepreneurs deployed images of, and material artifacts from, pharaonic Egypt in support of their claims to religious and temporal authority.[13] Nor has the role of pharaonic Egypt in modern Egyptian consciousness gone unremarked, as scholars have recently highlighted the role of pharaonic imagery and claims to pharaonic descent within the early twentieth-century Egyptian nationalist movement and beyond.[14]

Hieroglyphs and the Memory of Egypt

The study of the hieroglyphic script and the path to its eventual decipherment represents a significant theme within the larger academic conversation concerning pharaonic Egypt's reception history. Carved or painted on tomb and temple walls, stelae, statues, and other artifacts, hieroglyphic inscriptions were one of the most distinctive features of ancient Egyptian visual culture, and throughout Egyptian history they served as an important marker of Egyptian cultural identity. For non-Egyptians, hieroglyphs came early on to represent the "otherness" of Egypt, and authors from the classical period onward struggled to comprehend the nature of the hieroglyphic system—a question that became all the more difficult to answer after genuine knowledge of the script died out in the late Roman period. Over the past century, scholars have catalogued references to Egyptian hieroglyphs in classical literature and have begun to characterize the various interpretive methodologies by means of which ancient, medieval, and early modern authors, primarily from Western traditions, tried to explicate the hieroglyphic script. Erik Iversen's *The Myth of Egypt and Its Hieroglyphs in European Tradition*, first published in 1961 and reissued in 1993, is particularly significant in this context, offering as it does a detailed study of classical speculation on hieroglyphs and the legacy of that intellectual tradition in Renaissance and early modern Europe. The author intended his work to stand as a corrective to the attitude, prevalent among early twentieth-century classicists, that cultural influence in the ancient Mediterranean world was unidirectional, flowing from Greece to Egypt but not vice versa. Consequently, Iversen focused his attention on the Greek and Roman authors, their often-misguided attempts to interpret hieroglyphs, and the remarkably long afterlife of their misinterpretations in the period leading up to the early nineteenth-century decipherment of the Rosetta Stone.[15]

Since the publication of *The Myth of Egypt*, a number of other works have appeared that also address the later history of the hieroglyphic tradition. Both Erik Hornung and Brian Curran discuss hieroglyphs in the context of the Hermetic revival in the Italian Renaissance, and Richard Parkinson and John Ray treat classical accounts of hieroglyphic writing as a preliminary stage in the lengthy history of attempts at decipherment. Most recently, Jean Winand's brief but insightful history of hieroglyphic interpretation sets the classical commentaries on hieroglyphs firmly within the context of the script's ongoing development in the Ptolemaic and Roman periods, noting that the observations of the Greek and Roman authors, incorrect though they may be with respect to the conventions of classical Middle Egyptian, frequently do reflect aspects of Ptolemaic and Roman hieroglyphic usage.[16] This attempted rapprochement of "classical interpretation" and "Egyptian reality" is also apparent in much of the recent scholarship on the preeminent late antique commentator on hieroglyphs, the fifth-century Egyptian scholar Horapollo. Often derided by modern Egyptologists for his attempts to interpret hieroglyphs according to an elaborate allegorical methodology, Horapollo's work has recently been subject to a reappraisal of sorts, which seeks to identify the authentic Egyptian roots of the information he presents and to draw parallels between the way he talks about hieroglyphs and the way the script is presented in Egyptian-language reflections on the scribal tradition such as the Demotic Book of Thoth.[17]

Although this impressive body of scholarship deals with sources spanning a period of more than two thousand years, from the *Histories* of Herodotus in the fifth century B.C.E. to the works of Champollion and his fellow philologists in the nineteenth and early twentieth centuries C.E., Christian sources from the late antique period (ca. 250–700 C.E.) are almost entirely absent from the discussion. Iversen, for example, covers in a mere three pages the thousand-year gap between Horapollo's composition of the *Hieroglyphica* and the rediscovery and dissemination of that same work in the Italian Renaissance. Winand is even more dismissive; his history of decipherment moves briskly from classical antiquity (Chapter 1) to the Renaissance and early modern period (Chapter 2) with the observation that "during the Middle Ages, Egypt was decidedly out of fashion. . . . It is necessary to wait for the work of the humanists beginning in the fifteenth century . . . to see the rebirth of interest in ancient Egypt."[18]

What is lost by ignoring the late antique Christian sources on hieroglyphs? There is no direct Christian counterpart, in scope or focus, to Horapollo's *Hieroglyphica*, and anyone wishing to study late antique Christian attitudes toward hieroglyphic writing is forced to glean information from passing references in works devoted to other subjects altogether. But ignoring those brief references and skipping, as earlier studies have done, from the representation of hieroglyphs in the classical sources to the intense philological inquiry and avid Egyptomania of the Italian Renaissance risks writing late antique Christian authors out of the history of Egyptology altogether. Such a practice makes the implicit argument that for a period of nearly a thousand years, Christians in Egypt and elsewhere, their intellectual curiosity shackled by the dictates of their faith, simply closed their eyes to the visual evidence of Egypt's pharaonic traditions, reading the Scriptures but demonstrating no interest in reading or otherwise interpreting the enigmatic hieroglyphic inscriptions that fascinated countless generations both before and after them. As we shall see over the next several chapters, this view is demonstrably false. Christian authors *did* discuss the hieroglyphic tradition, both as they saw it with their own eyes and as they encountered it through their reading of a handful of more-or-less canonical classical accounts. This book examines the phenomenon of late antique Christian engagement with hieroglyphs with a view toward answering three principal questions: What did late antique Christian writers actually know about hieroglyphs? How and to what ends did they adopt (or adapt) the Egyptian and classical discourses on hieroglyphic writing? And what do their comments on hieroglyphs reveal about their attitudes toward the pharaonic Egyptian culture those hieroglyphs represented? Answers to these questions offer a new window into the relationship between late antique Christian communities and the rich cultural legacy of pharaonic Egypt.

Scope and Method of this Study

Let us return once again to the image of the nervous monk, Jacob, writing his graffito in the entryway of KV2. Ray claims that Jacob's pious fear of the hieroglyphic inscriptions found in the tomb prompted the monk to conceal them from his sight with some kind of covering.[19] Some works of late antique Christian literature do preserve traces of a belief that hieroglyphs might represent a spiritual danger, as we shall see in Chapter 4, but a closer look at this particular inscription suggests that Jacob was actually concerned *not* with the hieroglyphs in the tomb, but with another inscription that he himself had written. The relevant portion of Jacob's graffito reads, "I concealed some names as if with a veil (ⲁⲓϩⲱⲃⲥ̄ ϩⲉⲛⲣⲁⲛ ⲛ̄ⲑ[ⲉ ⲛ̄ⲟ]ⲩⲕⲁⲗⲗⲏⲙⲙⲁ) . . . but God knows that I did not know the power of the words which I concealed. I wrote them in good faith at that time."[20] Although some passages of the graffito are obscure because of sizeable lacunae, the phrase "*as if* with a veil" clearly indicates that the concealment referred to is metaphorical, rather than physical. Moreover, Jacob's claim that he "wrote them in good faith" argues against the ancient tomb-inscriptions being the object of his actions; he certainly did not write those, in good faith or otherwise.

Alain Delattre has proposed to see a link between this inscription and a nearby cryptographic Coptic graffito written, it would seem, by the same Jacob. According to Delattre's reading, the "concealment" Jacob speaks of here refers to the composition of the cryptographic text, which the monk wrote but later came to regret.[21] Jacob may have feared the inscriptions adorning the walls of Ramesses IV's tomb; he may have admired their aesthetic value; he may have ignored them completely as he went about his daily routine. His graffito, however, is mute on this subject. Indeed, even the editor of the Greco-Roman graffiti in the Valley of the Kings, who staunchly maintained that late antique Christians could not possibly have visited the tombs as tourists, was forced to concede that those same Christians typically did not try to destroy the reliefs and inscriptions they encountered in the tombs.[22] Further complicating the picture—and validating the need for a reevaluation of the available sources—is the recent discovery outside Theban Tomb 1152 of a sherd from a late Roman amphora dating to the sixth or seventh century c.e. and bearing incised hieroglyphic characters, seemingly sketched from memory. The excavators have interpreted this unique object as "a monk's random fancy and a simple sketch drawn during or after a walk around the Sheikh Abd el-Gurna necropolis, which should rather be perceived as a testimony of his fascination or curiosity about a part of the scenery."[23]

From a nervous monk allegedly concealing hieroglyphic inscriptions with a veil to an antiquarian hermit doodling hieroglyphs on a potsherd—where do we go from here? How can we access late antique Christian attitudes toward hieroglyphic writing? As noted above, there is no direct Christian equivalent to the *Hieroglyphica* of Horapollo or the lost work of Chaeremon on hiero-glyphs. References to hieroglyphic inscriptions, and to Egyptian writing more generally, are dispersed throughout the vast corpus of late antique Christian literature, written over a span of several centuries and in more than half a dozen languages and at least as many genres. For obvious reasons, then, the present study does not pretend to be an exhaustive catalogue of such refer-ences. Rather, it proceeds thematically, examining the motif of hieroglyphs as an element of Christian discourse in four major subject areas: late antique discussions of universal history and the role of Egyptian record keeping in reconstructing antediluvian chronologies; the question of how Christians should understand the "wisdom of Egypt," thought to have been encoded in hieroglyphic inscriptions and studied, then rejected, by Moses; the perceived relationship between hieroglyphs and the Judeo-Christian tradition that rep-resented Egypt as the quintessential land of idolatry; and late antique debates over the nature of translation and the possibility (and propriety) of cultural appropriation across linguistic and religious boundaries. Although the specific comments made about hieroglyphs differ widely across these subject areas and from one author to another, one of the main themes that emerges from these individual case studies is the fact that certain late antique Christian authors actively sought to advance their theological and political agendas by claiming the power to represent and interpret hieroglyphic inscriptions, that most tra-ditional marker of Egyptian cultural identity.

The majority of the Christian sources examined in this book come from the period stretching from the mid-third century to the mid- to late seventh century, although a few texts fall outside these parameters. Pushing the end-point of this study into what is, politically speaking, the early Islamic period is roughly consistent with the concept of a "long" late antiquity first espoused by Peter Brown and since adopted in a number of important volumes, nota-bly Bowersock, Brown, and Grabar's *Interpreting Late Antiquity: Essays on the Postclassical World.*[24] The notion of a late antiquity beginning in the mid-third century and extending beyond the establishment of the Islamic caliphate in the mid-seventh century is not universally accepted. However, I believe it is justified for the purpose of the present work, as the discourse under discussion here draws heavily on sources from the classical tradition and, at the other end of the chronological spectrum, is itself in dialogue with the nascent genre of early medieval Islamic historiography.

Because much of the present volume deals with the various ways in which hieroglyphic writing was *mis*interpreted by late antique authors, Chapter 1 offers a brief overview of the current Egyptological understanding of the origins and nature of the script, focusing on the different categories of hieroglyphic signs and the ways in which they combine to form larger syntactic units. The chapter also introduces the reader to Egypt's complex linguistic and graphic environment, in which multiple languages and scripts were employed concurrently. In the final section of the chapter, I explore the role of hieroglyphic writing as a marker of Egyptian religious and cultural identity and consider the role of the indigenous priesthood in preserving knowledge of the script. I argue that the obsolescence of hieroglyphic writing is closely linked to the decline of temple-centered Egyptian religion and the diminishing ranks of the priesthood under Roman imperial rule.

Chapter 2 takes as its starting point some of the most common themes in the classical accounts of hieroglyphic writing—the great antiquity of hieroglyphs, the attribution of their invention to the god Thoth-Hermes, and their use in historical record keeping—and examines the ways that the classical discourse on hieroglyphs is adapted (or subverted) in the works of church fathers such as Eusebius and Augustine. These authors were closely concerned with the relationship between Christian learning and the traditions of Hellenic and Near Eastern *paideia*, and their comments on hieroglyphs must be understood in the context of larger late antique arguments over biblical chronology and the existence of authoritative sources for antediluvian history.

Chapter 3 also considers the relationship between classical and patristic sources, looking specifically at the perceived link between hieroglyphs, esotericism, and the preservation of Egyptian priestly knowledge. The belief that hieroglyphs are a fundamentally symbolic system of communication, originally devised to encode the mysteries of Egyptian religion, is one of the most tenacious ideas to emerge from the classical discourse on hieroglyphs, and it was an idea that many of the church fathers shared. It is also a notion that resonates with very deep-seated Egyptian scribal traditions and ways of speaking about scripts and writing. Whereas the Egyptian and Greco-Roman sources privilege Egypt as a fount of primordial wisdom, however, in the Judeo-Christian tradition Egypt is excoriated as the land of oppression and idolatry. The "wisdom of Egypt" and its visual marker, hieroglyphic writing, are consequently problematized in the works of many late antique Christian commentators. Moses emerges as a key figure in these discussions, as he was said to have been educated in the Egyptian tradition but to have bested the wisest of all Egyptians—the magicians of Pharaoh—*not* by drawing on his intellectual formation, but by relying instead on divine assistance.

Hieroglyphs are further problematized in Chapter 4, which focuses on a unique text, a polemical sermon by the fifth-century abbot Shenoute of Atripe. Shenoute was outspoken in his desire to stamp out traditional Egyptian religion in the region of Panopolis, in Upper Egypt, and a fragmentary sermon attributed to his authorship provides us with the most detailed description of Egyptian hieroglyphs to survive in the Coptic language. In the sermon, Shenoute applies a reductionist mode of interpretation to the hieroglyphic inscriptions on the walls of a local temple, identifying them as foolish and misleading images, and denying any possibility that they could be "read" or reinterpreted in a Christian light. By emphasizing the many animal hieroglyphs used in the inscriptions, Shenoute situates hieroglyphic writing within the broader Christian discourse on Egyptian idolatry, which condemned the worship of cult images and the veneration of sacred animals, both key features of traditional Egyptian religious practice. This line of argumentation provides Shenoute with strong theological justification to support his ultimate goal, the transformation of the temple into a Christian church, and it also serves as a refutation of more conciliatory modes of interpreting the hieroglyphic legacy of pharaonic Egypt.

Modes of interpretation are also the focus of Chapter 5, which examines the tension between the claim, articulated in the *Corpus Hermeticum* and in the works of some of the late antique Neoplatonists, that Egyptian hieroglyphs could not be translated, and countervailing claims by Christian historians and ecclesiastical leaders to have translated hieroglyphic inscriptions. The chapter centers on a very high profile incident in which the Christian interpretation of hieroglyphs played a small but important role—the destruction of the Alexandrian Serapeum during the patriarchate of Theophilus. The accounts of this event by Rufinus, Socrates Scholasticus, and Sozomen are contrasted with the account of hieroglyphic translation preserved in the *Res Gestae* of Ammianus Marcellinus and with a cycle of later Coptic homilies in which the interpretation of a hieroglyphic inscription is likewise of central importance. In these homilies, multiple aspects of the Christian discourse on hieroglyphs converge, including the themes of esotericism and concealment, the importance of the act of translation, and the desire to control and/or appropriate Egypt's pre-Christian past.

In a seminal article from 1984, Klaas Smelik and Emily Hemelrijk argue that animal worship functioned as a kind of "national symbol" for Egypt from the Late Period onward, something that marked the Egyptians as unmistakably alien in the eyes of other nations and that, moreover, cemented the Christian church fathers' generally negative attitude toward Egypt.[25] I contend that, in the classical discourse on Egypt, hieroglyphs served as another major symbol of Egyptian identity, and, by engaging with that discourse and commenting on the hieroglyphic script, late antique Christian authors were afforded an opportunity to discuss not just Egypt's distinctive writing system, but also the larger culture that that writing system symbolized.[26] Considering the various forms of late antique engagement with the hieroglyphic tradition is unlikely to lead to any new understanding of the hieroglyphs themselves, nor is that the goal of this book. Rather, examining the ways in which hieroglyphs appear in the works of late antique Christian authors allows us to reflect on the ways in which Egypt's pharaonic past could be used in the construction of Christian identity and ecclesiastical authority in late antiquity. Ancient Egyptian religious texts long maintained that to know the name of something was to have power over it, and in the Christian discourse on hieroglyphs, with its concern for the issues of translation and interpretation, we see a lingering echo of that ancient attitude. Being able to stand in front of hieroglyphic inscriptions and interpret them (even if the resulting interpretations bore little or no relation to the texts' original meaning) gave Christian leaders like Shenoute and Theophilus a measure of authority over the spaces in which those inscriptions were carved and, by extension, the pharaonic Egyptian culture that they represented.

Note on Terminology

Finally, it is necessary to say a few words about some of the terms employed throughout this book. Categorization is often fraught with difficulty, all the more so when the terminology used for the purpose of categorization is drawn from tendentious sources. Early twentieth-century scholarship, heavily influenced, as we have seen, by polemical early Christian literary sources, routinely sorted late antique individuals and communities (along with their texts, cult places, and ritual practices) into broad categories: "Christian," "Jewish," "pagan," and so forth. A significant body of recent scholarship, however, has rightly problematized the uncritical use of the terms "pagan" and "paganism," requiring scholars to either relinquish these terms or to defend their continued usage.[27]

What makes the usage of these terms so controversial? "Pagan" derives from the Latin *paganus*, which in early Roman usage could refer to country dwellers or "rustics" in contrast to urbanites, or to "civilians" in contrast to soldiers. By the fourth century C.E., the term had been adopted in Christian usage as a "social classifier," used to designate—and, ultimately, to stigmatize and criminalize—non-Christians and non-Jews, worshippers of the traditional Greco-Roman and Near Eastern gods.[28] In the Christian sources, it is unquestionably a term of opprobrium, and its use by modern scholars to designate past individuals or social groups has consequently been called into question. Usage of the cognate "paganism," is, if anything, even harder to justify, as it risks imposing an artificial uniformity and systematization on an extremely diverse religious landscape and implies an acceptance of a triumphalist Christian point of view.[29]

What are the alternatives to this problematic (but highly convenient) terminology? Some historians have acknowledged the issues inherent in these terms but have continued to employ them anyway, while others have tested out various alternatives. "Polytheist" and "polytheism" have frequently been proposed as less ideologically fraught substitutes, although this is not altogether satisfying either. Hellenistic Jewish and early Christian authors utilized "polytheist" as a pejorative alongside "pagan," and "polytheism," like "paganism," risks lending a false appearance of unity to otherwise independent cults; it also fails to acknowledge trends toward monotheistic thought that existed in certain Greek, Roman, and Near Eastern religious traditions (what is sometimes characterized as "pagan monotheism").[30]

The approach I have taken in this book is as follows. In recognition of the issues outlined above, I have eschewed the use of "paganism" altogether and have tried to be cautious in my use of "polytheism" and "polytheist." I have, however, continued to employ "pagan" in certain circumstances: in translations, to render *paganus*, Ἕλλην, ϩⲈⲗⲗⲏⲚ, and their derivatives;[31] in representing the work of other scholars who make use of the term; and in representing the arguments of late antique Christian authors themselves. Wherever possible, I have tried to employ more context-specific terminology: "practitioners of traditional Egyptian religion," and the like.

Chapter 1

From Sign to Symbol in Roman Egypt

On the twenty-fourth of August in the year 394 C.E., a man stood before the north wall of the Gate of Hadrian on the island of Philae and carved three columns of rather crude hieroglyphic signs to the right of a now-mutilated relief depicting the Nubian god Mandulis (Figure 2). This ancient graffiti writer identified himself in his hieroglyphic text as Smet, son of Smet, the Second Prophet of Isis. In an accompanying Demotic inscription, he further described himself as "the scribe of the House of Writings (?) of Isis," and he claimed to have carved his graffiti to honor Mandulis because that god had been favorable ("fair of face") toward him. As a priest and scribe, Smet would have been uniquely capable of producing texts in both the ancient hieroglyphic and the more recent Demotic scripts. In fact, by the late fourth century he was likely one of only a handful of individuals in all of Egypt who possessed that ability.[1]

This priestly scribe, chiseling his brief inscriptions into the stone of Hadrian's Gate, stood unwittingly at a critical juncture in the history of Egypt's already-ancient writing system; the three short columns of hieroglyphs he carved on that August day are considered by scholars to be the last known hieroglyphic inscription ever produced in Egypt.[2] Smet and his graffiti are thus a logical starting point from which to begin a discussion of hieroglyphs and their reception in late antique Egypt, for they raise two very critical questions. First, how did the knowledge of Egypt's hieroglyphic writing system, in use for some three thousand years by the fourth century C.E., come to reside solely in the hands of Smet and his priestly brethren? And second, how and why did that knowledge finally die out? It is only in view of the obsolescence of the hieroglyphic script that we can begin to make sense of late antique attempts to "read" or otherwise interpret it. First, however, it is necessary to say a few words about the origins and nature of Egyptian hieroglyphs, and

Figure 2. Hieroglyphic inscription of Smet, son of Smet (*I.Philae.Dem.* 436), from the Gate of Hadrian, Philae. Photo courtesy of Peter Dorman.

about the contexts in which they were used and studied. The following does not pretend to be a comprehensive account of Egyptian writing from the Predynastic period through to late antiquity; rather, it is intended to provide an overview of some of the key features of the hieroglyphic script, the practicalities of its use, and the circumstances leading to its eventual abandonment.

Origins of the Hieroglyphic Writing System

The term "hieroglyphic" is not a native designation for the Egyptian writing system but rather a term applied to that system by Greek visitors to Egypt.[3] The Egyptians themselves referred to hieroglyphs as *mdw nṯr*, "god's words," a term that refers not to the sacral use of the script, but that rather reflects the long-standing belief that writing was the creation and gift of the god Thoth.[4] Although hieroglyphs are often taken as the paradigmatic form of all ancient Egyptian writing, the hieroglyphic script was in fact just one of several scripts used at different times and in different contexts to record the spoken Egyptian language.

The development of Egyptian hieroglyphic writing took place in the late Predynastic and Early Dynastic periods (ca. 3250–2700 B.C.E.), a time of increasing social complexity when many of the defining characteristics and institutions of Egyptian culture first came into being. It has been suggested that the abundant rock art found along routes in the Eastern and Western Deserts may represent an early stage in the development of written communication in Egypt, as may the pictorial motifs and incised pot marks found on some types of Predynastic ceramics, but it remains unclear what specific meaning these various images held for their creators and viewers.[5] Rock art, pot marks, and other types of figural representations may well have had some sort of communicative purpose, and some of the motifs employed therein resemble signs that later appear in the corpus of standardized hieroglyphic signs, but they cannot be considered to represent "writing" in the accepted modern sense of "visible speech."[6]

The earliest artifacts that clearly mark the origins of Egyptian writing derive from the Predynastic cemetery of Umm el-Qa'ab at Abydos, in Upper Egypt. Abydos was one of three major centers of power in the Predynastic period, alongside the cities of Hierakonpolis and Naqada, and the elite burials at the site attest to the developing social hierarchy and institutionalization of power that characterized the Predynastic. One of these elite tombs, designated

U-j by its excavators, is distinguished by its size, its architecture, and the extensive assemblage of valuable grave goods it once contained. All these factors have led archaeologists to speculate that the tomb owner was an individual of some importance, perhaps a proto-king who presided over the growing regional influence of Abydos during the Naqada III period.[7] Three classes of artifacts found in Tomb U-j seem to reflect early efforts at administrative record keeping: sherds of ceramic vessels bearing markings in ink, sealings (impressions left in clay by cylinder seals), and ivory tags or labels with incised symbols. Some of the signs on the tags seem to represent numerals, and others have been interpreted as indicating the place of origin of the material to which the label was originally affixed. Later labels from Abydos are explicitly royal in character, and close connections between the development of writing and the origins of the centralized, monarchical Egyptian state are commonly assumed.[8]

The earliest symbols depicted on the ivory labels from Tomb U-j do not yet represent a mature system for rendering continuous speech, and it has been suggested that they should be understood rather as "a marking system with a highly restricted scope of applications," which "displayed formal features typical of later writing and emergent representation of language" and was oriented primarily toward expressing the names of persons and places.[9] The Egyptian writing system continued to evolve over the next several centuries, expanding in both its functionality and in the range of sign forms it employed. By the late Second Dynasty (ca. 2690 B.C.E.), the hieroglyphic writing system was capable of expressing complete clauses with subject and predicate, and lengthier continuous texts began to appear in the Third and Fourth Dynasties. Most signs achieved their canonical form during the Early Dynastic period, and the corpus of hieroglyphs remained quite stable until the Ptolemaic period, when there was extensive experimentation with sign forms and many new signs were introduced.[10]

Types of Hieroglyphic Signs

In its classical Middle Kingdom form, the hieroglyphic script comprised some seven hundred distinct signs, conventionally divided by scholars into three categories: logograms or ideograms (signs that represent entire words), phonograms (signs that represent sounds), and determinatives or semagrams (signs that mark word breaks and provide metalinguistic information about the classification of the words to which they are attached). These categories are not absolutely fixed—the interpretation of a sign as an ideogram, phonogram, or determinative rests on its context—but these different types of signs combine to form syntactic units within the Egyptian writing system.[11]

Ideograms are signs that represent whole words or concepts; so, for example, the Egyptian word for "house," *pr*, can be written using the ideogram depicting the schematic floor plan of a house. A single stroke is written after or beneath the sign to indicate that it is meant to be read as an ideogram. Contrary to the views of late antique Neoplatonists like Plotinus, whose theories on hieroglyphic writing are discussed in Chapter 3, ideograms do not refer directly to reality, but to reality as mediated by language. That is, the ideogram for "house" refers not to the physical reality of a particular house or to some Platonic ideal of "house," but to the specific Egyptian word for house, *pr*.[12] Being tied to the spoken Egyptian language gives individual hieroglyphs phonetic value, and the phonetic value of individual signs enabled the Egyptians to use the rebus principle to write words that were difficult to depict graphically, but that sounded like words that could be represented. So, for example, the house hieroglyph, with its phonetic value of *pr*, could also be used to write the homonymous verb of motion *prỉ*, "to go out" (Table 1).

Phonograms are signs that represent sounds, rather than entire words. As noted above, some signs can act as both ideograms and phonograms; so, in the first example in Table 1, the house sign serves as an ideogram, connoting the word *pr*, or "house," while in the second example, the same sign acts as a phonogram with the phonetic value $p + r$. As the examples in Table 2 illustrate, phonograms may be "alphabetic" or monoconsonantal (representing a single consonant sound), biliteral (representing two consonants) or triliteral (representing three consonants). In theory, the corpus of monoconsonantal signs could have been used to spell out any word in the Egyptian language, and those signs were in fact commonly used to transliterate foreign names. The fact that

Table 1. Ideograms and the Rebus Principle

Hieroglyphic Sign(s)	Phonetic Value	Meaning
⌐⌐ ।	*pr*	"house"
⌐⌐ ◯Λ	*prỉ*	"to go out"

Table 2. Phonograms

Hieroglyphic Sign	Type	Phonetic Value
⌡	alphabetic	b
▭	biliteral	$m + n$
🪲	triliteral	$\underline{h} + p + r$

purely "alphabetic" writing of this sort never became the norm in Egypt, how-ever, suggests that the high value placed on the hieroglyphic script in Egyptian culture went beyond the script's immediate communicative function.[13]

Determinatives make up the third major category of hieroglyphic signs. They do not convey phonetic information but stand at the end of a word to mark the word break. They also serve as classifiers, providing metalinguistic information about the semantic category to which the word belongs. So, for example, the walking legs sign is used to determine verbs of motion such as "walk" and "run," while the house sign is used to determine words for types of buildings. Recent studies have drawn on insights from the field of semiotics to emphasize the range of culturally specific information that can be conveyed by determinatives and, conversely, the insight that determinatives can give us into the Egyptians' conceptual universe. For example, Orly Goldwasser has noted that the use of a depiction of a man lying on a bed to determine the word *sḏr*, "to lie down, spend the night," suggests that the writing of that word was codified in elite circles, as beds would have been status items unavailable to the majority of the Egyptian population.[14] Determinatives can also illuminate unexpected con-ceptual categories very specific to the Egyptian thought world. A good example of this is the image of a female breast, which is used to determine words as seemingly unrelated as "sky," "cow," and "flood"—terms that a recent study has shown to be conceptually linked by the notion of nourishment.[15]

The Egyptian language is classified as Hamito-Semitic, related to both the family of languages spoken in northern and eastern Africa and to Semitic languages such as Akkadian, Hebrew, and Arabic. One of the features that Egyptian shares with the Semitic languages is a consonantal root system, in

Table 3. Use of Determinatives

Hieroglyphic Sign(s)	Phonetic Value	Meaning
	pr	"house"
	prỉ	"to go out"
	pr.t	"winter"
	pr.t	"fruit, seed"

which groups of related words are constructed based on a root of (typically) three consonants in a fixed order. Grammatical inflection and variations in meaning can be indicated by changing the vowels that separate the consonants or by adding prefixes and suffixes to the root. Vowels were not normally written in Egyptian until the advent of Coptic (see below), but the correct vocalization of a given word would have been determined by the native Egyptian speaker from contextual clues. Table 3 demonstrates how the different types of hieroglyphs combine to form syntactic units and how the triconsonantal root system can be used to derive word groups.

In the first example in Table 3, the house sign is used as an ideogram, to write the word *pr*, "house." In the second example, the same sign is used as a phonogram, representing the biconsonantal phoneme *p + r*. This is followed by an alphabetic sign, the open-mouth hieroglyph that stands for the consonantal value *r*. This sign acts as what is known as a "phonetic complement," repeating the second consonant of the preceding biliteral sign and emphasizing that the previous sign is meant to be read as a phonogram rather than as an ideogram. The walking-legs determinative follows, indicating that the word in question is the verb of motion *prỉ*, "to go out." Examples three and four are homonyms with identical consonantal structure (*p + r + t*); in spoken Egyptian they would presumably have been differentiated by interpolated vowel sounds, but the hieroglyphic script differentiates them graphically by means of determinatives. *Pr.t*, the season of "winter," receives the sun disk determinative indicating that the word represents a unit of time, while *pr.t*, the noun "fruit, seed," is determined by a plough and three seeds. Both phonetic complements and determinatives serve the purpose of disambiguation, specifying precisely how individual signs and sign groups are meant to be read. In the absence of punctuation and word spacing, neither of which was commonly used in Egyptian, determinatives also signal to the reader that the end of a word has been reached.

From the perspective of modern Egyptology, most of the classical and late antique interpretations of hieroglyphs that will be discussed in the following chapters are quite simply incorrect. Many of these later misinterpretations derive from a fundamental misunderstanding of the nature and function of the three types of hieroglyphic signs outlined above. Prior to the discovery of the Rosetta Stone and the nineteenth-century decipherment of the hieroglyphic script, the phonetic value of hieroglyphic signs was not recognized by most scholars, and it was widely believed that hieroglyphs functioned on a purely symbolic level.[16] That is, rather than representing the spoken Egyptian language made visible, hieroglyphs were thought to transcend linguistic differences and to participate in a universal language of symbols, the meaning of which was accessible only to those initiates who possessed the proper hermeneutic tools. The signal contribution of scholars like Thomas Young and Jean-François Champollion was the recognition of hieroglyphs' phonetic value, which liberated the script from purely symbological interpretations and permitted subsequent generations of philologists to begin reconstructing the underlying grammatical structures of the Egyptian language.[17]

Scripts and Their Uses

The aesthetic value of the hieroglyphic script, which made it so beautifully suited for use on monumental temples, tombs, and stelae, also made it cumbersome to use in more mundane contexts. A scribe who had to painstakingly detail all the feathers of his bird hieroglyphs—a practice seen in many monumental inscriptions—would soon find his bookkeeping in arrears and clients demanding to know why their letters had not yet been sent. Early on in the development of the Egyptian writing system, therefore, a cursive script known as hieratic was developed for use in nonmonumental contexts, typically written in ink on papyrus or ostraca.[18] "Hieratic" was, like "hieroglyphic," a Greek term applied to the Egyptian writing system. Although the literal meaning of the word, "priestly," implies that texts written in hieratic necessarily have religious content, the script in fact had a very wide range of possible uses, from personal letters to legal records, as well as literary and religious texts, and the hieroglyphic and hieratic scripts were used in parallel throughout much of Egyptian history.[19] In hieratic, the hieroglyphic prototypes of many of the signs can still be recognized, but the signs themselves have been somewhat stylized so as to render them quicker and easier to write; some hieroglyphic signs are reduced to little more than strokes or squiggles in the hieratic script. As John Baines notes, the early development and widespread use of hieratic was likely critical in allowing the hieroglyphic script to retain its representational character and its preeminence as what he calls the "vehicle of public writing, and more generally of written display."[20]

Toward the middle of the seventh century B.C.E., a third and even more cursive script developed out of hieratic. Called "demotic" or "common" by the Greeks, it was initially used for mainly administrative purposes (hence its Egyptian designation, sḫ n šꜥ.t, or "document writing"), although its usage later expanded to include religious and literary texts as well. In Demotic, unlike in hieratic, the hieroglyphic prototypes of individual signs are often unrecognizable, and there is a strong tendency for signs to be combined or "ligatured" together.[21] Demotic eventually supplanted hieratic as the principal script used in administration and daily transactions and pushed hieroglyphs even further out of the realm of common knowledge.[22] The Demotic script remained in use for roughly eight hundred years; the last known inscriptions written in Demotic are graffiti from the temple of Isis at Philae dated to the year 452 C.E., approximately fifty years after Smet son of Smet composed his own graffiti, in both hieroglyphs and Demotic, at the same site.[23]

The abandonment of the Demotic script did not mean the death of the Egyptian language, however. Already in the Ptolemaic period, scribes had begun experimenting with the possibility of rendering the Egyptian language phonetically using Greek letters. This experimentation intensified in the early Roman period, particularly in the context of the production of ritual texts. Because the Greek alphabet, unlike the Egyptian scripts, indicates vowel sounds, this system of notation was used to gloss obscure words and magical names, the pronunciation of which was seen as being of the utmost importance for effective ritual performance.[24] By the third or fourth century C.E., this experimental system had been codified into an alphabet consisting of the twenty-four letters of the Greek alphabet plus a handful of additional signs (six or seven depending on the dialect) derived from Demotic and used to represent sounds that do not occur in Greek. This distinctive script and latest phase of the Egyptian language, known as Coptic (the term is derived via Arabic from the Greek Ἀιγύπτιος, or "Egyptian"), was adopted early on by Egypt's nascent Christian communities and was used, among other purposes, for translating the New Testament from Greek into Egyptian.[25] By the time of the Arab conquest in the mid-seventh century, the use of Coptic was widespread for both religious and secular purposes, and under the Umayyad and Abbasid caliphs Coptic was commonly used for administrative and legal documents. Arabic supplanted Coptic as the principal language of administration and day-to-day life only in the eleventh century c.e., and Coptic survives to this day in a fossilized form as the liturgical language of the Egyptian Christian church.[26]

Multilingualism

In addition to the Egyptian language and the multiplicity of scripts employed at any given time to render that language in writing, numerous other languages and scripts were used in Egypt at different times. Some, such as Akkadian and Aramaic, were relatively restricted in their scope and influence, employed for a specific purpose (diplomatic correspondence, in the case of Akkadian) or by members of a particular ethnic group (Jewish mercenaries, in the case of Aramaic). Others, such as Greek and, later, Arabic, would spread widely and serve many different purposes. Throughout the pharaonic period, Egyptian remained the language of business, administration, religion, and daily life for the vast majority of the population. By the Byzantine period, however, following the Macedonian and Roman conquests, Egypt had become a profoundly bilingual society, one in which both Egyptian and Greek were widely spoken and written. In the centuries following the Arab conquest the spread of Arabic would complicate the country's linguistic situation even further.

Greek speakers, mainly Ionians and Carians, first began to arrive in Egypt during the seventh century b.c.e. as merchants and as mercenaries in service to the Egyptian pharaohs. The royal policy of bestowing land grants on soldiers upon their retirement from military service resulted in the first wave of Greek settlement in the area of Pelusium on the Mediterranean coast, and the establishment of the city of Naucratis as the main locus of commerce between Greeks and Egyptians in the late seventh century b.c.e. led many Greek merchants to settle in that area as well, further expanding the Greek population base in Egypt. However, it was not until the conquest of Alexander the Great in 332 b.c.e., and the subsequent establishment of the Greek-speaking

Ptolemaic dynasty (305–30 B.C.E.), that the use of Greek became widespread outside of ethnic Greek enclaves. The Ptolemaic rulers, themselves of Macedonian descent, made Greek the official administrative language of the country, and according to Plutarch (*Vita Antonii* §27) only Cleopatra VII, last of her dynasty, made any attempt to learn Egyptian. In practical terms, Greek became the status language of Ptolemaic Egypt, and Egyptians who wished to participate in the political system were effectively required to learn that language, whatever level of literacy they might have already attained in Demotic. (Evidence for Greeks learning Demotic also exists, but this practice seems to have been considerably less common.) As Greeks and Egyptians intermarried and as Egyptians of the upper classes learned Greek in order to seek a greater voice in the country's economy and administration, a bilingual elite came into being, conversant in both Greek and Egyptian and able to adapt their language use to particular circumstances and situations.[27]

In 30 B.C.E., Egypt came under Roman control following the defeat of Cleopatra and Mark Antony at the battle of Actium and their subsequent suicides. Administered as the "private estate" of Octavian and the emperors who followed him, Egypt followed a slightly different path than many other Roman provinces, although many of these administrative differences vanished following the reforms of Diocletian in the late third century.[28] As in the other eastern provinces, Roman administration in Egypt was carried out largely in Greek, and the country's Greco-Egyptian bilingualism became even more deeply entrenched during the first centuries of Roman rule. In contrast, the use of Latin in Roman Egypt was quite restricted, and the language had little impact outside of military circles.[29] By the time of the Arab conquest in 642 C.E., Coptic had long since supplanted the Demotic script as the principal vehicle for writing the Egyptian language, and the conquerors inherited a strong tradition of Greco-Egyptian bilingualism. It took more than three centuries for Arabic to overtake Greek and Coptic to become the country's dominant language, and even into the nineteenth century it was rumored that there existed villages in remote parts of the country where Coptic was still spoken on a day-to-day basis, the last surviving vestige of the ancient Egyptian language.[30]

Literacy, Status, and the Priesthood

"See, there is no office free from supervisors, except the scribe's. He is the supervisor!" This claim, one of many set forth in the Middle Kingdom text now known as The Satire on the Trades or The Instruction of Dua-Khety, was intended as an exhortation to a trainee scribe, who is encouraged to complete his education because every other trade is deemed inferior to that of the scribe.[31] The privileged position of scribes within the Egyptian social hierarchy was recognized already in the Old Kingdom, and the genre of didactic or "Instruction" texts that developed in that period has plausibly been linked to an apprenticeship model of scribal training. Sources from the Middle and New Kingdoms point to the existence of scribal schools associated with both the royal palace (as in the introduction to The Satire on the Trades, where Dua-Khety is said to have "sailed southwards to the Residence to place him [his son] in the school of writings among the children of the magistrates, the most eminent men of the Residence") and with certain of the major temples, such as those of Amun and Mut at Karnak. Beginning in the Old Kingdom, scribal training was seen a necessary prerequisite for advancement in the county's burgeoning administration, a fact that would hold true in subsequent periods of Egyptian history as well.[32]

The process of learning to read and write in Egyptian during the pharaonic period can be reconstructed to some extent based on surviving didactic literature and school texts, which are abundantly preserved in certain contexts, especially from the New Kingdom.[33] From this material, it appears that students would begin their studies not, as one might suppose, by learning individual hieroglyphic signs, but rather by memorizing entire words and phrases in the hieratic script, learning to break them down into their component signs only later in the educational process. Given that hieratic was the script most commonly used for bureaucratic purposes and that many apprentice scribes were undoubtedly training for a position in the central administration, it is hardly surprising that the curriculum would have privileged hieratic over the more formal hieroglyphic script. Indeed, individuals who attained literacy in hieratic were not necessarily literate in hieroglyphs as well. Instruction in the hieroglyphic script, if it were undertaken at all, would have taken place during a student's secondary education, after he had already achieved a certain level of proficiency in hieratic and had studied the classics of the Middle Egyptian literary canon.[34]

For the Ptolemaic and Roman periods, education in Greek (and later, Coptic) has received extensive discussion on the basis of papyrological documentation, but somewhat less is known about instruction in the Egyptian language during the same periods. Based on surviving documents tentatively identified as school texts, it has been suggested that instruction in Demotic focused primarily on the acquisition of the vocabulary and formulae needed to compose administrative texts, but this remains a matter of some debate.[35] Less still is known about education in the hieroglyphic script in Hellenistic and Roman Egypt, but it seems likely that it took place within the context of the Egyptian temples and, more specifically, in the institution known as the House of Life (on which see below).[36]

Given the centrality of the written word both within the Egyptian administration and in Egyptian culture more broadly, an important question to consider is the extent to which Egypt's population was literate at any given time. Inscriptions covered the walls of the country's temples, stelae and funerary papyri were commissioned for placement in the tombs of those who could afford them, and contracts and deeds were written in ink on papyrus rolls and ostraca. But how likely was it that any given Egyptian was capable of engaging with the textual material that crossed his or her line of sight on a daily basis? Studies on literacy in the ancient world emphasize that literacy must be seen as a "highly variable package of skills in using texts"; the ability to read does not necessarily imply the ability to write, and writers might only be able to produce texts in a single genre.[37] This is indeed the picture that emerges from the Egyptian sources of the New Kingdom and Late Period. Although precise statistics are still a matter of considerable debate, the estimate of 1 percent literacy proposed by John Baines and Christopher Eyre in the early 1980s is still widely accepted, although it has been argued that the rate of literacy rose to perhaps as high as 10 percent of the population during the Ptolemaic and Roman periods with the increased use of Greek in Egypt. Baines and Eyre insist on the fact that "literacy" in this context does not necessarily imply that a literate individual was fully conversant with the several scripts and phases of the Egyptian language; their discussion of witnessing and signing documents, in particular, emphasizes the highly variable skill set encompassed by the term "literate."[38]

Although royal officials and members of the administration would have been required by the demands of their profession to attain a certain level of competence in hieratic (or Demotic, beginning in the Late Period), the need for proficiency in hieroglyphs would have been significantly more restricted, and literacy in that script consequently lower overall. As noted above, from fairly early on the use of hieroglyphs was largely limited to the realms of monumental display and the study, transmission, and production of sacred texts. As a result, instruction in the hieroglyphic script would likely have taken place as a type of vocational training required of young men seeking to attain high standing within the priesthood.[39] Literacy was not an absolute necessity for priestly service prior to the professionalization of the priesthood in the Late

Period, and the level of literacy among the low-ranking priests who served in monthly rotations and then returned to their ordinary lives outside the temple must have depended heavily on the exigencies of their nonsacerdotal professions.[40] That said, however, the office of the "lector-priest" (ḫrj-ḥb) is attested as early as the Old Kingdom, and the temples were important loci for the production and consumption of written material. Lector-priests, members of the temple personnel responsible for the recitation or reading aloud of ritual texts, came to be closely associated with magical practice and the production of magical texts, both within the context of the temple itself and for private clients.[41] It is likely to these ritual specialists that we owe not only the extensive corpus of religious literature dating to the later periods of Egyptian history but also much of the linguistic and graphic experimentation that characterizes texts of the Late Period and the Greco-Roman era.[42]

By the Roman period, literacy in the Egyptian language had become one of the fundamental requirements for priestly hopefuls, together with circumcision and documented descent from a priestly family. The requirement of literacy is attested by a judicial report on papyrus from Tebtunis, dated to 162 C.E., in which it is remarked that a priestly candidate by the name of Marisouchos has been admitted to the ranks of the priesthood, "having given proof of a knowledge of [hie]ratic [and] Egyptian writ[ing] ([ἱε]ρατικὰ [καὶ] Αἰγύπτια γράμ[ματ]α) from a hieratic book (βίβλου ἱερατικῆς) produced by the sacred scribes (οἱ ἱερογραμματεῖς)" (P.Tebt. II 291, fragment B 2, lines 41–43).[43] The document demonstrates the necessity for priests to be familiar with the hieratic script, which accords well with the widespread use of hieratic for religious literature from the late New Kingdom onward.[44] The phrase "hieratic [and] Egyptian writing" may refer to the candidate's proficiency in both the hieratic and Demotic scripts; Αἰγύπτια γράμματα was sometimes used in documentary texts to refer to the latter (cf. P.Vind.Tand. 26, line 20), and Demotic would have been commonly used by Egyptian priests of the Roman period. It is less clear whether priests were also expected to show proficiency in hieroglyphic writing at this time. With the shift to composing ritual texts in hieratic and then in Demotic, knowledge of hieroglyphs would have become increasingly recherché even among the educated priestly elite, and education in hieroglyphs, if it took place at all, would probably have begun only after a candidate's admission to the priesthood.

An institution known as the House of Life (pr-ꜥnḫ) is of critical importance for our understanding of Egyptian scribal traditions, particularly in the later periods that concern us here. The term is attested as early as the Old

Kingdom, but references are most numerous from the middle of the New Kingdom to the Roman period. In the surviving documentation, the House of Life appears to be the place of production of a wide range of religious and ritual texts, including hymns, spell books, and medical texts. Although the scope of activities carried out in the House of Life has been much debated—some have argued for seeing this institution as a type of early university, while others have taken a more conservative view and understood it as primarily a workshop for the production of religious documents—there is widespread agreement that the House of Life was a center of Egyptian scribal culture and a vital force in the preservation and promulgation of ritual knowledge.[45] Archaeological evidence for Houses of Life is limited, but several are attested in textual references, and it is believed that many of the major Egyptian temples would have had such an institution associated with them.[46] As the text of the Canopus Decree (238 B.C.E.) makes clear, the "Scribes of the House of Life" who are attested in numerous texts were priests in their own right, so a close link between temple and House of Life is hardly surprising.[47] In his study *Religion in Roman Egypt*, David Frankfurter allocates a central role to the House of Life in not only the preservation of Egypt's scribal traditions, but also in the presentation of those traditions to Greek and Roman visitors to Egypt, a fact that undoubtedly affected the impression such visitors received of the hieroglyphic writing system.[48] The linkage between the hieroglyphic tradition and the House of Life was so strong, in fact, that the Coptic term for "hieroglyphic characters," ϨⲈⲚⲤϨⲀⲓ ⲚⲤⲀϨⲠⲀⲚϢ, literally "letters of a scribe of the House of Life," makes explicit reference to that institution.[49]

Script Obsolescence

The city of Oxyrhynchus, a regional capital and thriving metropolis during the first several centuries of Roman rule, still counted five professional hieroglyph carvers on its tax rolls in the early second century C.E.; less than three hundred years later, by the time of Smet of Philae, the carving of monumental hieroglyphic inscriptions in public venues had been discontinued, and knowledge of hieroglyphs was restricted to the repetition of a few fossilized phrases by a member of the priestly elite.[50] How did this state of affairs come about? Studies of language and script use in late Roman Egypt have pointed to a number of causal factors, which must be examined in turn: the disconnect between hieroglyphs and the spoken vernacular, which, by the fourth century

C.E., was profound; the existence of a higher-status language, Greek, that was potentially easier to learn and use; the changing functionality of hieroglyphs as markers of cultural identity; and finally, the impact on the native priesthood of diminishing imperial support for the temples, which ultimately bankrupted the very communities that had preserved the knowledge of the hieroglyphic script over the preceding two millennia.[51]

As noted above, already in the Old Kingdom there existed a functional divide between hieroglyphs, which were used principally in religious contexts and for display by the king and members of the elite, and hieratic, which was widely used for administrative purposes. Through the Middle Kingdom, however, these two different scripts were still writing what was, grammatically, the same language. This began to change in the New Kingdom, as the spoken language continued to evolve, while the grammatical forms of the Middle Kingdom, fossilized as the "classical" stage of the language, were still used for the composition of monumental inscriptions. Script and language continued along these divergent paths into the Late Period, when the development of the Demotic script, in which ligatured sign groups cannot always be traced back to a hieroglyphic original, drove a final wedge between hieroglyphs and the language of daily life. By the end of the Late Period, monumental hieroglyphic inscriptions were still being composed in a form of the language that had not been spoken in a thousand years, and the vigorous experimentation with the hieroglyphic script that took place in the Ptolemaic period, with its expansion of the corpus of signs, frequent wordplay, and esoteric theological references, only increased the distance between hieroglyphs and the Egyptian language as it was spoken in the streets. Ptolemaic hieroglyphs were beyond question the province of the priestly elite, inaccessible both to bureaucrats versed in Demotic and Greek and to lower-ranking priests who used Demotic and hieratic in reading and composing ritual texts, and this state of affairs continued through the Roman period into late antiquity. The effect of this divergence was to progressively reduce not only the number of people who could read hieroglyphs, but also the number of people who would have any reason for doing so. As we shall see, when hieroglyphs became inextricably tied to the priesthood, their fates became linked as well, and the story of the obsolescence of hieroglyphs is, in a very real sense, the story of the radical transformation of Egypt's priestly tradition.[52]

It has long been acknowledged that with the establishment of the Greek-speaking Ptolemaic dynasty in the late fourth century B.C.E., Egypt's linguistic environment changed dramatically. As discussed above, emigration swelled the

ranks of native speakers of Greek residing in Egypt, and the use of Greek as
the main language of administration offered a powerful incentive for ambitious Egyptians to learn the language of the ruling elite. However, the impact
of Greek on the hieroglyphic tradition is less clear-cut. Several studies have
emphasized the limited influence Greek had on Demotic, even in administrative contexts where the Greek and Egyptian languages and scripts were used
side by side. Hieroglyphs, employed primarily in the rarefied environment of
temple scriptoria, seem to have been even less affected.[53] Additionally, it has
been noted that although Greek can be considered a status language from the
perspective of upwardly mobile members of the Egyptian elite, who needed to
learn the language in order to participate in their country's governance, hieroglyphic Egyptian retained its status as a conveyer of cultural meaning, particularly in the religious sphere.[54] Indeed, the graphic exuberance of Ptolemaic and
Roman hieroglyphic inscriptions may be seen, on some level, as a celebration
of that role.[55] That hieroglyphs continued to be privileged as a medium of religious expression into the Roman period is suggested by treatise 16 in the *Corpus
Hermeticum*, which includes a meditation on the perceived impossibility of
translating Egyptian religious concepts into the Greek language (further on
this text, see Chapter 5 below).[56] Thus, it appears that, notwithstanding Greek's
privileged position as an administrative language and its close association with
the ruling elites, the widespread adoption of that language in Ptolemaic and
Roman Egypt is not in itself sufficient to explain the eventual abandonment of
hieroglyphs in late antiquity. We must look instead to other factors.

In their 2003 study of script obsolescence in Egypt, Mesopotamia, and
Mesoamerica, Houston, Baines, and Cooper note that the preservation or
obsolescence of a script is strongly correlated to that script's functionality; they
go on to observe that in the case of Egypt, the functionality of hieroglyphic
texts was not always—or even necessarily—dependent on their legibility.[57]
In making this statement, the authors draw on the work of Heike Sternberg
el-Hotabi, whose study of Ptolemaic and Roman Horus-*cippi* revealed the
use of what the author termed "pseudo-hieroglyphic inscriptions," in which
hieroglyphic signs do not necessarily represent readable letters or graphemes,
but rather serve to signal the *presence* of sacred text.[58] The existence of such
pseudoinscriptions, which are also attested on a variety of Ptolemaic- and
Roman-period funerary objects such as the shroud depicted in Figure 3, suggests that for the individuals who commissioned the objects on which these
"texts" appear, the legibility of the inscriptions was of secondary importance to
their mere presence on the object.[59] If this is in fact the case, it could suggest

Figure 3. Funerary shroud of Tasheretwedjahor. Egyptian, Greco-Roman period, first or second century C.E. Museum of Fine Arts, Boston, Gift of the Class of the Museum of Fine Arts, Mrs. Arthur L. Devens, Chairman, 54.993. Photo © 2019 Museum of Fine Arts, Boston.

that the arduous process of attaining proficiency in the hieroglyphic script—already effectively useless in the administrative sphere—was being further disincentivized. If a pseudohieroglyphic inscription, or even an empty field on a coffin or shroud, could be functionally equivalent to a text composed according to the rules of Egyptian grammar and orthography, why bother to learn those rules in the first place? This point should not be pressed too far, particularly in light of the skillful composition of certain Roman-period hieroglyphic temple inscriptions, as David Klotz has observed, but it does raise the possibility that the functionality of hieroglyphs as a viable writing system, rather than simply a marker of sacrality, was being impinged even in the realm of religion, where hieroglyphs had long retained much of their ancient cultural cachet.[60]

In the scholarship of the early twentieth century, it was common to call on the "rise of Christianity" to explain various phenomena observed in the late antique period, including the eventual abandonment of the hieroglyphic script. The hostility of early Christians toward any vestige of "pagan" practice was taken as a given, and it was assumed that the ancient writing system, bound as it was to Egyptian religious concepts and to the milieu of the temples, was one more casualty of the shifting religious tide.[61] As discussed above in the Introduction, however, the rise-of-Christianity model of historiography has come under a great deal of criticism in recent decades for its heavy reliance on tendentious early Christian sources, and historians have continued to seek deeper, systemic causes for the major religious changes that took place in late antique Egypt. Much of the recent scholarship on this topic has highlighted the crucial significance of economic factors leading to the closure of Egypt's temples and the eventual abandonment of many of the practices supported by those temples and their priesthoods.[62] The Ptolemies saw a clear political benefit to promoting the traditional Egyptian cults, and the major temples of Edfu, Esna, Dendera, and Philae stand as a testament to their financial support. The economic situation of the temples changed dramatically over the course of the Roman period, however, as Roman fiscal policy increasingly aimed at maximizing the tax base and shrinking the size of nontaxable landholdings. As we have already seen, admission to the priesthood (and thereby to tax-exempt status) became more restrictive, priests were forbidden to engage in business, and temple landholdings were diminished.[63] As David Klotz emphasizes in his study of Roman-period temple construction at Thebes, however, this must be seen as a very gradual process, and he notes that many of the first- and second-century emperors, including even the famously anti-Egyptian Tiberius, were responsible for carrying out a fairly extensive program of temple construction and decoration in the province.[64] Direct imperial support for the construction, embellishment, and maintenance of the temples did start to decrease after the reign of Antoninus Pius in the mid-second century C.E., however, and it had dried up almost completely by the crisis years of the mid-third century; the last known hieroglyphic attestation of an emperor's name is a cartouche of Maximin Daia, dating to the early fourth century and preserved on blocks from a now-destroyed temple at Tahta, in Middle Egypt.[65]

The closure of the Egyptian temples did not automatically mean the abandonment of all the rites and traditions supported by those temples, as David Frankfurter has shown. Certain observances might move from the public sphere to the domestic, ritual specialists might take to the road as itinerant holy men, and some Egyptian cultural forms might quietly reappear with minimal differences in a newly Christian context.[66] The hieroglyphic script, however, long restricted in its use to a small circle of priestly individuals and incomprehensible to the vast majority of the population, did not survive the loss of institutional support occasioned by the closure of the last temples. What *did* survive was a tradition, already more than half a millennium old by the fourth century C.E., of trying to interpret what had become, by that time, mysterious symbols of Egypt's ancient past. It is to those interpretive efforts, in all their various forms, that we shall now turn.

Chapter 2

Hieroglyphs, Deep History, and Biblical Chronology

Beginning at least as early as the work of Herodotus in the fifth century B.C.E., descriptions of hieroglyphs and other Egyptian scripts became a literary commonplace in Greek and Roman geographic and historical accounts of Egypt, where they were often deployed as signs of Egypt's alterity. As discussed in the previous chapter, hieroglyphic writing served as an important marker of Egyptian cultural identity among the Egyptians themselves. For outside observers, unfamiliar with the hieroglyphic script and possessing only a limited understanding of how the writing system functioned, hieroglyphs served as a convenient shorthand marking Egypt as unmistakably foreign. Many of the early classical authors were writing in a time when hieroglyphs were still in active, if increasingly restricted, use and their Egyptian interlocutors might have been able to provide accurate information about the script. However, their works betray a kind of complacent intertextuality, as a number of well-worn tropes about the nature and meaning of hieroglyphs are repeated from one text to another. Writers such as Herodotus, Diodorus Siculus, Strabo, and Tacitus essentially defined the terms in which hieroglyphs would be discussed in Greco-Roman circles for centuries to come, and a few major themes run throughout their works, including the great antiquity of the hieroglyphic script, the attribution of its invention to the god Thoth, and the use of the script to record Egypt's deep history.

Many of the same themes also appear in the writings of the church fathers; in fact, it is virtually impossible to read the patristic sources that deal with the hieroglyphic tradition in isolation from the classical discourse on hieroglyphs, as Christian and non-Christian authors alike frequently drew on the same source material. When the church fathers took up the subject of hieroglyphs, however, it was often in an attempt to debunk or at least problematize the classical authors' claims about Egypt's great antiquity and esoteric wisdom. Hence the preponderance of negative formulations that we see in the Christian texts: Egyptian writing is not a gift from the gods, but a human invention; Hebrew, not Egyptian, is the most ancient written language; the Egyptians possess not real wisdom, but some doctrine which is *like* wisdom; and their ancient hieroglyphic temple inscriptions and sacred books preserve not the true history of the world, but the misguided and dangerous teachings of an idolatrous society. This chapter examines three of the major themes that run throughout the classical discourse on hieroglyphs—the divine origins of the writing system, its antiquity, and its connection to Egyptian historical record keeping—and the way that those themes were reshaped by Christian authors such as Eusebius and Augustine in their discussions of world chronology and the authority of the biblical tradition. Although the church fathers did not produce any extended treatises on hieroglyphs comparable to the *Hieroglyphica* of Horapollo, the ways in which they deployed their limited knowledge of the hieroglyphic script offer a window not only into late antique views of Egyptian writing, but also into larger Christian debates about the value of classical and Near Eastern paideia and the relationship of those traditions to scriptural authority.

The Invention of Hieroglyphs in Classical Sources

Although Herodotus is widely credited with laying the foundation for several centuries' worth of Hellenic Egyptomania, his remarks about the Egyptian writing system are actually quite limited. He notes the existence of two distinct scripts, which he characterizes as "sacred" and "common" (that is, hieroglyphic and Demotic), but he does not offer any detailed description of hieroglyphs or speculate on their origins, either historical or mythic.[1] Of critical importance for later commentators, however, is his assertion that Egypt was the birthplace of many different arts and technologies. He reports being told by his local informants that the Egyptians were, among other things, the first to establish temples and cultic ceremonies for the gods, and this notion of Egypt's cultural primacy is reiterated in numerous subsequent accounts.[2]

It fell to later Greek and Roman authors to elaborate in greater detail on the specific origins of the Egyptian writing system, and those writers who comment on the subject are in substantial (though not unanimous) agreement that writing in Egypt was the invention of the god Thoth, identified with Greek Hermes and Roman Mercury. So, for example, Plato writes in the *Phaedrus* that "at Naucratis, in Egypt, was one of the ancient gods of that country, the one whose sacred bird is called the Ibis, and the name of the god himself was Theuth. He it was who invented numbers and arithmetic and geometry and astronomy, also draughts and dice, and, most important of all, letters (γράμματα)." This origin myth is seconded by Cicero, Diodorus, and Plutarch, among others.[3] Like Plato, Diodorus posits that Thoth-Hermes was the inventor, not only of the *Egyptian* writing system, but of human language more generally. He writes, "it was by Hermes, for instance, according to them, that the common language (κοινὴ διάλεκτος) of mankind was first further articulated, and that many objects which were still nameless received an appellation, that the alphabet was invented, and that ordinances regarding the honours and offerings due to the gods were duly established."[4]

Naucratis is an unlikely birthplace for the Egyptian scribal arts, having been established as a Greek trading depot only in the late seventh century B.C.E., but for Plato to attribute the invention of writing to the figure of Thoth-Hermes is perfectly consistent with Egyptian mythology, which had long identified Thoth as the scribe of the gods and the "lord of hieroglyphs (*nb mdw nṯr*)." Although the archaic origins of Egyptian devotion to Thoth remain somewhat obscure, a cult of Thoth seems to have been in existence at least as early as the Fourth Dynasty, and he appears in the Pyramid Texts. From the Middle Kingdom onward the association of Thoth with knowledge, wisdom, and the invention of technologies such as writing was well established.[5] In the Egyptian sources, Thoth is reckoned as "excellent of speech (*iḳr dd*)," "lord of script (*nb sḫ*)," "lord of books (*ḥḳȝ mḏȝt*)," "excellent scribe (*sḫ iḳr*)," and "he who gave words and script (*rdi mdw drf*)," among other titles.[6] Unlike the Mesopotamian scribal tradition, which preserves a narrative account of the invention of cuneiform and the creation of the first cuneiform tablet in the tale of *Enmerkar and the Lord of Aratta*, the Egyptian sources do not record at any length the story of Thoth's invention of hieroglyphs, which must rather be gleaned from the cumulative evidence of his many epithets. So, for example, a late Ptolemaic text from the temple of Edfu refers to Thoth as "the heart of Re, *who first wrote in the beginning*, lord of script, who reckons lifetimes (*ib n rˁ šȝˁ-sphr m-šȝˁ nb sḫ ḥsb-ˁḥˁw*)."[7] Thanks to his identity as the inventor of hieroglyphs and the scribe of the gods, Thoth is also associated with administration, law, and magic, frequently combining these capacities when he appears in the mortuary literature. For example, in a first-century C.E. funerary papyrus from Thebes, the deceased is told, "the letter of breathing of Thoth is your protection, which was written with his own fingers. He will cause your speech to be eloquent in the presence of Osiris [after] you [have come] to the hall of the righteous."[8] Accompanying vignettes in the funerary papyri frequently depict Thoth in his scribal guise, proffering a rolled-up papyrus scroll or holding a reed pen and scribal palette as he does in the Book of the Dead fragment shown in Figure 4.

Just as the classical authors' claim that Thoth-Hermes was the inventor of hieroglyphs can be traced back to long-standing ancient Egyptian traditions, the notion that Thoth was the originator of all human language also finds some validation in the Egyptian sources. In addition to being recognized as the "lord of hieroglyphs," as we have already seen, in the New Kingdom Thoth was credited as the one who "distinguished the tongue of one land from another (wp ns ḫꜣst r kt)," a function that has led some modern scholars to suspect the existence of an Egyptian parallel to the story of the confusion of languages recorded in Genesis 11:1–9.[9] Even if such a theory may be pushing the limits of the available evidence, references to Thoth differentiating foreign languages from one another do appear to reflect Egypt's increasingly cosmopolitan outlook during the New Kingdom and suggest a growing belief in Thoth's power to transcend the borders of Egypt and act on an international scale.

Although the belief that Thoth-Hermes was the inventor of writing was widespread among both Egyptian and non-Egyptian commentators, the sources do record a few dissenting voices. Pliny the Elder, for example, observes that although some of his sources posit an Egyptian origin for the art of writing, his personal belief is that the Assyrians got there first, and Pomponius Mela credits the Phoenicians with the invention of "the alphabet, literary pursuits, and other arts."[10] The latter does concede, however, that the Egyptians "are, as they declare, the oldest human beings, and they refer in unambiguous annals to three hundred and thirty pharaohs before Amasis and to a history of more than thirteen thousand years."[11] It was toward the agency of Thoth-Hermes as the inventor of writing, however, that the majority opinion inclined, supported by a plethora of references in the Egyptian sources themselves to Thoth as the patron of scribes and of the scribal arts.[12]

The impressive longevity of Thoth's status as a kind of culture hero for his role in the invention of Egyptian writing is further attested by a composition that has come to scholarly attention relatively recently and may represent a bridge of sorts between the Egyptian and Greco-Roman traditions. This text, published as the Book of Thoth, has been reconstructed by its editors from approximately thirty Demotic manuscripts dating mainly from the first

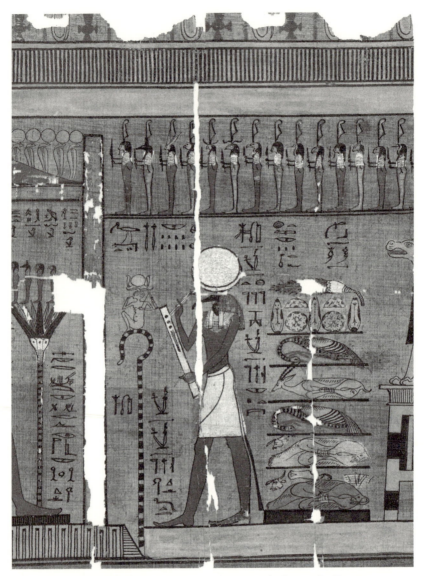

Figure 4. Book of the Dead fragment depicting Thoth as scribe. Egyptian, Ptolemaic period, ca. 320 B.C.E. Toronto, Royal Ontario Museum 910.85.236.10. With permission of the Royal Ontario Museum © ROM.

century B.C.E. to the second century C.E.; it is almost certainly the product of the type of priestly scriptorium known as the House of Life, discussed above in Chapter 1.[13] Formatted as a dialogue between master (*Ḥs-rḫ*, "The-one-who-praises-knowledge," probably to be identified with Thoth himself) and disciple (*Mr-rḫ*, "The-one-who-loves-knowledge"), the Book of Thoth allows us a glimpse of how the Egyptian scribes themselves conceptualized their own writing system. As the editors note, "the author of this book manifestly aimed to give to the engaged reader a deep understanding about the symbolic and religious aspects of writing within the Egyptian world view."[14] The text celebrates the role of Thoth, the "great, great, great one" not only as the master of hieroglyphs but also as their inventor. This creative process is alluded to in the following terms: "The signs revealed their forms. He called to them. They answered him. / He knew the form of speech of the baboons and the ibises. / He went about truly in the path of the dog. He did not restrain their barkings. / He understood the barking of these and these cries of the Vizier (= Thoth)."[15] As Richard Jasnow has observed, animal imagery is frequently used in the Book of Thoth to describe the repertoire of hieroglyphic signs, and the metaphors of hunting and trapping are used to represent the scribe's mastery of that repertoire. Hence we read that "The Ba-souls of Re (that is, hieroglyphs), they are possessors of wings. They fly to the Wise-One (that is, Thoth). / He is their herdsman who makes for them sustenance. They are quiet so as to place themselves by him. / The document is a nest. The books are its nestlings. That is, t[hey are] in his shade (?)."[16] Thoth's mastery over hieroglyphs is asserted throughout the text and, via the medium of the dialogue, this wisdom is conveyed to the disciple as well.

The *editio princeps* of the Book of Thoth was published with the subtitle *An Egyptian Pendant to the Classical Hermetica*, and speculation on the possible relationship between the Demotic composition and the Greek- and Latin-language compositions of the *Corpus Hermeticum* represents an important area of emerging scholarship. Although the editors themselves caution that "there are no obvious verbal 'parallels' between the Book of Thoth and the Classical *Hermetica*," they do note that the Book of Thoth shares a number of common features with the *Hermetica*, including the use of the dialogue format; the prominent role accorded to Thoth-Hermes, described in both as "thrice-great"; and the heavy emphasis placed on the notion of Egyptian wisdom, particularly as it is encoded in hieroglyphic texts.[17]

Jean-Pierre Mahé, in his preliminary commentary on the Book of Thoth, goes a step further, proposing that the text should be seen as "pre-hermetic" in nature and noting that "since we now have, within the same Demotic writing, a dialogic framework and wisdom instructions, we may fairly assume that this provides a very close antecedent to the Greek *Hermetica*."[18] Mahé also notes that the existence of Greek and Old Coptic glosses in some manuscripts of the Book of Thoth could point to a bilingual readership for the text, which would go a step further in cementing a link between the milieu of composition of the Book of Thoth and that of the Hermetic tractates.[19] Most importantly for the present chapter, although the Book of Thoth and the Hermetic corpus represent fairly esoteric intellectual traditions, they both attest to a very strong belief in the role of Thoth-Hermes as the creator of the Egyptian writing system and in the centrality of that writing system within Egyptian culture. Moreover, these beliefs are in substantial harmony with the views expressed in the broader classical discourse on Egyptian hieroglyphs, stretching back to Diodorus and forward to Ammianus Marcellinus. It remains to be seen, however, to what extent they are congruent with the views expressed in the works of the Christian church fathers and ecclesiastical historians, and it is to these sources that we shall now turn.

The Invention of Hieroglyphs in Christian Sources

Given the indebtedness of the early Christian literary tradition to earlier classical works, which provided Christian authors with both stylistic exemplars and content to be discussed (or disputed), it is not surprising that Thoth-Hermes-Mercury does indeed appear as the inventor of writing in the works of several of the church fathers.[20] Eusebius, for example, quotes Diodorus' statement that Thoth was the inventor of letters, and Lactantius paraphrases Cicero's *De natura deorum* to say the same in his *Divinae institutiones*, writing:

> In Cicero the pontifex C. Cotta . . . says that "there are five
> Mercuries" and, after listing four of them in a row, that "the fifth
> is the killer of Argus; that is why he fled to Egypt and established
> laws and literature (*leges ac litteras*) among the people there. The
> Egyptians call him Thoyth; from him the first month of their year"
> (which is September) "got its name." He also built a town, which
> in Greek is still called Mercury's city, and the people of Faenia
> worship him very devotedly. Though he was a man, nevertheless

he was so very old and so very learned in all manner of scholarship
that his knowledge of many facts and skills gave him the extra name
of Trismegistus. He wrote many books in great quantity which
are relevant to knowledge of things divine; in them he asserts the
supremacy of the one and only God most high, and calls him by the
titles that we do, "lord and father."[21]

Although he denies the divinity of Thoth-Hermes-Mercury ("he was a man"),
Lactantius seems to have greatly respected the figure he called "Trismegistus"
as a philosopher, and in his apologetic works he makes extensive use of Hermetic texts that he thought bore witness to the Christian message, especially
the so-called *Perfect Discourse* or *Asclepius*.[22] So, for example, he argues that the
existence of an all-powerful Son of God "is demonstrated not just by what the
prophets say, which is unanimous, but also by the predictions of Trismegistus
and the prophecies of the Sibyls." He goes on to support this claim with quotations drawn from the *Asclepius*, the Sibylline oracles, and Proverbs 8:22–31.[23]
A similar approach is taken by Cyril of Alexandria in his apologetic work
Contra Julianum, in which he claims that "the Egyptian Hermes," despite
being a priest (τελεστής) and an inhabitant of the temple-precincts of the
idols (τῶν εἰδώλων τεμένη), was nonetheless acquainted with the teachings
of Moses and had profited from them.[24] Like Lactantius, Cyril proceeds to
include quotations from the *Hermetica* in his collection of pagan testimonia
to the Christian message.[25]

Lactantius was not alone among the church fathers in his reliance on
Cicero's *De natura deorum* for the link between Thoth-Hermes-Mercury and
the development of writing. In *Adversus nationes*, Lactantius' teacher Arnobius
also offers an extended paraphrase of the same passage from Cicero, although
unlike Lactantius, he does not identify its source, referring only in general
terms to "authors on unknown antiquity."[26] The influence of Cicero not only
on Arnobius and Lactantius, but on the overall development of Christian literature in Latin, is suggested by Jerome's famous self-condemnation (*Ep.* 22.30)
as an unregenerate Ciceronian. *De natura deorum*, with its debate over the
existence of the gods and the proper interpretation of Greco-Roman mythology, was of particular interest to Christian authors who wished to find arguments against the gods from within the classical tradition itself.[27] Moreover,
Cicero's characterization of the inventor of writing as a murderer and exile
provided fertile ground to Christian authors seeking to discredit traditional

Greek, Roman, and Near Eastern mythology by highlighting the immoral actions of the gods recounted in those myths. Hence, for example, the apologist Aristides writes, "they bring forward Hermes as a god, representing him to be lustful, and a thief, and covetous, and a magician (and maimed) and an interpreter of language. But it cannot be admitted that such an one is a god."[28] Despite the euhemeristic reevaluation of his divinity in the patristic sources, however, the position of Thoth-Hermes-Mercury as the inventor of writing generally remained secure.

Elsewhere in the patristic corpus, brief remarks by Tertullian and Eusebius, among others, testify to just how widely diffused this tradition was.[29] Many of these comments are made only in passing and often appear in the context of critiques of classical mythology and historiography. Tertullian, for example, argues in *De testimonio animae* that people spoke of God "before letters had sprung up in the world, before Mercury, I suppose, was born," and Eusebius uses the example of Hermes to explicate the process by which Greeks and Romans were wont to deify abstract concepts, writing that they "shrank not from labelling gods even the calculations of their own minds or even the language by which they gave expression to these, naming the mind 'Athena' and speech 'Hermes.'"[30] The extent to which this association had become common cultural currency among both Christian and non-Christian authors is indicated by Augustine's dry remark in *De doctrina Christiana*, where he notes that "we (Christians) were not wrong to learn the alphabet just because they say that the god Mercury was its patron."[31]

Augustine's position on the invention of writing in Egypt is worth considering in more detail, as his work demonstrates the way in which theories about the origin of letters could feed into larger Christian debates about world chronology, universal historiography, and the nature of the Greek, Roman, and Near Eastern gods. As his comment in *De doctrina Christiana* indicates, Augustine was well aware of the tradition that situated Thoth-Hermes-Mercury as the originator of both writing and human speech more generally. This tradition is also alluded to at various points in *De civitate Dei*, where Augustine argues that although Mercury is often identified as having power over speech, and as having been "noted for his skill in many arts," which he taught to mankind around the time of Moses, he was not in fact divine. Rather, Augustine writes, "weighty historians who have committed these ancient tales to writing agree" that Mercury was originally human, and that he was awarded divine honors in recognition of the fact that his many gifts to mankind made human life more pleasant. This euhemeristic interpretation allows Augustine simultaneously to retain the ancient tradition linking Thoth-Hermes-Mercury with the invention of writing and to demote the latter figure to the ranks of human culture heroes.[32]

Elsewhere in *De civitate Dei*, however, Augustine records an alternative tradition which he seems to prefer, according to which writing was the invention not of Thoth-Hermes-Mercury, but of Isis. This view is articulated on four separate occasions in book 18, where it serves to underpin Augustine's presentation of world chronology from the time of Abraham to that of Christ. In an attempt to harmonize biblical chronology with that of the Greeks (an endeavor of which more will be said below), Augustine writes that Inachus, the first king of Argos, rose to power "at the time of Abraham's grandsons." He goes on to state that "it is also said that Io was the daughter of Inachus: Io, who, afterwards called Isis, was worshipped in Egypt as a great goddess. Other writers, however, say that she came to Egypt from Ethiopia as queen, and that, because her government was both broad and just, and because she instituted many beneficial things, *especially the art of writing*, divine honours were accorded to her there after her death."[33]

Returning to this notion later in book 18, Augustine uses both the humanity of Io/Isis and the chronological position of Inachus as a contemporary of Abraham's grandsons as a convenient means of refuting the Egyptians' claims to primordial wisdom. He writes, "not even the wisdom of the Egyptians could have preceded in time the wisdom of our prophets; for Abraham himself was also a prophet. Moreover, what wisdom could there be in Egypt before the art of letters had been taught by Isis, whom the Egyptians, after her death, thought worthy to be worshipped as a goddess?"[34] In a stringent critique of the Egyptians' claims to expertise in the astronomical sciences, which was much vaunted in classical sources, Augustine goes on to say, "it is futile, therefore, for certain persons to babble with most vain presumption and say that Egypt has understood the pattern of the stars for more than 100,000 years. For in what books could they have collected so much information, who learned the art of writing from their teacher Isis not much more than two thousand years ago? That is what Varro informs us, who is no mean authority in the field of history; and, moreover, his statement is not at variance with the truth of the Divine Scriptures."[35] In other words, if the goddess Isis could be equated with the human figure of Io, thought to have lived not in the dim, primordial past but a mere two millennia before Augustine's own time, and if it was Io/Isis who introduced writing to Egypt, then the Egyptians' claims to possess a scientific tradition stretching back several tens of thousands of years could not be valid.[36]

The conflation of the Greek Io and the Egyptian Isis was an ancient notion by Augustine's time. The iconographic similarity between the two figures—Io said in Greek mythology to have been changed by Hera into a cow and Isis commonly depicted with the Hathor-headdress of cow's horns surmounted by a moon disk—was noted already by Herodotus. Diodorus likewise affirms a congruence between Io and Isis, as do Lucian and Juvenal, among others. That this connection was also known to early Christian authors is confirmed by Clement of Alexandria, who writes that "Isis, who is the same as Io, is so called, it is said, from her going roaming over the whole earth."[37] But where does Augustine's contention that Io/Isis invented Egyptian writing originate? Although Egyptian mythology presents Isis as a wise woman and a skilled magician, she is not traditionally credited with the invention of writing itself in Egyptian thought.[38] Nor do the earlier classical sources typically accord her such a role, preferring, as we have seen, to confer that honor on Thoth-Hermes-Mercury. Moreover, although Plutarch acknowledges Isis' "knowledge and understanding" in *De Iside et Osiride*, he explicitly *dissociates* her from the discovery of writing, observing that "many have related that she was the daughter of Hermes, and many others that she was the daughter of Prometheus, believing the latter to be the discoverer of wisdom and forethought, and Hermes to be the discoverer of writing and of music and poetry."[39]

Augustine claimed to owe his information about Io/Isis' invention of writing to the Roman writer Varro, who was active in the first century B.C.E. and whom later authors, both Christian and non-Christian, cited widely as an authority on everything from agriculture to Latin linguistics and Greco-Roman mythology. Unfortunately, only fragments of various works from Varro's sprawling and diverse oeuvre survive, making it difficult to obtain a clear sense of where this most erudite of Roman scholars obtained his information.[40] We may nevertheless speculate that Varro was drawing on the traditions preserved in the Greek-language Isis aretalogies. These praise hymns developed during the Hellenistic period and continued to be produced as late as the third century C.E.; they celebrate Isis as a universal goddess and culture hero, responsible for the development of numerous technologies and attributes of advanced civilization, including writing.[41] In the best-preserved example, a first- or second-century C.E. inscription from Kyme in Asia Minor, the goddess states, "I am Isis, the ruler of every land; I was taught by Hermes (ἐπαιδεύθην ὑπὸ Ἑρμοῦ), and with Hermes I devised letters, both the sacred and the common, that all might not be written with the same (καὶ γράμματα εὗρον μετὰ Ἑρμοῦ, τά τε ἱερὰ καὶ τὰ δημόσια, ἵνα μὴ τοῖς αὐτοῖς πάντα γράφηται)."[42] The fact that the invention of the hieroglyphic and Demotic Egyptian scripts stands at the very start of the long list of Isis' achievements recounted in the aretalogy suggests its signal importance for the text's author, who also attributes to Isis a number of deeds more traditionally credited to Thoth-Hermes, including the distinguishing of Greek and other "barbarian" languages.

The cultural and linguistic background of the Isis aretalogies has, not surprisingly, been the object of intense scholarly interest since the genre was first identified in the first decades of the nineteenth century. Although the Kyme aretalogy purports to be "copied from the stela in Memphis that stands before the temple of Hephaestus (τάδε ἐγράφη ἐκ τῆς στήλης τῆς ἐν Μέμφει ἥτις ἕστηκεν πρὸς τῶι Ἡφαιστιήωι)," arguments have been made for greater or lesser Egyptian influence on the development of the text.[43] Some scholars have proposed to see the aretalogy as fundamentally Egyptian in nature, representing the more-or-less literal Greek translation of phrases and concepts native to Egyptian mythology. Others have claimed that the text is squarely rooted in Greek thought, leavened with a handful of identifiably Egyptian notions for the sake of exoticism. Although the debate remains open, in recent years scholarly opinion has tended toward the middle ground, recognizing that although some of the individual statements in the Kyme aretalogy and the other related inscriptions can indeed be traced back to specific Egyptian-language models, some of them are equally clearly Greek in origin. Thus, the aretalogies may best be seen, in Žabkar's words, as "composite" in nature, deriving, as Dieleman and Moyer argue, from the "mixed cultural milieu of Ptolemaic Egypt in the second century B.C.E. or earlier."[44]

The striking claim that Isis was educated by Hermes and was his collaborator in the invention of the hieroglyphic and Demotic Egyptian scripts has been taken by some scholars as evidence of the aretalogies' composite character. Although Isis is not traditionally identified with the invention of writing in Egyptian sources, Dieter Müller has noted the existence of a few Egyptian texts in which Isis is credited with the same close connection to the writing system that is normally reserved for Thoth. Thus, in inscriptions from the Ptolemaic-period temple of Horus at Edfu, Isis is identified with the epithets "excellent of writing" (mnḫ sš) and "lady of writing" (nb.t sš); the latter title, in its masculine form, is very commonly borne by Thoth, as we have seen above.[45] Müller proposes that the attribution of these titles to Isis may result from the assimilation of Isis to the goddess Seshat, who is attested as early as the Pyramid Texts as the companion of Thoth and the goddess of writing and arithmetic. Also from Edfu comes a text stating that "Isis is at his (Thoth's) side like Seshat" (*Is.t r-gs=f m Sš.t*), and a close parallel to this phrase is known from the temple of Isis at Philae as well.[46] Isis' connection to Seshat (and her assumption of the latter's epithets, including "lady of writing" (*nb.t sš*), is even more pronounced in texts from the Ptolemaic temple of Hathor at Dendera, as Dagmar Budde has shown.[47]

Whatever its precise point of origin may have been in the multicultural context of Ptolemaic Egypt, the genre of the Isis aretalogy was, by the first century B.C.E., widely diffused in the Mediterranean world. As noted above, Diodorus preserves a portion of the Kyme aretalogy, or a version thereof, in his writings. In terms strongly reminiscent of the claim that the Kyme aretalogy had been copied from a Memphite stela, Diodorus writes of a stela "bearing an inscription in hieroglyphs (ἐπιγεγραμμένην τοῖς ἱεροῖς γράμμασιν)" that was said to have marked the purported tomb of Isis. That stela, he says, read as follows: "I am Isis, the queen of every land, she who was instructed of Hermes, and whatsoever laws I have established, these can no man make void. I am the eldest daughter of the youngest god Cronus; I am the wife and sister of the king Osiris; I am she who first discovered fruits for mankind; I am the mother of Horus the king; I am she who riseth in the star that is in the Constellation of the Dog; by me was the city of Bubastus built."[48] This passage corresponds very closely to lines 3a–11 of the Kyme aretalogy; interestingly, however, two lines from the latter text are omitted in Diodorus' account: line 3c, which relates Isis' collaboration in the invention of the hieroglyphic and Demotic scripts, and line 10, which states "I am the one called goddess by women." Diodorus himself states that the original text was considerably longer, remarking "so much of the inscriptions on the stelae can be read, they say, but the rest of the writing, which was of greater extent, has been destroyed by time."[49]

This comment offers an important clue as to the transmission of the aretalogy tradition; Diodorus does not claim to have seen the stela himself, but to have accessed the text at second or third hand. He opens his discussion of the text with the statement "I am not unaware that some historians give the following account of Isis and Osiris," and his use of the phrase "they say" in 1.27.6 gives a further indication that Diodorus accessed this tradition by means of one or more copies of the Kyme aretalogy that were circulating during his lifetime.[50] If Žabkar is correct in asserting that the praises of Isis contained in

Apuleius' *Metamorphoses* represent a Latin translation of concepts originating in the Greek-language aretalogy tradition, it can be argued further that such texts were still being shared in the first centuries of the Roman empire and that they were, moreover, being transmitted between different linguistic communities.[51] For the purposes of the present discussion, this is significant because it offers a glimpse of the mechanism by which the motif of Isis as the student of Thoth and the inventor of hieroglyphs might have reached the Latin-speaking Varro in the first century B.C.E. Even if Diodorus himself does not transmit line 3c of the Kyme aretalogy, his testimony indicates that the text of the inscription was being circulated, perhaps in multiple versions, among scholars during his lifetime; Varro, Diodorus' slightly older contemporary, would presumably have had access to this material as well.

From the aretalogy tradition, then, the attribution of Egyptian writing to Isis seems to have passed to Varro and from Varro to Augustine. Although this motif is not widely repeated in the church fathers—as we have seen, those few Christian authors who speak of the invention of hieroglyphs typically attribute it to the agency of Thoth-Hermes-Mercury—it does appear in a late and highly influential context, the seventh-century *Etymologiae* of Isidore of Seville. Isidore, writing in the late antique encyclopedic tradition and drawing heavily on the works of both Varro and Augustine, among other authorities, claims that "in the language of the Egyptians, the earth is called Isis, and they mean by this the person Isis. Now Isis, daughter of king Inachis, was a queen of the Egyptians; when she came from Greece she taught the Egyptians literacy and established cultivation of the land, on account of which they call the land by her name."[52] In Isidore, then, we find not only the conflation of Isis and Io, but also the euhemeristic assertion that Isis was a human who received divine honors based on her benefactions for mankind and the claim that she was responsible for two of the quintessential hallmarks of Egyptian civilization—the agricultural economy and the highly distinctive writing system. Nor does Isidore represent the endpoint of this particular tradition. Io and Isis are connected to each other and to the invention of writing in such late medieval and early Renaissance works as Boccaccio's *De mulieribus claris* and Christine de Pizan's *Epistre Othéa*, whence the remarkable scene of Io presiding over a scriptorium from the early fifteenth-century Harley MS 4431, depicted in Figure 5.[53] With Christine de Pizan's treatment of Io/Isis, the Christianization of this complex character is complete; as one recent commentator on the text has noted, the "letters" with which Io is associated in *Epistre Othéa* are not hieroglyphs or Greek, but rather the Holy Scriptures.[54]

Figure 5. Manuscript illumination showing Io presiding over a scriptorium.
Detail of Harley MS 4431 f.109r (ca. 1410–14) © The British Library Board.

Egyptian Historical Records in Classical Sources

In the earliest classical sources, the claim that the art of writing was an Egyptian innovation frequently went hand in hand with the assertion that the hieroglyphic script was of tremendous antiquity and that its quintessential purpose was to preserve Egyptian historical records, particularly records of *royal* history. Herodotus himself claimed that the Egyptians are "great in cultivating the memory of mankind and are far the greatest record-keepers of any people with whom I have been in contact."[55] The link between the Egyptians' ancient writing system and their ancient tradition of historical record keeping is stated even more explicitly in Plato's *Timaeus*. In that text, the author reports a meeting between the Athenian lawgiver Solon, who was widely reputed to have visited Egypt, and the priests of Athena (that is, the Egyptian goddess Neith) at Sais. The priests tell Solon,

> And if any event has occurred that is noble or great or in any way
> conspicuous, whether it be in your country or in ours or in some
> other place of which we know by report, all such events are recorded
> from of old and preserved here in our temples; whereas your people
> and the others are but newly equipped, every time, with letters
> and all such arts as civilized States require; and when, after the
> usual interval of years, like a plague, the flood from heaven comes
> sweeping down afresh upon your people, it leaves none of you but
> the unlettered and uncultured, so that you become young as ever,
> with no knowledge of all that happened in old times in this land or
> in your own.[56]

The notion that the priests of Egypt were the custodians, not just of Egyptian history, but of world history more generally, is articulated in a number of other classical sources, including Diodorus, who claimed that the priests maintained royal annals "which were regularly handed down in their sacred books (ἐν ταῖς ἱεραῖς βίβλοις) to each successive priest from early times, giving the stature of each of the former kings, a description of his character, and what he had done during his reign," and Strabo, who found it curious that the Egyptian priests did not know the source of the Nile flood, because they "rather meticulously record in their sacred letters (εἰς τὰ ἱερὰ γράμματα), and thus store away, all facts that reveal any curious information."[57] Dio Chrysostom similarly claimed that "a certain very aged priest" had given him the true history of the Trojan War, telling him that "all the history of earlier times was recorded in Egypt, in part in the temples, in part upon certain columns, and that some things were remembered by a few only as the columns had been destroyed, while much that had been inscribed on the columns was disbelieved on account of the ignorance and indifference of later generations."[58] In the same vein, whole sections of Josephus' *Contra Apionem* read like a historian's paean to the scrupulous record keepers of earlier generations. Closely echoing Plato's observations in the *Timaeus*, Josephus draws a sharp contrast between the Greeks, whose memory of the past has been obliterated by war and natural disaster, and the Egyptians, Chaldeans, Phoenicians, and Jews, whose "extremely ancient and extremely stable tradition of memorialization," is the happy result of temperate climatic conditions and a conscientious approach to record keeping, these peoples having "applied great forethought to leaving nothing of what happens among them unrecorded, but to have them consecrated continuously in public records composed by the wisest individuals."[59] As William Adler has argued in his study of Christian chronography, by praising these ancient Near Eastern chroniclers, Josephus was attempting both to highlight the great antiquity of the Jews and simultaneously to problematize the Greek historiographic tradition and, by extension, the Greeks' claim to cultural primacy. As we shall see below, Christian authors like Eusebius developed these same themes (and engaged with many of the same sources) in their own disputations with the Greeks.[60]

Given the common late antique assertion that hieroglyphs had a purely *religious* function (discussed below in Chapter 3), the extent to which the earlier classical commentaries dwell on hieroglyphs as a means of conveying *historical* information is quite striking. It is also in substantial, if fortuitous, agreement with modern Egyptological theories about the fundamentally royal context of the earliest experimentation with hieroglyphic writing.[61] Some ancient authors go so far as to suggest that hieroglyphs were developed specifically for the purpose of recording historical events; such a view is articulated in Tacitus' *Annals*: "The Egyptians, in their animal-pictures, were the first people to represent thought by symbols: these, the earliest documents of human history, are visible today, impressed upon stone. They describe themselves also as the inventors of the alphabet: from Egypt, they consider, the Phoenicians, who were predominant at sea, imported the knowledge into Greece, and gained the credit of discovering what they had borrowed."[62] Such a focus on the annalistic use of the hieroglyphic script is wholly in keeping with the Egyptians' very ancient tradition of maintaining king lists and royal annals and their practice of preserving those documents in monumental form, as in the famous example of the king list from the temple of Seti I at Abydos.[63] Although it is unclear whether Greco-Roman visitors to Egypt would have had any knowledge of the Abydos king list (which is not mentioned in Strabo's description of the important monuments at Abydos, although he knew of the building in which it was found), general awareness of the Egyptians' historiographic traditions would have come down to them from Greek-language sources such as Herodotus, who relates how the priests of Thebes confronted Hecateus of Miletus with the visual representation of 345 priestly generations, and later Manetho, who claimed to have written his history of Egypt on the basis of "sacred writings (ἐκ τῶν ἱερῶν γραμμάτων)" to which he had access by virtue of his position as an Egyptian priest.[64]

The early classical authors' focus on the use of hieroglyphs for the writing of historical records is underscored by the fact that many of the specific inscriptions they describe purport to be historical accounts of royal activities. Some of these inscriptions are either wholly apocryphal or, at the very least, egregious misinterpretations of real monuments. For example, one of the inscriptions of "Sesostris" that Herodotus claims to have seen in Ionia, carved "in sacred Egyptian script (γράμματα ἱρὰ Αἰγύπτια)" across the breast of a monumental relief depicting the king, has long been identified with a Hittite relief from the Karabel Pass, carved with an inscription, not in Egyptian hieroglyphs, but in hieroglyphic Luwian.[65] Traces of "Sesostris"—the heavily mythologized composite of the Twelfth Dynasty pharaohs Senusret I and III—were said to have been found throughout the eastern Mediterranean and are referred to not only by Herodotus but also by Diodorus and Strabo.[66] These claims may in part be a reflection of the long-standing Egyptian tradition of erecting commemorative stelae along campaign routes; the Beth Shan stelae of Seti I stand as notable examples from the New Kingdom, and the Adulis inscription of Ptolemy II suggests that this practice continued at least into the early Hellenistic era.[67] However, as Deborah Steiner argues in *The Tyrant's Writ*, for Herodotus the writing of monumental royal inscriptions is also a sign of "Oriental" despotism, both Egyptian and Persian; moreover, she proposes that in Herodotus' discussion of the various inscriptions he claims to have seen, "accuracy does not seem to be the historian's chief aim; instead the inscribed monuments may form part of a larger motif that associates the tyrant with the written word." Thus, by insisting on the act of writing (royal) records as a distinctive feature of Egyptian culture, Herodotus and his fellow Greek writers were also emphasizing the stark political contrast between Egypt's absolute monarchy and classical Greek experimentation with more representative forms of government.[68]

This perceived connection between Egyptian record keeping, the carving of monumental inscriptions, and the various manifestations of despotic power may also underlie the references, in Herodotus and elsewhere, to Egyptian inscriptions not directly connected to the figure of Sesostris. Herodotus claims, for example, to have seen an inscription carved on the pyramid of Khufu at Giza that recorded "the amounts spent on radishes, onions, and garlic for the workmen"—the equivalent, according to his interpreter, of sixteen hundred talents of silver. This claim is repeated almost verbatim by Diodorus, who adds the homely detail that the workmen were furnished not only with vegetables but also with "purgatives." Khufu appears as a tyrant in the accounts of both authors, much as he does in the Middle Kingdom tales of Papyrus Westcar, and the purpose of this epigraphic excursus is seemingly to emphasize the massive and, to critical eyes, wasteful expenditure associated with constructing the pyramids.[69]

Although the notion of ration lists carved into the facing stones of the Giza pyramids is presumably apocryphal—such accounts were kept, but on papyrus, as shown by the administrative documents from the reign of Khufu recently discovered at the site of Wadi al-Jarf—other inscriptions referenced by classical authors do have clear parallels within the Egyptian epigraphic tradition.[70] This is the case, for example, of the Theban inscriptions described by Tacitus, which clearly echo the bombastic military records of New Kingdom pharaohs like Thutmose III and his Ramesside successors. In describing Germanicus' visit to Thebes, Tacitus observes that "on piles of masonry Egyptian letters (*litterae Aegyptiae*) still remained, embracing the tale of old magnificence. . . . The tribute-lists of the subject nations were still legible: the weight of silver and gold, the number of weapons and horses, the temple-gifts of ivory and spices, together with the quantities of grain and other necessities of life to be paid by the separate countries; revenues no less imposing than those which are now exacted by the might of Parthia or by Roman power."[71] Such a display, down to the enumeration of booty garnered by Egypt's imperial expansion, is completely consistent with the form and content of existing New Kingdom royal inscriptions, most notably the Karnak annals of Thutmose III (which, it is worth noting, record the collection of plunder and tribute paid in precisely the kinds of materials listed here by Tacitus). For example, the spoils collected by Thutmose III's forces in the aftermath of the siege of Megiddo included nearly two thousand prisoners of war and "additionally, precious stones, gold, bowls, and a variety of vessels. [. . .], a large jar of Syrian workmanship, vases, bowls, plates, a variety of drinking cups, [x+]27 knives, adding up to 1784 deben. Golden disks which were hand crafted and many silver disks, adding up to 966 *deben* and one *kite*." The list goes on to record additional plunder in the form of statues, walking sticks, carrying chairs, furniture, and clothing, among other goods.[72]

Significantly, neither Strabo, writing in the age of Augustus, nor Tacitus, compiling his *Annals* under the Nerva-Antonine dynasty, betrays any particular anxiety about the role of writing in documenting (and supporting) an imperial regime. In fact, Tacitus draws an explicit parallel between the Theban tribute lists and the revenues exacted by the Roman Empire. Under the bureaucratic Roman state, the use of writing was no longer the clear signifier of alterity that it had been for earlier Greek commentators like Herodotus and Diodorus, and in the later Roman commentaries the focus of attention shifts from the use of writing to support the Egyptian monarchy to the character of the writing system itself and its purported religious function, as we shall see in Chapter 3.[73]

Egyptian Historical Records in Christian Sources

Like the classical authorities on whose work they drew so heavily, the church fathers were clearly aware of the long-standing tradition associating Egyptian writing, and especially the production of hieroglyphic inscriptions by the Egyptian priesthood, with the keeping of historical records. The second-century apologist and theologian Tatian, for example, claims that the Greeks learned to write history from the Egyptians' annals, and Christian chronographers from Julius Africanus in the third century to George Syncellus in the ninth made use of the Egyptian historiographic tradition in their efforts to reconstruct a universal chronology stretching back to the dawn of time (in the case of Syncellus) or, more modestly, to the birth of Abraham (in the case of Eusebius).[74] Claims about the antiquity and authority of the Egyptian sources, however, were not unproblematic for these Christian writers, who struggled to harmonize the lengthy chronologies calculated on the basis of Egyptian king lists with the considerably shorter chronologies that could be reconstructed from biblical genealogies.

This divergence of Egyptian and Judeo-Christian chronography was all the more troubling given that many of the Christian writers recognized the methodological need to consult sources outside the scriptural canon in order to flesh out a picture of truly universal history. Thus, Eusebius writes at the very beginning of his *Chronicle* that he thinks it would be appropriate to summarize the "diverse histories of the past which the Chaldeans and Assyrians have recorded, which the Egyptians have written in detail, and which the Greeks have narrated as accurately as possible" and to place this information alongside "the history of the Hebrew patriarchs." When the information provided by these Near Eastern chronicles fails to support the chronological and cultural primacy of the Hebrews (and, by extension, their Christian heirs), however, Eusebius is forced to denigrate the very sources whose utility he has just defended, remarking that "the Egyptians relate many fabulous accounts [about ancient times], as do the Chaldeans, since they reckon their literacy embraces more than 400,000 years. The Egyptians have written extensively . . . in fable-like, delirious ravings."[75] As William Adler has observed, "the presumed antiquity of the Chaldean and Egyptian chronicles was a double-edged sword"; it helped the Christian chronographers to stake their claim to greater antiquity than the Greeks, but it also opened up biblical chronology to unwelcome scrutiny.[76] The following pages will examine this tension over the Egyptian historiographic sources as it is expressed in two major works of late antique Christian chronography and history: the fourth-century *Chronicle* of Eusebius and Augustine's early fifth-century *De civitate Dei*.

Eusebius' *Chronicle* and the Value of Egyptian Historiography

Eusebius of Caesarea—bishop, bibliophile, and pioneering church historian—produced his *Chronicle* in Caesarea during the first decade or so of the fourth century. The work, which has survived to the present day via a patchwork collection of translations, expansions, and excerpts in the works of other writers, was originally composed in two parts. Part 1, the *Chronographia*, offered a narrative of world chronology going back to the time of Abraham and highlighting the various synchronisms that could be drawn between the historiographic traditions of different nations, including the Greeks, Hebrews, Egyptians, and Chaldaeans. Part 2, the *Chronici canones*, laid out this cross-cultural timeline in a tabular format, offering a kind of quick visual overview of the material contained in part 1.[77] As already noted, Eusebius himself highlighted the value of utilizing historiographic sources outside the scriptural canon in his attempt to reconstruct a universal chronology. Hence in addition to its intrinsic interest as a work of Christian historiography and polemic, one of the most important aspects of Eusebius' *Chronicle* from the perspective of modern scholarship is the fact that it preserves a massive amount of material quoted from earlier sources, some of which have since been lost.[78] These sources include earlier chronographers such as Alexander Polyhistor and Julius Africanus, both of whom, in turn, drew on the work of earlier Hellenistic annalists such as the Egyptian Manetho and his Babylonian counterpart Berossus.[79]

In introducing the section of his *Chronicle* that is based primarily on Egyptian sources, Eusebius quotes Diodorus on the quality and significance of the Egyptian historiographic tradition, noting that "the priests kept records about all of them (that is, the Egyptian kings) in their temple archives, which were transmitted continuously from ancient times from generation to generation."[80] Written in the Egyptian language and scripts, these "temple archives" of the priests would have been as incomprehensible to Eusebius as they had been to Diodorus. Consequently, Eusebius and his fellow Jewish and Christian chronographers were forced to access Egyptian historiographic sources through the mediation of authors competent to work in both Egyptian- and Greek-language milieus. Such an individual was Manetho, the Hellenistic Egyptian author of the *Aegyptiaca*, a Greek-language history of Egypt purportedly written for Ptolemy II. The text of the *Aegyptiaca* now survives only in fragments quoted by later writers, notably Josephus, Julius Africanus, Eusebius, and George Syncellus.[81] Manetho claimed (and was widely believed by later epitomizers) to have had direct access to ancient Egyptian-language sources; consequently, his reconstruction of Egyptian chronology, particularly royal history, was highly influential. Despite the fact that Manetho did not achieve any great popularity in his own time, his work was widely used, if not universally accepted, by Christian chronographers in late antiquity.[82]

Manetho's identity as an Egyptian and, more particularly, as an Egyptian *priest*, is referenced at various points in the surviving fragments of his work and in the Jewish and Christian commentary on that work. Flavius Josephus, who relied heavily on Manetho in his apologetic efforts to establish the great antiquity of the Jews, identifies him as "an Egyptian by descent, a man steeped in Greek culture, as is clear: for he wrote his national history in the Greek language, having translated, as he himself says, from the sacred tablets (ἐκ δέλτων ἱερῶν)."[83] Although the earliest testimonia to Manetho (Josephus, Aelian, Tertullian, and Eusebius) do not specifically identify him as a priest, the fourth-century *Expositio totius mundi et gentium* refers to him as "the Egyptian prophet," and the ninth-century Byzantine chronographer George Syncellus adds the information that Manetho was from the Delta city of Sebennytus, a contemporary of Ptolemy II, and "high priest of the polluted temples in Egypt (ἀρχιερεὺς τῶν ἐν Αἰγύπτῳ μιαρῶν ἱερῶν)."[84] Given that the association of the indigenous priesthood with the maintenance of historical records was deeply entrenched in the classical discourse on Egypt from a very early date, the identification of Manetho as an Egyptian priest serves to support the claim that he had privileged access to authoritative and restricted source material.[85]

In addition to preserving significant fragments of Manetho's widely known *Aegyptiaca*, Syncellus' *Ecloga Chronographica* also points to the existence of a work entitled the *Book of Sothis*, which seems also to have circulated under the name of Manetho. Syncellus introduces this text with a brief description of Manetho's purported sources and methodology. He writes:

> At the time of Ptolemy Philadelphos, he (Manetho) was serving as a high priest of the temples of idols (ἀρχιερεὺς τῶν ἐν Αἰγύπτῳ εἰδωλείων) in Egypt, [and wrote a work] on the basis of monuments lying in the Seriadic land (ἐκ τῶν ἐν τῇ Σηριαδικῇ γῇ κειμένων στηλῶν),[86] inscribed, he says, in a sacred language and priestly characters (ἱερᾷ φησι διαλέκτῳ καὶ ἱερογραφικοῖς γράμμασι κεχαρακτηρισμένων) by Thoth, the first Hermes, and translated after the Flood from the sacred language into Greek wording {with hieroglyphic characters} (καὶ ἑρμηνευθεισῶν μετὰ τὸν κατακλυσμὸν ἐκ τῆς ἱερᾶς διαλέκτου εἰς τὴν Ἑλληνίδα φωνὴν {γράμμασιν ἱερογλυφικοῖς}).[87] They were committed to books (ἀποτεθέντων ἐν βίβλοις) by the second Hermes, the son of Agathodaimon and the father of Tat, in the shrines of the holy places of Egypt (ἐν τοῖς ἀδύτοις τῶν ἱερῶν Αἰγύπτου).[88]

As represented by Syncellus, then, Manetho's work in the *Book of Sothis* was not merely derived from hieroglyphic Egyptian temple records (as is claimed for the *Aegyptiaca*). Rather, Manetho is said to have had access to antediluvian sources written, in hieroglyphs, by Thoth-Hermes himself.

This Hermetic connection is further elaborated as Syncellus goes on to quote the dedication of the *Book of Sothis*, which takes the form of a letter from Manetho to Ptolemy II. In this document, Manetho identifies himself as "high-priest and scribe of the sacred shrines of Egypt, born at Sebennytus and dwelling at Heliopolis" (ἀρχιερεὺς καὶ γραμματεὺς τῶν κατ᾽ Αἴγυπτον ἱερῶν ἀδύτου).[89] This claim of a Heliopolitan connection is no idle remark; not only was the city a very ancient center of Egyptian cult practice, but Greek tradition going back to Herodotus had identified the Heliopolitan priesthood as particularly wise. Thus, Herodotus writes that "the Heliopolitans are said to be the greatest chroniclers among the Egyptians," and Strabo claims to have seen the house where Plato himself lived during the fourteen years he allegedly spent studying with the priests of Heliopolis.[90] Having thus established his priestly bona fides, and his connection to this well-known ancient cult site, Manetho addresses the king: "as you are doing research about the future of the universe, in response to your request, I will produce for you those sacred books composed by our forefather, Hermes Thrice-Greatest." Shifting back into his own voice, Syncellus concludes, "this is what he says about the translation of the books by the second Hermes. Now after this, he also narrates about the five Egyptian classes [of kings], in thirty dynasties, called by them gods, demigods, spirits of the dead, and mortal men."[91]

As we have already seen, the connection between Thoth-Hermes and the Egyptian writing system was well established in both the classical and the patristic traditions, as was the belief that the Egyptian priests used the hieroglyphic script to maintain meticulous genealogical and historical records in inscriptions and "sacred books." The *Book of Sothis*, as presented by Syncellus, takes these associations a step further, linking the presentation of Egyptian history with the Hermetic tradition and with the legend, also reported by Josephus and Ammianus Marcellinus, that maintained that inscribed stelae had been erected prior to the Flood in an attempt to preserve the wisdom of Egypt for subsequent generations.[92] In both tone and content, the dedication of the *Book of Sothis* is strongly reminiscent of the claims made in some of the Greek magical papyri, which likewise purport to have been translated from hieroglyphic originals.[93] Although such claims were most commonly associated with texts from the magical and scientific, rather than historiographic, traditions, such was the vaunted authority of the Egyptian priests and their written sources that they could evidently be used to bolster the authority of texts in other genres as well.

So what did Christian chronographers like Eusebius and his later counterparts, including Syncellus, actually take from Manetho, whether from the *Aegyptiaca* or from the so-called *Book of Sothis*? Manetho's *Aegyptiaca*, described by Eusebius as "a three-volume work about the gods, demi-gods, spirits, and the mortal kings who ruled over the Egyptians, to the time of the Persian king Darius," furnishes the basic framework for much of the portion of Eusebius' *Chronicle* that deals with Egypt. Indeed, as a glance at any modern history of pharaonic Egypt can confirm, Manetho's division of pharaonic history into a sequence of dynasties, stretching from Menes in the First Dynasty to the last native Egyptian kings of the Thirtieth Dynasty, continues to serve as a fundamental organizing principle for the reconstruction of ancient Egyptian political history. In *Chron.* 1.44–54, Eusebius reproduces Manetho's dynastic schema with relatively little comment, seemingly content to accept the accuracy of his source, which is supported by Manetho's priestly credentials and by Diodorus' identification of the Egyptian priests as the individuals most responsible for the maintenance of historical records. As Eusebius himself remarks, "it is fitting and proper to add to this Manetho's account of the Egyptians, since his history seems quite reliable."[94] Following the conclusion of the third book of the *Aegyptiaca* with the reign of Darius, Eusebius proceeds to quote an extended passage of Josephus' *Contra Apionem* in which Josephus presents Manetho's account of the Hyksos kings.[95] In his *Ecloga Chronographica*, Syncellus likewise utilizes Manetho's dynastic framework in discussing Egyptian political history; indeed, he makes a side-by-side comparison of the epitomes of Manetho preserved in both Julius Africanus and Eusebius, generally viewing the former as the more accurate.[96]

Eusebius' decision to make such heavy use of Egyptian source material like Manetho's *Aegyptiaca* in his reconstruction of world chronology—and to accord such respect to those sources—was really a remarkable one, given the apologetic nature of the genre in which he was writing.[97] The respective value of Hebrew and other Near Eastern sources for the establishment of a universal chronology from the time of Creation was hardly an academic question for Christian chronographers, as claims to Hebrew (and thus, by extension, Christian) cultural and chronological primacy played a critical role in Christian apologetics. As one modern commentator writes, "from early on, Christianity was locked in an argument with Greco-Roman culture about the antiquity of its traditions. . . . Platonist and Stoic philosophers in this period widely adhered to the idea that earliest mankind had discovered philosophical knowledge about [the] cosmos and had hidden this in the symbolism of religion. The older a tradition was, the closer it therefore was to that primitive wisdom."[98] Christian chronographers, then, had a strong vested interest in demonstrating that Hebrew patriarchs and prophets such as Abraham and Moses predated the rise of the Greek philosophical and legal traditions. Chroniclers from the Egyptian and Near Eastern traditions, who were, as we have just seen, widely acknowledged as skilled record keepers, could offer support for the Christian effort to challenge Greek cultural primacy. However, those same chroniclers could also challenge the Hebrews' own claim to primeval antiquity.

With his extravagant claims of a 150,000-year recorded history for the Chaldaeans, Berossos was a notably difficult source for Christian authors to deal with, but his Egyptian counterpart, Manetho, presented challenges of his own.[99] Although Eusebius' predecessor and major source, Julius Africanus, utilized both Berossos and Manetho in his *Chronographiae*, his adherence to a rigid millennialist conception of history virtually obligated him to cast aspersions on the accuracy and authority of the two Hellenistic historians. Thus, he speaks critically of those Egyptians who, "in order to make something of an impression, have set forth outlandish cycles and myriads of years according to some sort of system based on astrological calculations made by them." He goes on to mention Manetho by name, stating that he was engaged in "telling falsehoods himself just like Berossos." The problem with both Berossos' and Manetho's accounts of history, in Africanus' view, is that they are simply too outrageously long to be harmonized with the "more modest and moderate" six-thousand-year chronology that could be reconstructed based on the Scriptures and that underpinned his calculation of the coming end times.[100] Grafton and Williams, in their discussion of Africanus, suggest that the chronicler brought Berossos and Manetho into his chronological discussion specifically in order to prove them wrong: "He wished to protect his readers from the infectious pagan belief in the deep antiquity of the world—a belief that could lend support to the popular view that the Chaldeans and Egyptians had cultivated the sciences for thousands of years."[101] Africanus, then, was seemingly unmoved by claims that the cuneiform sources utilized by Berossos and the hieroglyphic sources underlying Manetho's *Aegyptiaca* held any claim to greater authority (or antiquity) than the Hebrew Scriptures.

Although Eusebius himself did not adhere to such a rigid chronological model as Julius Africanus—in fact, he was willing to concede that even the Scriptures themselves could not always provide an accurate chronological record—he nonetheless shared Africanus' belief in the primacy of the Hebrews and his concerns with the overly lengthy chronologies of the Egyptians and Babylonians. For this reason, although he shows himself more willing than Africanus to make use of Berossos and Manetho, Eusebius finds himself needing to modulate those chroniclers' claims in an effort to harmonize them with the biblical tradition. This could result in some questionable argumentation; hence, for example, Eusebius' dubious contention that the "years" recorded in Egyptian historical records are actually "lunar years," or months. The remaining discrepancy, Eusebius goes on to say, can be explained by the phenomenon of coregency and the tendency of Egyptian chroniclers to treat contemporaneous kings as if they had reigned sequentially: "if the number of years seems excessive, we must examine the reasons for it. It is conceivable that there were many kings ruling in Egypt simultaneously."[102] Although Eusebius was not alone in these contentions—the theory that Egyptian regnal "years" were actually lunar months had already been proposed by Diodorus in an attempt to rationalize the extremely long life spans credited to Egypt's archaic rulers—they were not universally accepted, even by other Christian commentators.[103] Particularly outspoken in their criticisms of Eusebius' sources and methodology were his fifth-century Alexandrian successors, the chronographers Annianus and Panodorus; their lost chronicles, now known principally from quotations in Syncellus, were sharply critical of what Annianus called Eusebius' "deranged thinking," which caused his chronology to differ from theirs by some 290 years.[104] Syncellus inherited this particular critical stance, and although he did on occasion defend his illustrious Caesarean predecessor, he also criticized Eusebius on various grounds, including erroneous calculations, faulty logic, and failure to properly vet his sources.[105]

What can we conclude about the significance of Egyptian hieroglyphs for Eusebius and for the Christian chronographic tradition more generally speaking? It is clear that the Christian chronographers, like their Jewish forebears, were well aware of the tradition that positioned Egyptian priests as the keepers of their country's ancient historiographic legacy. Consequently, Egyptian historiographic texts are variously described in the Jewish and Christian sources as "priestly writings" and "sacred books," among other designations.[106] These sources were obviously not accessible to Greek- and Latin-speaking chronographers in their original form, thus we encounter them in the chronographic tradition principally as mediated by Manetho's *Aegyptiaca* and the various epitomes of the latter which were in circulation by late antiquity. Like the *Babyloniaca* of Berossus, Manetho's work offered both promise and danger to authors seeking to challenge Greek claims to cultural and chronological primacy. It is by now well established that chronography played an integral role in both Jewish and, later, Christian polemic against the Greeks and in the efforts of Christian apologists to establish the antiquity of their religious traditions.[107] Eusebius consequently made extensive use of Manetho in his efforts to reconstruct a universal chronology from the time of Abraham. However, as William Adler has noted, the access to deep history provided by Berossus and Manetho was, in some respects, "too much of a good thing," as the lengthy chronologies that both authors offered threatened the primacy of Greek and biblical traditions alike."[108] Cautious in his approach to source material that diverged so significantly from chronological calculations based on Scripture, but still wishing to utilize it, Eusebius equivocated, proposing various strategies for harmonizing the Manethonian and biblical chronological systems but stopping short of fully accepting or rejecting either one. Although such an

approach left Eusebius open to significant criticism, as noted above, it indicates that the Egyptian historiographic tradition, as represented by Manetho,
was an integral part of late antique chronographic thinking and could not be
simply dismissed or ignored. Indeed, the fifth century saw Augustine confronted with similar concerns and forced to grapple with the question of the
nature and authority of Egyptian source material in his own historical and
chronographic writings.

Augustine's *De civitate Dei* and the Problem
of Egyptian Historiography

Although Augustine is not typically counted among the ranks of late antique
Christian chronographers, he devoted a significant amount of space in *De
civitate Dei* to the question of world chronology and the age of the earth.
Relying heavily on Jerome's Latin translation of Eusebius' *Chronici canones*
for his understanding of chronological synchronisms, Augustine inherited
the same fundamental problem that had plagued Africanus, Eusebius, and
their fellow Christian chronographers: that is, the vast discrepancy between
the chronological span provided by Near Eastern authorities such as Berossos and Manetho and the much shorter scripturally based chronologies that
placed the creation of the universe circa 5500 B.C.E.[109] Augustine's dependence
on and engagement with Eusebius is especially pronounced in book 12, which
deals with the creation of mankind and with various theories of human history, and in book 18, which outlines a series of synchronisms between biblical
and secular histories.

Despite his apparent regard for Eusebius' *Chronicle* (or, more precisely, for
the *Chronici canones*), and his willingness to make use of chronological arguments for his own apologetic purposes—as, for example, in *Civ.* 18.37, where
he utilizes Eusebius' synchronism of Pythagoras with the date of the Exodus
to argue for the chronological precedence of Hebrew prophecy over the Greek
philosophical tradition—Augustine was highly conscious of the dangers posed
by the acceptance of Near Eastern historiographic records over and against
scriptural authority. His stance in this regard is more rigid than Eusebius' own
approach. Eusebius was willing to allow for a certain amount of chronological
ambiguity, accepting that even the biblical tradition itself could not produce
an absolutely reliable chronology for the earliest ages of human existence and
acknowledging that it might never be possible to fully reconcile the biblical

chronological tradition with the various Near Eastern chronologies. Augustine, however, absolutely rejects such equivocation. In his view, when the various chronographic traditions diverge, scriptural chronology is automatically to be preferred, "for the truth of the account of the past given in these books is shown by the very fact that their predictions of future events have been so entirely fulfilled."[110]

The three-way comparison of the Egyptian, Greek, and biblical chronologies for the Persian and Macedonian empires that Augustine outlines in *Civ.* 12.11 clearly demonstrates that he was aware of some of the methods by which earlier chronographers had attempted to harmonize divergent chronological traditions, including the argument that the regnal "years" attested in the ancient Egyptian historiographic sources actually represent a period shorter than the full solar year. However, when such methods fail to produce agreement among the sources, Augustine argues that the shorter Greek chronology should be preferred to the longer Egyptian one because it yields a result closer to that provided by the Scriptures: "we must be more ready to have faith in the former, for it does not exceed the true account of the years contained in our writings, which are truly sacred."[111] The sacred origins of biblical chronology, in Augustine's assessment, trump any possible authority that might be vested in the chronographic traditions and historiographic records of other nations, and any notion that biblical chronology might be checked against or corrected by these outside sources is utterly rejected.

Augustine returns to this theme of problematizing the antiquity and authority of Near Eastern historiographic sources multiple times in *De civitate Dei*, and he reserves special scorn for the widely held notion that the Egyptian priests transmitted accurate historical information via their hieroglyphic records. In introducing the chronographic argument of *Civ.* 12.11, discussed above, he directly refutes what he calls "certain wholly untruthful writings which purport to contain the history of many thousands of years of time." These sources are automatically suspect because they contradict the much shorter biblical chronology: "for *we* compute from the sacred writings that six thousand years have not yet passed since the creation of man. Hence, the writings which make reference to far more thousands of years than there have been are vain, and contain no trustworthy authority on the subject."

As his chief exemplar of such a misleading document, Augustine cites a letter purportedly written by Alexander the Great to his mother, Olympias, detailing "the narrative which he had received from a certain Egyptian priest, which the latter had taken from writings held to be sacred among the Egyptians, and which contained an account of kingdoms known also to Greek history."[112] Augustine is clearly aware of the long-standing tradition associating Egyptian priests with historical record keeping, but the theological imperative of his work, which is aimed at the validation of his scripturally based chronology, precludes him granting any authority to the Egyptian sources.

The purported letter of Alexander to Olympias is referenced at two other points in *De civitate Dei*, and in those references Augustine provides some additional information about the nature and content of this document. In *Civ.* 8.5, where Augustine argues that the Platonists have come closer than any other philosophical school to a correct understanding of God, he speaks of written sources dealing with the "sacred rites" devoted to the various gods and notes that "to this same class of writings belong the letters which Alexander of Macedon wrote to his mother." He goes on to say that "in them, he (Alexander) relates what had been revealed to him by the Egyptian high priest Leo" and that this same Leo, fearful "because he had revealed a mystery, . . . adjured and admonished Alexander that, when he had communicated these things in writing to his mother, he was to command that the letter should be burnt." The content of the letter, according to Augustine, demonstrated that various mythological figures honored with cultic rites, including Romulus, Hercules, and Aesclepius, were in fact mortal men.

Although such a euhemeristic interpretation of classical mythology is not inconsistent with Augustine's own views, he objects to the notion that such individuals should be accorded cultic honors and prefers the Platonic theory of an incorporeal deity as theologically closer to the Christian understanding of divinity. Augustine returns to this same theme later when he differentiates between the respect paid to Christian martyrs and the sacred rites of the polytheistic traditions. Singling out Egyptian religious practices for particular scorn, he writes,

> It is written that Isis, the Egyptian goddess and wife of Osiris, and
> all their ancestors, were royal personages. . . . All the great evils
> which she wrought were recorded for posterity not by poets, but in
> the mystic writings of the Egyptians. Let those who will and can
> do so read the letter written by Alexander to his mother Olympias
> in which he relates the things revealed to him by the priest Leo;
> and let those who read reflect upon it and see what manner of men

they were, and what their deeds were, for whom sacred rites were
instituted after their death as if they were gods.[113]

In Augustine's account, then, the "letter of Alexander" appears to serve as a
convenient shorthand for the transmission of two different Egyptian textual
traditions: ritual texts detailing the cultic honors paid to the gods, and historiographic sources extending into the distant past and cataloguing the deeds of
famous men and women who were later deified; needless to say, the Christian
theologian finds both to be equally objectionable.

That a letter pertaining to theological matters did indeed circulate under
the name of Alexander is known from a number of attestations in the works of
various Christian apologists, who cite it (or at least its existence) in support of
their larger euhemeristic arguments against pagan mythology and cult practice.
Minucius Felix writes, for example, that "the famous Alexander the Great, of
Macedon, in a remarkable letter to his mother, wrote that his power had awed a
priest into unfolding to him the secret concerning deified men; in it, he makes
Vulcan first of the line, followed by the family of Jupiter." Athenagoras adds the
detail that Alexander is to be trusted in this because he, like Herodotus, had as
his interlocutors the priests of Heliopolis, Memphis, and Thebes.[114]

The identity of "the high priest Leo," said by Augustine to be Alexander's Egyptian source, has long been the subject of debate, with some scholars
taking Augustine's statement essentially at face value, and others preferring to
see Leo as the actual author of the letter that subsequently circulated under
Alexander's name.[115] Whichever of these roles the historical Leo may have fulfilled, the testimonia to the letter, in Augustine's oeuvre and elsewhere, utilize a
number of common tropes pertaining to Egyptian source material that were in
wide circulation in late antiquity. These include the recognition that Egyptian
priests, particularly those attached to prominent cultic sites like Heliopolis and
Thebes, were the guardians of Egypt's literary and historiographic heritage, and
the notion that these priestly records were bound up in a tradition of secrecy
and arcane wisdom that could be transmitted to outsiders only at great risk
(witness, for example, the anxiety of Alexander's priestly informant in *Civ.* 8.5).

The problematization of Egyptian source material like the purported letter of Alexander goes hand in hand with Augustine's claim that the Egyptian
writing system was a relatively recent invention, attributable to Isis rather than
to Thoth-Hermes-Mercury. Although the classical discourse on hieroglyphs
had enshrined the notion that Egyptian priestly records preserved accurate
historiographic information stretching back into the primordial past, leading

Christian chronographers to try and mine this information for ammunition in their polemic against the Greeks, the lengthy king lists provided by Manetho and subsequently transmitted by Africanus and Eusebius in their chronographic studies threatened the fundamental Judeo-Christian belief in the chronological primacy of the Hebrews and therefore had to be approached with caution, if at all. For Augustine, who argued much more strongly than Eusebius for the absolute authority of scriptural chronology, the Egyptian historiographic sources (like their Babylonian counterparts, transmitted by Berossus) could not be used independently to verify scriptural chronology but could only be checked against that standard and rejected when they diverged from it. The attribution of the invention of hieroglyphs to Isis "not much more than two thousand years ago" (*Civ.* 18.41) vitiates the claim that the Egyptian historiographic tradition, as preserved in hieroglyphic "priestly writings," could have extended into an earlier period than the Hebrew scriptures and allows Augustine to ignore the Egyptian material when it suits him to do so. His approach is not entirely consistent, however, as we can see in the case of the letter (or letters?) of Alexander. As an exemplar of the euhemeristic reinterpretation of the pagan gods, Augustine cites this pseudepigraphic work as an authoritative source (*Civ.* 8.5 and 8.27); as a representative specimen of the Egyptian historiographic tradition, however, Augustine classifies the same text as "wholly untruthful" and discounts it entirely (*Civ.* 12.11).

Conclusion

Although many of the classical authors who discuss hieroglyphs seem to have been content to follow Egyptian tradition and acknowledge "the famous old god whose name was Theuth" as the inventor of the hieroglyphic script, this view posed a certain conundrum for the church fathers in their efforts to challenge Greek cultural primacy and to assert the antiquity of the Jews and thus, by extension, that of the Christians as heirs to the Hebrew biblical tradition. On the one hand, if hieroglyphic sources existed that reached back into the primordial past, such documents might allow Christian chronographers to extend their accounts of world history back to a much earlier point than was possible on the basis of the Greek historiographic record—a fact that was seen as vindicating the (Judeo-)Christian claim that the Greeks were a young civilization with respect to their Near Eastern forebears. On the other hand, the great antiquity claimed for the hieroglyphic and cuneiform traditions represented a real challenge to the church fathers' reconstruction of world chronology computed on the basis of Scripture, which produced a timeline of only about six thousand years from creation to late antiquity.

The church fathers responded to these challenges in a few different ways. Eusebius' *Chronicle* represents one possible approach. Although he acknowledged the antiquity and, to some extent, the authority of the Egyptian historiographic tradition and made extensive use of Egyptian historical records as mediated by Manetho, he also recognized that those records had the potential to challenge scriptural chronology and offered a variety of possible methodologies for harmonizing the divergent traditions, including recalculating the length of Egyptian regnal years and compressing the Egyptian king lists by looking for cases of coregency or simultaneous dynasties. In his assessment, Manetho's account is a "fitting and proper" source for Christian historiography, even if it must be used cautiously. Augustine's approach to the same material is, in contrast, simultaneously more critical and less scholarly. Although he acknowledged that the Egyptian priests were known for keeping extensive historical records, when those records failed to harmonize with the scriptural tradition he saw no reason to make use of them. He also called into question the widely held tradition that Thoth-Hermes-Mercury was the inventor of hieroglyphs, which placed the invention of writing in Egypt in the depths of the mythical past. Such a tradition, which would seem to validate the common notion that the Egyptians possessed a particularly ancient historiographic tradition, did not serve Augustine's apologetic purposes. Far more congenial, from his perspective, was an alternative tradition that identified Isis as the inventor of Egyptian writing. Granting this role to Isis, who in Augustine's euhemeristic reworking of Egyptian mythology was a queen of Egypt approximately two thousand years before his own time, undercut the claims to great antiquity conventionally accorded to the hieroglyphic writing system and ensured that the historiographic sources emanating from that tradition could be dismissed as needed when they conflicted with scriptural chronology.

As the examples of Eusebius and Augustine demonstrate, the church fathers typically expressed little intellectual interest in the actual history of the hieroglyphic script, nor (with a few exceptions that will be discussed in Chapter 3) were they especially concerned with understanding how that script functioned. They received from the classical historians and geographers a well-defined and well-rehearsed discourse on hieroglyphs whose salient points—invention by Thoth-Hermes-Mercury, great antiquity, connection to the Egyptian priesthood, use for writing historical records—they redeployed as they saw fit in their own works. And when those tropes failed to conform to the dictates of their apologetic or polemical writings, they could either seek out variant traditions that better suited their line of argumentation (as Augustine did in the case of Isis), or dismiss the Egyptian material entirely (as he did in his defense of scriptural chronology). In the end, these patristic sources tell us very little about hieroglyphs themselves, but a great deal about both the persistence and, crucially, the malleability of the classical discourse on hieroglyphs that the church fathers had inherited.

Chapter 3

Encoding the Wisdom of Egypt

In the fifth book of his *Stromateis*, the Christian theologian Clement of Alexandria (ca. 150–ca. 215 C.E.) offers a famously enigmatic description of the three principal ancient Egyptian scripts, which he identifies as epistolographic (ἐπιστολογραφική), hieratic (ἱερατική), and hieroglyphic (ἱερογλυφική). After discussing the different types of hieroglyphic signs and explicating, or attempting to explicate, a handful of Egyptian symbols, Clement goes on to speak more generally about the Egyptians' motivation for using hieroglyphs. "All then," he says, "in a word, who have spoken of divine things, both Barbarians (Βάρβαροι) and Greeks ("Ελληνες), have veiled the first principles of things, and delivered the truth in enigmas, and symbols, and allegories, and metaphors, and such-like tropes."[1] Although Clement's presentation of the various scripts, which will be discussed in more detail below, suggests that he had access to some accurate information about Egyptian writing systems, his contention that hieroglyphs served the explicit purpose of concealing information about the divine betrays his equal indebtedness to the classical discourse on hieroglyphs. The ideas about the hieroglyphic script that Clement articulates in *Stromateis* 5—notably, that it has a fundamentally symbolic quality and that it is intimately connected to the religious and intellectual traditions of the indigenous Egyptian priesthood—have roots that reach at least as far back as the work of Diodorus two centuries earlier and branches stretching as far forward as the Renaissance humanists who prized hieroglyphs as a universal means of symbolic communication.

In the previous chapter, we saw that the classical authors who first wrote about hieroglyphs established a series of tropes about Egyptian writing that proved to be remarkably stable over time—so much so that the Christian writers who later turned their attention to the subject of hieroglyphic writing were essentially forced to deal with the same themes, which they adapted to suit their individual theological agendas. The present chapter likewise examines two of the most tenacious ideas about hieroglyphs ever to emerge from the classical sources, the symbolic nature of the hieroglyphic script and its use to conceal Egyptian priestly wisdom, and it considers the way that these themes are dealt with in late antique Christian sources. As we shall see, the notion of the "wisdom of Egypt," encoded in hieroglyphic inscriptions and carved on temple walls, represented something of a conundrum to Christian theologians. Christian and non-Christian sources alike tend to agree that hieroglyphs were used to conceal esoteric Egyptian knowledge, but they place a very different premium on that knowledge. Moreover, although church fathers like Augustine roundly condemned the "great evils . . . recorded for posterity not by poets, but in the mystic writings of the Egyptians," they were simultaneously forced to confront the claim, irrefutable because grounded in Scripture, that Moses himself was "instructed in all the wisdom of the Egyptians." Moses' connection to the wisdom of Egypt meant that Christian authors could not dismiss or reject the concept entirely, so in the late antique sources various strategies were deployed to problematize the wisdom tradition passed down by means of hieroglyphic texts. Among other charges, "Egyptian wisdom" is linked to boastfulness, corruption, and heresy; it is said to conduce to idolatry; and, perhaps most important, it is ultimately said to have been rendered unnecessary by new Christian modes of learning and understanding, which privilege the notion of wisdom "taught by the Spirit" over human wisdom passed down through mundane processes of textual transmission.[2]

Egyptian Scripts in Classical and Christian Sources

As described above in Chapter 1, the Egyptians utilized three principal scripts to render their language in written form: hieroglyphic, hieratic, and, beginning in the seventh century B.C.E., Demotic. The majority of ancient commentators, however, followed Herodotus in recognizing only a broad division between "sacred" (hieroglyphic) and "common" (Demotic) scripts. Diodorus echoes this view, while providing additional information about the educational process; he states,

> In the education of their sons the priests teach them two kinds
> of writing (γράμματα διττά), that which is called "sacred" (τά

τε ἱερὰ καλούμενα) and that which is used in the more general instruction (καὶ τὰ κοινοτέραν ἔχοντα τὴν μάθησιν). . . . As to the general mass of the Egyptians, they are instructed from their childhood by their fathers or kinsmen in the practices proper to each manner of life as previously described by us; but as for reading and writing, the Egyptians at large give their children only a superficial instruction in them, and not all do this, but for the most part only those who are engaged in the crafts.[3]

Later, he observes that "of the two kinds of writing (γράμματα) which the Egyptians have, that which is known as popular (δημώδης) is learned by everyone, while that which is called sacred (ἱερά) is understood only by the priests of the Egyptians, who learn it from their fathers as one of the things which are not divulged (ἐν ἀπορρήτοις μανθάνοντας)." This correlates well with the information on scribal pedagogy provided by the Egyptian sources, which indicate that apprentice scribes typically began their training with hieratic (later Demotic) and advanced to the study of the hieroglyphic script only if they intended to pursue a career in the priesthood.[4]

Only two ancient authors are known to have acknowledged the existence of not two, but *three* Egyptian scripts, and even then the distinctions that they draw do not always align perfectly with the modern tripartite classification of hieroglyphic, hieratic, and Demotic.[5] The Neoplatonist philosopher Porphyry of Tyre (ca. 234–ca. 305 C.E.) writes in his *Vita Pythagorae* that the philosopher traveled to Egypt, where "he lived with the priests, and learned the language and wisdom of the Egyptians, and three kinds of letters, the epistolic, the hieroglyphic, and symbolic (γραμμάτων δὲ τρισσὰς διαφοράς, ἐπιστολογραφικῶν τε καὶ ἱερογλυφικῶν καὶ συμβολικῶν), whereof one imitates the common way of speaking, while the others express the sense by allegory and parable."[6] For Porphyry, therefore, although he claims to recognize three scripts, the primary distinction is actually between the script he calls "epistolic" (a reference to Demotic, known in Egyptian as *sẖ n šꜥ.t*, or "document-writing") and two forms of hieroglyphic scripts; the existence of hieratic is thus elided completely. Interestingly, however, later medieval Arabic sources that speak of Pythagoras' studies in Egypt do appear to refer to hieratic as one of the objects of the philosopher's learning. For example, the tenth/eleventh-century writer Ibn Fatik states that Pythagoras "attached himself to the priests in Egypt and learned wisdom from them. He excelled in the language of the Egyptians with the three types of script: the script of the commoners, the script of the elite which is the cursive one of the priests, and the script of the kings."[7]

The distinction Porphyry draws between "hieroglyphic" and "symbolic" characters echoes the work of the second-century church father Clement of Alexandria, whose discussion of Egyptian writing appears in the *Stromateis*, a compilation of observations on a diverse array of religious subjects including, but not limited to, the relationship between Christianity and Greek philosophy.[8] Book 5 of the *Stromateis* deals with the role of faith (πίστις) and knowledge (γνῶσις) in the individual seeker's efforts to grasp the truth of God. In this book, as in the rest of the text, Clement is concerned with the tension between the notions of revelation and concealment; this leads him to examine the various means by which religious truths have been expressed in figurative language not only in Hebrew prophecy but also by Greeks and Egyptians. This leads him to expound at some length on the nature, as he understood it, of the Egyptian writing system. He writes, "those who, among the Egyptians, receive instruction learn firstly the style of Egyptian writing called epistolographic (ἐπιστολογραφική); and secondly, the hieratic (ἱερατική) style, which the sacred scribes practice." He goes on, in a difficult passage that has generated a great deal of philological commentary, to distinguish between different types of hieroglyphic signs:

> Lastly, the hieroglyphic type, which, in part, expresses things literally by means of primary letters and which, in part, is pictographic (ἧς ἡ μέν ἐστι διὰ τῶν πρώτων στοιχείων κυριολογική, ἡ δὲ συμβολική). In the pictographic method (τῆς δὲ συμβολικῆς), one sort expresses things literally by imitation (ἡ μὲν κυριολογεῖται κατὰ μίμησιν), another sort writes, so to speak, in a metaphorical fashion (ἡ δ' ὥσπερ τροπικῶς γράφεται), while a third is frankly allegorizing by means of certain enigmas (ἡ δὲ ἄντικρυς ἀλληγορεῖται κατά τινας αἰνιγμούς).[9]

Clement then attempts to explain in more detail the system he has just outlined. He writes, "thus, wishing to express 'sun' in writing, they make a circle, and for 'moon,' the form of a crescent, according to the 'literal' type (κατὰ τὸ κυριολογούμενον εἶδος). In the 'metaphorical' type (τροπικῶς), they carve (signs), transferring and transposing (them) on the basis of their affinity (κατ' οἰκειότητα μετάγοντες καὶ μετατιθέντες), in part substituting them (for other signs) and in part changing their shapes entirely (τὰ δ' ἐξαλλάττοντες, τὰ δὲ πολλαχῶς μετασχηματίζοντες)." Although he does not provide specific examples of this "tropic" or "metaphorical" style of writing, he notes that "it is in this way that, wishing to transmit praises of their kings by means of religious myths, they inscribe (them) in bas-reliefs (ἀναγράφουσι διὰ τῶν ἀναγλύφων)." Finally, Clement offers a series of examples of what he refers to as the "enigmatic" type of hieroglyphs, in which the stars are represented by serpents "because of their sinuous paths" and the sun is represented by a scarab because of that creature's natural qualities.[10]

The potential significance of this passage as a key to the decipherment of hieroglyphs was recognized early on, and Clement figures prominently in several of the notable early modern studies of hieroglyphs, including William Warburton's lengthy excursus on Egyptian writing in *The Divine Legation of Moses Demonstrated* and Georg Zoega's *De origine et usu obeliscorum*.[11] In many respects, however, the text represents a false signpost on the route to decipherment. The rather obscure terminology that Clement uses to characterize the different types of hieroglyphic signs, coupled with his insistence on the symbolic qualities of the script, largely frustrated attempts to use *Stromateis* 5 as a means of explaining how hieroglyphs functioned. Rather than Clement providing the key to decipherment, in the end it was Champollion's decipherment of the Rosetta Stone that provided the key to reading Clement, and modern reinterpretations of this passage were, in turn, swiftly deployed to support Champollion's radical new theories.[12]

The most convincing reassessment of Clement's description of hieroglyphs in light of the modern Egyptological understanding of the script is that of Jozef Vergote.[13] Unlike earlier scholars such as Albert Deiber and Pierre Marestaing, who felt that Clement possessed, at best, incomplete and secondhand knowledge of the hieroglyphic writing system, Vergote argues that Clement's understanding of hieroglyphs was highly accurate, and he takes the outline of the hieroglyphic system presented in *Stromateis* 5 as an essentially faithful representation of the various types of signs now known to have existed in the hieroglyphic repertoire.[14] In his analysis of this passage, which forms the basis of the translation given above, Vergote identifies references not only to ideograms (which "express things literally by imitation") and cryptograms (which function "by means of certain enigmas"), but also to alphabetic signs ("primary letters") and bi- or triliteral phonograms (signs that function "in a metaphorical fashion"). Vergote's reading of πρῶτα στοιχεῖα as a reference to the corpus of alphabetic signs is particularly significant, insofar as this makes Clement the only surviving ancient author to clearly acknowledge the existence of hieroglyphs that functioned on a phonetic, rather than symbolic, basis.[15]

The similarity between Clement's characterization of hieroglyphs and that of Porphyry, already mentioned above, has frequently been noted. Although it is not impossible that Porphyry drew on the text of *Stromateis* 5, it is more commonly held that Porphyry and Clement both depended on a common source for their understanding of the various Egyptian scripts, and the most likely candidate for that source is the *Hieroglyphica* of the Alexandrian Stoic philosopher and *hierogrammateus* Chaeremon.[16] This first-century source, now lost but for scattered quotations preserved in the works of other authors, circulated widely in the ancient world, and its author was respected as a major authority on the nature and use of hieroglyphs.[17] It is worth considering, however, that if Clement did owe his knowledge that some hieroglyphs functioned phonetically rather than symbolically to Chaeremon, this information is not explicitly mentioned in either the surviving fragments of Chaeremon's own work or in any of the secondary works that are known to have relied on his *Hieroglyphica*, all of which insist on the fundamentally *symbolic* character of the hieroglyphic script.[18] The equivocation of the sources on this point calls into question whether or not Vergote's reading of this passage actually reflects the way Clement and Chaeremon were being understood in antiquity. That is, Vergote may have succeeded in reconstructing the intended meaning of Clement's description of hieroglyphs, but this reconstruction may not fully align with the text's ancient reception. A number of factors could have contributed to this mismatch, including Clement's obscure terminology and the fact that he himself seems to have been much more interested in the symbolic and cryptographic uses of hieroglyphs than in their phonetic function.[19] As noted above, Clement's discussion of the Egyptian writing system appears in a chapter of the *Stromateis* devoted to the use of figurative or enigmatic language for the concealment of religious knowledge, and after he outlines the different types of Egyptian writing, Clement goes on to say that hieroglyphs are one mechanism among many for "deliver[ing] the truth in enigmas."[20] In other words, even if he may have been better informed than most of his contemporaries about the different types of hieroglyphic signs, Clement still seems to have been working very much within the parameters of the classical discourse on hieroglyphs, which insisted on the notion the hieroglyphs were, above all, a means of rendering in written form the secrets of the Egyptian priesthood, while at the same time protecting those secrets from the uneducated majority of the population. It is to these notions of

symbolism and secrecy that we must now turn, as they are a critical factor in
the development of the late antique discourse on hieroglyphs.

Hieroglyphs as Symbols from Diodorus to Horapollo

The first author to claim that hieroglyphs functioned as a fundamentally symbolic script, rather than a phonetic one, was Diodorus. He highlights the non-
syllabic nature of Egyptian writing in a lengthy passage to which he adduces
multiple examples of hieroglyphs and their purported meanings:

> Now it is found that the forms of their letters (τύπος) take the
> shape (ὁμοίους) of animals of every kind, and of the members
> of the human body, and of implements and especially carpenters'
> tools; for their writing (ἡ γραμματικὴ παρ' αὐτοῖς) does not
> express the intended concept (οὐ γὰρ . . . τὸν ὑποκείμενον λόγον
> ἀποδίδωσιν) by means of syllables joined one to another (ἐκ τῆς
> τῶν συλλαβῶν συνθέσεως), but by means of the significance
> of the objects which have been copied (ἐξ ἐμφάσεως τῶν
> μεταγραφομένων) and by its figurative meaning which has been
> impressed upon the memory by practice (καὶ μεταφορᾶς μνήμῃ
> συνηθλημένης) . . . for by paying close attention to the significance
> which is inherent in each object (ἐν ἑκάστοις ἐνούσαις ἐμφάσεσι
> συνακολουθοῦντες) and by training their minds through drill and
> exercise of the memory over a long period, they read from habit
> (ἀναγινώσκουσι) everything which has been written.[21]

The implications of Diodorus' remarks are clear; in his view, hieroglyphs do
not represent individual phonemes or syllables, nor does he acknowledge
any connection between the script and the spoken Egyptian language. Signs,
which he emphasizes are primarily depictions of animals, body parts, and
other material objects, obtain their meaning from the characteristics or "significance" (ἔμφασις) of the items they represent, and Diodorus highlights the
key role of memory and convention in the practical application of this system.
Because of the nonphonetic nature of the script, texts cannot be sounded out
syllable by syllable, so the meaning of each individual sign must be memorized
in order for trained scribes to be able to "read from habit everything which
has been written."

Within the Egyptian writing system as it is now understood, the closest parallel to the kind of symbols Diodorus describes here are determinatives, signs that are not read phonetically but that serve as metalinguistic classifiers to identify semantic categories and parts of speech. When Diodorus writes, for example, that "the hawk signifies to them everything which happens swiftly, since this animal is practically the swiftest of winged creatures. And the concept portrayed is then transferred (μεταφέρεταί τε ὁ λόγος), by the appropriate metaphorical transfer (ταῖς οἰκείαις μεταφοραῖς), to all swift things and to everything to which swiftness is appropriate, very much as if they had been named," it is possible to see a reference to the use of a sign (the hawk) as a determinative, applied to a group of words that share a common semantic or conceptual link (in this case, the notion of swiftness).[22] The problem is, of course, that Diodorus fails to recognize that determinatives are ordinarily used in conjunction with phonograms to form larger semantic units; they do not, in themselves, convey the full meaning of the words they are used to determine, and ideograms, which *do* have the potential to represent entire words, also *do* have a phonetic value, contrary to Diodorus' claims. Diodorus' failure to see the link between spoken and written Egyptian, coupled with his insistent claim that there was a direct link between the meaning of individual signs and the objects they represent, lays the foundation for the profound misunderstanding of the hieroglyphic system exhibited by later commentators.[23]

Diodorus' observations are echoed, in greater or lesser detail, in many subsequent Greek and Latin discussions of hieroglyphs. Lucan, for example, distinguishes between the Egyptians' symbolic writing system, which he seems to regard as an earlier and more primitive mode of communication, and the Phoenicians' discovery of the alphabet and its potential to record spoken language: "These Phoenicians first made bold, if report speak true, to record speech in rude characters for future ages, before Egypt had learned to fasten together the reeds of her river, and when only the figures of birds, beasts, and other animals, carved in stone, preserved the utterances of her wise men (*et saxis tantum volucresque feraeque / Sculptaquae servabant magicas animalia linguas*)."[24] Similarly, Lucian distinguishes between proper Greek letters and "signs and symbols (σημεῖα καὶ χαρακτῆρας) such as the many that the Egyptians use instead of letters—dog- and lion-headed men."[25] Perhaps the clearest statement of the difference between Egyptian writing and the phonetic alphabets of the Greeks and Romans is articulated by Ammianus, who writes, "For not as nowadays, when a fixed and easy series of letters (*litterarum numerus praestitutus et facilis*) expresses whatever the mind of man may conceive, did the ancient Egyptians also write; but individual characters stood for individual nouns and verbs (*singulae litterae singulis nominibus serviebant et verbis*); and sometimes they meant whole phrases (*non numquam significabant integros sensus*)."[26] Although it is true that in the Egyptian system individual signs (ideograms) can represent whole words, Ammianus, like Diodorus, ignored (or was unaware of) the underlying phonetic basis of the script, and both authors' insistence on the notion that entire phrases can be condensed into single signs played a major role in the hieroglyphic speculation of later centuries.[27]

Although there was widespread agreement among most Greek and Roman commentators that the Phoenicians should be credited with the discovery of the alphabet and its subsequent dissemination to the Greek-speaking world, a handful of sources suggest that the Egyptians themselves were the originators of alphabetic writing; ironically, this view is sometimes expressed by the very same authors who insist on the *symbolic* nature of Egyptian hieroglyphs. For example, although Tacitus states that "the Egyptians . . . were the first people to represent thought by symbols," he goes on to say that the Egyptians claimed to have invented the alphabet, an innovation that then spread to the Phoenicians and then the Greeks.[28] This view has some earlier precedents; Plato, in the *Philebus*, describes the creation by Thoth of a phonetic system of writing where individual sounds were assigned to individual letters, and Diodorus similarly reports that, according to the Egyptians, Hermes had invented the alphabet.[29] Pliny the Elder, although he considers the Assyrian writing system to be the most ancient, notes that one of his sources "records that a person named Menos invented the alphabet in Egypt 15,000 years before Phoroneus, the most ancient king of Greece, and he attempts to prove this by the monuments," and Plutarch suggests that the Egyptians had an alphabet of twenty-five letters, observing that "the number five forms a square of itself, which is the same number as the Egyptians have of letters and as the Apis had of years to live."[30]

Could any of these authors have been aware of the existence of phonetic signs in the hieroglyphic corpus, or even of the group of monoconsonantal hieroglyphs that modern Egyptologists designate as "alphabetic"? A somewhat enigmatic remark in the ninth book of Plutarch's *Quaestiones conviviales* suggests that he, at least, may have had access to some reliable information concerning the Egyptians' own system of classifying the hieroglyphic corpus. In his response to "Question Three," which deals with the number of letters in the (Greek) alphabet and the proportion of vowels to semivowels, the character Hermeias states the following: "Hermes . . . was, we are told, the god who first invented writing in Egypt (γράμματα πρῶτος εὑρεῖν). Hence the Egyptians write the first of their letters with an ibis, the bird that belongs to Hermes (διὸ καὶ τὸ τῶν γραμμάτων Αἰγύπτιοι πρῶτον Ἶβιν γράφουσιν, ὡς Ἑρμῇ προσήκουσαν), although in my opinion they err in giving precedence among the letters to one that is inarticulate and voiceless (οὐκ ὀρθῶς κατά γε τὴν ἐμὴν δόξαν ἀναύδῳ καὶ ἀφθόγγῳ προεδρίαν ἐγγράμμασιν ἀποδόντες)."[31] Although this remark greatly puzzled the editors of the Loeb volume, who noted that "the modern order of phonetic signs is . . . barely a hundred years old: there seems to be no evidence, unless it is to be found in this passage, to show which of these signs the Egyptians themselves placed first, or even that they had any fixed order of signs," evidence has since come to light that seems to validate Plutarch's remark.[32] A small group of papyri, probably school texts, provide alphabetical lists of terms in which the scribes "designated each letter of the alphabet by a bird name beginning with the letter in question." According to this system, which is documented from the fourth/third century B.C.E. into the Roman period, the first letter of the Egyptian alphabet, ḥ, is given the name ḥb, "ibis."[33] In his discussion of these alphabetical lists, François Gaudard notes further that Plutarch's claim that there were twenty-five letters in the Egyptian alphabet does, in fact, agree with the number of alphabetic signs in the standard hieroglyphic corpus.[34]

What should we make of this? Did Plutarch, alone of his compatriots, possess an accurate understanding of the hieroglyphic script? Despite his observations on the Egyptian alphabet, seemingly validated by the school texts just described, comments in Plutarch's other works seem to suggest that, on the whole, he subscribed to the majority view and understood hieroglyphs as a primarily symbolic mode of communication. This attitude is clearly apparent in the passages from *De Iside et Osiride* where Plutarch offers "readings" of various inscriptions. For example, he writes that

> in Saïs, at any rate, on the pylon in front of Athena's temple there had been engraved a child, an old man, and after this a falcon, and then a fish, and behind them all a hippopotamus. It meant symbolically (ἐδήλου δὲ συμβολικῶς), "O you who are coming into being and you who are passing away, <God hates shamelessness". For the child is a symbol of birth>, the old man <of death>; with a falcon they denote a god, with a fish hatred, as we have said, because of the sea, and with a hippopotamus shamelessness; for it is said to violate its mother after killing its father.[35]

As Griffiths notes in his commentary on this passage, "enough is right to show that [Plutarch] was in contact with a source to which the hieroglyphs were not unfamiliar." For example, the word "god," *nṯr*, can in fact be written with the sign of a falcon on a perch, and the fish sign is the regular determinative for the word "abomination," *bwt*.[36] However, Plutarch's use of the phrase "it meant symbolically" indicates that, like so many of his compatriots, he understood the hieroglyphic script to function as a symbolic, rather than a phonetic, system. A similar understanding seems to underlie many of the other passages where he discusses the meaning of individual signs; although he may correctly connect the signs to the words they are used to write (for instance, the use of the eye and scepter signs to write the name "Osiris"), his explanations remain firmly planted in the realm of allegory.[37]

Writing some 130 years after Plutarch, the Neoplatonist philosopher Plotinus (204/5–70 C.E.) offered an assessment of hieroglyphic writing in which we can see the development of some of the themes that had emerged from the earlier classical discourse on hieroglyphs. He writes,

> the wise men of Egypt (οἱ Αἰγυπτίων σοφοί) . . . when they
> wished to signify something wisely (περὶ ὧν ἐβούλοντο διὰ
> σοφίας δεικνύναι), did not use the forms of letters which follow
> the order of words and propositions and imitate sounds and the
> enunciations of philosophical statements (μὴ τύποις γραμμάτων
> διεξοδεύουσι λόγους καὶ προτάσεις μηδὲ μιμουμένοις φωνὰς
> καὶ προφορὰς ἀξιωμάτων κεχρῆσθαι), but by drawing images
> and inscribing in their temples one particular image of each
> particular thing, they manifested the non-discursiveness of the
> intelligible world (ἀγάλματα δὲ γράψαντες καὶ ἓν ἕκαστον
> ἑκάστου πράγματος ἄγαλμα ἐντυπώσαντες ἐν τοῖς ἱεροῖς
> τὴν ἐκείνου <οὐ> διέξοδον ἐμφῆναι), that is, that every image is
> a kind of knowledge and wisdom and is a subject of statements, all
> together in one, and not discourse or deliberation (ὡς ἄρα τις καὶ
> ἐπιστήμη καὶ σοφία ἕκαστόν ἐστιν ἄγαλμα καὶ ὑποκείμενον
> καὶ ἀθρόον καὶ οὐ διανόησις οὐδὲ βούλευσις).[38]

The nondiscursive nature of reality, Plotinus argues, finds a particularly appropriate expression in the (purportedly) nondiscursive hieroglyphic script, which has the potential to represent the world more accurately than strictly glottographic writing systems. Plotinus' contention that each hieroglyphic sign represents, in a highly compressed form, the summation of accumulated wisdom or knowledge about a given subject would prove to be highly influential for later commentators on hieroglyphs, who sought, in their interpretive efforts, to "unpack" the information they believed to be encoded in each individual hieroglyph.

Nowhere is this mode of interpretation more central than in the composition known as the *Hieroglyphica* of Horapollo, which in many respects represents the apogee of late antique hieroglyphic speculation. Highly influential in the Renaissance and early modern period, following the discovery of a manuscript copy on the Greek island of Andros in 1419, the text played a central role in (unsuccessful) early attempts to decipher hieroglyphs, and for this reason it has also been central to modern histories of decipherment.[39] The composition of the *Hieroglyphica* is attributed to one Horapollo Nilous—that is, Horapollo the Egyptian—and is said, in its incipit, to have been composed by Horapollo in the Egyptian language and translated into Greek by a man identified only as "Philip."[40] The date of composition of the text and the precise identity of the author remain somewhat uncertain. Following Maspero as well as Masson and Fournet, Thissen has argued for a connection to a grammarian and philosopher named Horapollo who was born in the Panopolite nome and was active in Alexandria in the latter decades of the fifth century, and this view is widely followed.[41] The claim that the text represents the Greek translation of an Egyptian original is surely spurious, intended to enhance the authority of the text and its author. As Thissen states the introduction to his edition of the text, it is highly unlikely that Horapollo composed the text in Coptic, the vernacular Egyptian of his own time, and his clear incomprehension of how the hieroglyphic writing system actually functions precludes the (already remote) possibility that it was originally composed in hieroglyphs.[42]

The *Hieroglyphica* is divided into two books, the first of which appears to be the work of Horapollo himself, perhaps based on earlier source material, and the second of which may have been written partly by Horapollo (chapters 1–30) and partly by a second individual, perhaps the purported editor/translator, Philip (chapters 31–119).[43] As Thissen notes, the entries in book 1 of the *Hieroglyphica* tend to follow a predictable pattern, a statement along the lines of "if they want to write A, they draw B, because of C," where A is the word or subject to be expressed, B is the hieroglyphic sign, and C is an explanation of the connection between signifier and signified, which often takes an allegorical form.[44] A classic and much-discussed example is *Hieroglyphica* 1.26, which reads, "when they want to represent 'opening,' they paint a hare, because that animal always has its eyes open (Ἄνοιξιν δὲ θέλοντες δηλῶσι λαγωὸν ζωγραφοῦσι διὰ τὸ πάντοτε τοὺς ὀφθαλμοὺς ἀνεῳγότας ἔχειν τοῦτο τὸ ζῷον)." As numerous modern commentators have observed, although the hare hieroglyph, with its biconsonantal phonetic value of *w* + *n*, is indeed used to write the Egyptian verb *wn*, "to open," Horapollo's explanation of the conceptual link between signifier and signified completely ignores the underlying phonetic rationale for the use of that sign. Rather, it turns on a highly questionable zoological observation about the habits of hares.[45]

Many of the entries in the *Hieroglyphica* follow a similar pattern; Horapollo may correctly identify the hieroglyphs used to write certain words, but his explanation of *why* they are used has nothing to do with the spoken Egyptian language and everything to do with the qualities and characteristics of the objects the hieroglyphs represent. For this reason, much of the *Hieroglyphica* reads like an extended set of case studies where Diodorus' claim that hieroglyphs express meaning "by means of the significance of the objects which have been copied" is tested against a series of individual hieroglyphic signs. What the *Hieroglyphica* fails to offer, of course, is any coherent explanation of how individual signs might be combined into larger syntactic units; for this reason, the text has long been seen as another false lead on the road to decipherment, which required modern scholars to look beyond the purported symbolic meaning of individual signs to grasp the underlying phonetic structure of the language.

No late antique Christian counterpart to Horapollo's *Hieroglyphica* is known to have existed, nor should we assume that there was any perceived need for such a composition; Christian scholars interested in the hieroglyphic script could consult Horapollo's text as well as other hieroglyphic treatises known to have circulated in late antiquity but that have not survived to the present day. Manuscript copies of Horapollo's work were still being produced as late as the sixteenth century, which suggests some degree of sustained interest in his subject matter, and the *Hieroglyphica* of Chaeremon, which may have been a source for Horapollo's own work, is known from references in John Tzetzes' scholia on the *Iliad* to have circulated in Byzantine intellectual circles as late as the twelfth century.[46] That Chaeremon, like Horapollo, adhered to the symbolic interpretation of hieroglyphs is illustrated by the statement, quoted by Tzetzes, that "since the more ancient of the sacred scribes wanted to conceal the theory about the nature of the gods (βουλόμενοι γὰρ οἱ ἀρχαιότεροι τῶν ἱερογραμματέων τὸν περὶ θεῶν φυσικὸν λόγον κρύπτειν), they handed these things down to their own children by way of such allegorical symbols and characters (δι᾿ ἀλληγορικῶν [καὶ] συμβόλων τοιούτων καὶ γραμμάτων τοῖς ἰδίοις τέκνοις παρεδίδουν αὐτά), as the sacred scribe Chaeremon says."[47] The symbolic or allegorical understanding of hieroglyphs, already established in the work of Diodorus and perpetuated by later classical authors, thus became ever more entrenched throughout the late antique period and thereafter, when it was accepted by Christian and non-Christian commentators alike.

Hieroglyphs, Secrecy, and Priestly Knowledge

Hand-in-hand with the prevailing Greco-Roman belief in the symbolic nature of the hieroglyphic script went the belief that hieroglyphs were, above all, a means of rendering in written form, and thus simultaneously concealing and revealing, the profound wisdom of the Egyptian priesthood. That the Egyptians had a reputation for knowledge, particularly of an arcane sort, is an observation that goes back at least to Herodotus and his claims that the Egyptians were the originators of many of the religious practices familiar to the Greeks of his own time.[48] This theme, which neatly complements the assertion, discussed above in Chapter 2, that the Egyptians were in possession of a particularly rich and ancient historical record, runs throughout the Greek and Latin commentaries on Egypt, and in many of these sources we encounter a direct correlation between Egyptian writing and the desire to both record and conceal Egyptian wisdom. A clear statement of this view is found in Apuleius' *Metamorphoses*, where the narrator describes his initiation into the mysteries of Isis:

> After the service of the opening of the temple had been celebrated with exalted ceremony and the morning sacrifice performed, he brought out from the hidden quarters of the shrine (*de opertis adyti*) certain books in which the writing was in undecipherable letters (*quosdam libros litteris ignorabilibus praenotatos*). Some of them conveyed, through forms of all kinds of animals (*figuris cuiusce modi animalium*), abridged expressions of traditional sayings (*concepti sermonis compendiosa verba*); others barred the possibility of being read from the curiosity of the profane (*a curiositate profanorum lectione munita*), in that their extremities were knotted and curved like wheels or closely intertwined like vine-tendrils (*nodosis et in modum rotae tortuosis capreolatimque condensis apicibus*).[49]

Apuleius appears to distinguish between two scripts in this passage, both of which he characterizes as "undecipherable letters." One script was almost certainly hieroglyphic; the author's reference to the conveyance of meaning using "forms of all kinds of animals" echoes, deliberately or unconsciously, Tacitus' claim that the Egyptians utilize "animal-pictures" in their monumental inscriptions. The second script Apuleius refers to may be hieratic; the ornate style of certain hieratic documents offers a good parallel for Apuleius' description of letters "knotted and curved like wheels or closely intertwined like vine-tendrils."[50] In both cases, the author claims a connection between the nature of the script and the books' content; the hieroglyphs are not merely symbolic, but liturgical in character, and the elaborate appearance of the second script is deliberately intended to protect the books "from the curiosity of the profane."

These dual themes of arcane wisdom and its concealment recur in many of the classical sources and become a dominant theme in Greco-Roman hieroglyphic speculation. In speaking of Pythagoras, for example, Plutarch, emphasizes the philosopher's supposed indebtedness to the Egyptian way of thinking, stating that he "imitated their symbolism and mysterious manner, interspersing his teaching with riddles (ἀπεμιμήσατο τὸ συμβολικὸν αὐτῶν καὶ μυστηριῶδες ἀναμίξας αἰνίγμασι τὰ δόγματα); for many of the Pythagorean sayings are not at all lacking in the lore of the writing which is called hieroglyphic (τῶν γὰρ καλουμένων ἱερογλυφικῶν γραμμάτων οὐθὲν ἀπολείπει τὰ πολλὰ τῶν Πυθαγορικῶν παραγγελμάτων).[51]

Plutarch's own work, particularly his *De Iside et Osiride*, is likewise riddled with references to Egyptian symbolism, as noted above. This arcane Egyptian lore, quite literally enshrined in temple inscriptions and temple libraries, was said to be of interest to kings as well as prophets and philosophers. Lucan, for example, imagines Julius Caesar exhorting an Egyptian priest to "expound . . . your forms of worship and the shapes of your gods; reveal all that is engraved upon your ancient shrines (*quodcumque vetustis / Insculptum est adytis profer*), and disclose your gods who are willing that they should be known" (*noscique volentes / Prode deos*), and Cassius Dio relates that Septimius Severus, on his visit to Egypt in 199/200 C.E., "inquired into everything, including things that were very carefully hidden (ἐπολυπραγμόνησε πάντα καὶ τὰ πάνυ κεκρυμμένα). . . . Accordingly, he took away from practically all the sanctuaries all the books that he could find containing any secret lore, and he locked up the tomb of Alexander (κἀκ τούτου τά τε βιβλία πάντα τὰ ἀπόρρητόν τι ἔχοντα, ὅσα γε καὶ εὑρεῖν ἠδυνήθη, ἐκ πάντων ὡς εἰπεῖν τῶν ἀδύτων ἀνεῖλε καὶ τὸ τοῦ Ἀλεξάνδρου μνημεῖον συνέκλεισεν); this was in order that no one in future should either view Alexander's body or read what was written in the above-mentioned books."[52] Although one must doubt the historicity of these accounts, they betray a common belief, especially prevalent in the later classical sources, that hieroglyphs were used to conceal secret knowledge from the uninitiated, particularly within the sacred precincts of Egyptian temples.

Did this reflect actual Egyptian practice? As Dieleman, Winand, and others have argued, the emphasis in the classical sources on the use of hieroglyphs to conceal knowledge actually parallels a major developmental trend in the use of hieroglyphs in the Ptolemaic and Roman periods, when the use of various forms of cipher-scripts reached unprecedented heights. A spectacular example of this style of graphic experimentation is provided by the famous Roman-period cryptographic hymns to Khnum from the temple of Esna, shown in Figures 6 and 7; in these texts, formulaic hymns of praise to the deity are rendered almost entirely through variations on ram and crocodile hieroglyphs.[53] However, as Dieleman has observed, in such temple contexts, "cryptographic texts were usually displayed at an eye-catching spot with free access, while the reading of the enigmatic signs was more often than not facilitated by the presence of ordinary hieroglyphs or by a parallel text recorded in regular script." So, although secrecy and the protection of ritual information was certainly a feature of Egyptian religious thought from very early periods, the connection between concealment and the cryptographic use of hieroglyphs was probably not as straightforward as the classical sources would seem to suggest. That said, in practical terms the very low level of hieroglyphic literacy among the general population (and the complete illiteracy in hieroglyphs of Greek and Roman visitors) would certainly have had the effect, intended or not, of concealing the meaning of hieroglyphic inscriptions from the vast majority of people who viewed them.[54]

Even if hieroglyphs were not always, or even usually, used with the intent to hide or encrypt information, the classical view of a nexus between hieroglyphs and the concealment of esoteric knowledge was strongly affirmed in both the Hermetic and Neoplatonic corpora (a fact that has contributed to the ongoing vitality of this notion up to the present day).[55] Particularly significant in this context is the work of the late antique Neoplatonist Iamblichus (245–325 C.E.), who offers a highly influential reading of Egyptian symbolism in his work De mysteriis. Like Plotinus before him, Iamblichus argues that hieroglyphic writing is essentially nondiscursive, claiming that the Egyptians, "imitating the nature of the universe and the demiurgic power of the gods, display certain signs of mystical, arcane and invisible intellections (τῶν

Figure 6. Cryptographic ram inscription (Esna II, 103) from
the temple of Esna. Photo courtesy of Foy Scalf.

Figure 7. Cryptographic crocodile inscription (Esna II, 126) from the temple of Esna. Photo courtesy of Foy Scalf.

μυστικῶν καὶ ἀποκεκρυμμένων καὶ ἀφανῶν νοήσεων εἰκόνας τινὰς . . . ἐκφαίνουσιν) by means of symbols (διὰ συμβόλων), just as nature copies the unseen principles in visible forms through some mode of symbolism." Moreover, Iamblichus continues, this semiotic system of the Egyptians is "a mode of concealment that is appropriate to the mystical doctrine of conceal- ment in symbols (τὸν πρόσφορον αὐτῆς τρόπον τῆς κεκρυμμένης ἐν τοῖς συμβόλοις μυσταγωγίας)."[56] Although, as the editors of the text point out, the examples that Iamblichus chooses to illustrate this system—"mud," "the lotus," "the solar barque," and "the zodiac"—are drawn from the realm of Egyptian iconography and are not, strictly speaking, actual hieroglyphs, Iam- blichus' remarks further promulgate the notion that the Egyptians were con- cerned not only with communication via symbols, but also with using those symbols for the purpose of concealment.[57]

One of the principal motifs that cuts across both classical and Judeo- Christian sources and unites the themes of concealment, revelation, and Egyptian wisdom is the tradition of the hieroglyphic stela (or stelae, or tab- lets) of Thoth-Hermes, said to have been engraved before the Flood with the accumulated arcane knowledge of the Egyptians. The notion of a compen- dium of knowledge, particularly knowledge of cosmic or astrological mat- ters, inscribed in stone so as to protect it from a coming cataclysm and later revealed/translated, has roots reaching back to Jewish pseudepigrapha of the Hellenistic period. The *Book of Jubilees*, for example, recounts the discovery, by Cainan, of "a writing which former (generations) had carved on the rock"; Cainan "read what was thereon, and he transcribed it and sinned owing to it; for it contained the teaching of the Watchers in accordance with which they used to observe the omens of the sun and moon and stars in all the signs of heaven."[58] Josephus, in his *Antiquitates Judaicae*, attributes the composition of a similar cosmological text to the descendants of Seth, who are said to have "discovered the science with regard to the heavenly bodies and their orderly arrangement." Having received the knowledge, from Adam, that the universe was to be destroyed by fire and deluge, "they made two pillars, one of brick and the other of stones and inscribed their findings on both, in order that if the one of brick should be lost owing to the flood the one of stone should remain and offer an opportunity to teach men what had been written on it and to reveal that also one of brick had been set up by them. And it remains until today in the land of Seiris."[59]

Adapted to an Egyptian context, these pillars of brick and stone become stelae, the author becomes Thoth-Hermes, and the script becomes hieroglyphic or hieratic. Thus, Iamblichus refers to a cosmological text passed down from Hermes and discovered by the prophet Bitys "inscribed in hieroglyphic characters (ἀναγεγραμμένην ἐν ἱερογλυφικοῖς γράμμασι) in a sanctuary (ἄδυτον) in Sais in Egypt."[60] Ammianus Marcellinus, in his description of the "syringes," or rock-cut tombs of western Thebes, writes that "those acquainted with the ancient rites, since they had fore-knowledge that a deluge was coming, and feared that the memory of the ceremonies might be destroyed, dug in the earth in many places with great labour; and on the walls of these caverns they carved many kinds of birds and beasts, and those count-less forms of animals which they called hierographic writing (*quas hierograph-icas litteras appellarunt*)."[61] As we have already seen, the same motif appears in George Syncellus' *Ecloga Chronographica*, in which the so-called *Book of Sothis* attributed to Manetho is said to have been based on antediluvian stelae writ-ten in hieroglyphs by Thoth.[62] One might also compare the command given by the master to his disciple in the *Discourse on the Eighth and Ninth*: "My son, write this book (ΠΕΕΙϪⲰⲘⲈ) for the temple at Diospolis in hieroglyphic characters (ϨⲚ ϨⲈⲚⲤϨⲀⲒ ⲚⲤⲀϨⲢⲀⲚⲰϢ) . . . write the language of the book (ΠϢⲀϪⲈ ⲘⲠⲬⲰⲰⲘⲈ) on steles of turquoise. My son, it is proper to write this book on steles of turquoise, in hieroglyphic characters (ϨⲚ ϨⲚⲤϨⲈⲈⲒ ⲚⲤⲀϨⲢⲀⲈⲒϢ). For Mind himself has become overseer of these. Therefore I command that this teaching (ΠΕΕΙϢⲀϪⲈ) be carved on stone, and that you place it in my sanctuary."[63] In his analysis of this motif, Christian Bull notes that the use of hieroglyphs in carving these inscriptions, a specific feature of the Egyptian variations on the theme, serves the dual purpose of revelation (the secrets of the universe were committed to writing in a monumental con-text) and concealment (few people could read hieroglyphs, therefore the infor-mation contained in the inscriptions was protected from the unworthy).[64] In some ways, this notion of simultaneous revelation and concealment is reminiscent of the inscriptions in cryptographic hieroglyphs discussed briefly above—simultaneously difficult to read, yet also prominently displayed and sometimes accompanied by a "key" facilitating their interpretation.

The church fathers generally concur with the classical sources in seeing Egyptian temples and their hieroglyphic inscriptions as the locus for the trans-mission of Egyptian wisdom, although as we shall see below, they tend to regard that "wisdom" from a sharply critical vantage point. Clement, for exam-ple, notes that Pythagoras underwent circumcision so that he might enter the sacred space of the Egyptian temples and learn from the priests there, and in his effort to refute the allegation that Jesus was a magician, the apologist

Arnobius clearly articulates the conceptual link between temples, hieroglyphs, and Egyptian wisdom (or "wisdom"). He writes, "my opponent will perhaps meet me with many other slanderous and childish charges which are commonly urged. Jesus was a magician; he effected all these things by secret arts. From the shrines of the Egyptians he stole the names of angels of might, and the religious system of a remote country (*Aegyptiorum ex adytis angelorum potentiam nomina et remotas furatus est discplinas*)."[65]

The claim that Jesus was a magician whose miracles were not fundamentally different from the ritual expertise attributed to Egyptian priests was, as Arnobius notes, a staple of anti-Christian polemic, and the details Arnobius provides reinforce the association between the Egyptian temples and the esoteric wisdom thought to be enshrined there. The reference to the "names of angels of might" purportedly stolen by Jesus from the Egyptian shrines is especially striking in its resonance with the passage from Lucan discussed briefly above (*Pharsalia* 10.176–81), in which Caesar asks the Egyptian priest to disclose what is written on the temple walls and, in so doing, to reveal the identities of the gods. In the Christian sources as in the classical works dealing with Egypt, Egyptian temples are repositories of arcane knowledge, including the names of supernatural beings, and at least some of this information is difficult of access, concealed the in form of hieroglyphic texts.

Moses and the "Wisdom" of Egypt

Just as Christian authors like Eusebius and Augustine were forced to confront the common belief that Egyptian hieroglyphic inscriptions might preserve the historical records of the antediluvian past, they also had to respond to the assertion that hieroglyphs, particularly those carved on temple walls, served as a means of transmitting an ancient and powerful esoteric tradition. The biblical claim that Moses had been "educated in all the wisdom of the Egyptians (πάσῃ σοφίᾳ Αἰγυπτίων) and was powerful in his words and deeds" precluded the wholesale rejection of the concept, so we find Christian authors simultaneously acknowledging and problematizing the tradition of Egyptian wisdom as expressed in hieroglyphic sources. Although, as Clement acknowledges, "barbarian" arts might be "inventive and practically useful" insofar as they could lead to the invention of scientific disciplines such as geometry and metallurgy, several of the church fathers associate the wisdom of Egypt with a variety of negative qualities, including boastfulness, corruption, heresy, and idolatry. Some also claim that it is fundamentally *unnecessary* under the new Christian dispensation, worldly wisdom having given way before the wisdom of God, taught by the Holy Spirit.[66]

At the heart of any discussion of Christian views on the "wisdom of Egypt" must be the claim about the education of Moses recorded in Acts 7:22. As Ton Hilhorst has observed in his commentary on this passage, the author of Acts was here amplifying the brief comment in Exodus 2:10 that states only that Moses had been adopted by Pharaoh's daughter, without further commenting on his upbringing.[67] Acts 7:22 also echoes the wording of 1 Kings 4:30, where it is stated that "Solomon's wisdom surpassed the wisdom of all the people of the east, and all the wisdom of Egypt."[68] Although the author of Acts does not further specify the precise nature of Moses' education, other Jewish and Christian commentators filled this lacuna on the basis of existing notions of what training in "wisdom" might look like in the context of an Egyptian upbringing. Particularly influential was the account of Philo, whose *De vita Mosis* provides a vivid picture of the young Moses at his lessons: "Arithmetic, geometry, the lore of metre, rhythm and harmony, and the whole subject of music as shown by the use of instruments or in textbooks and treatises of a more special character, were imparted to him by learned Egyptians. These further instructed him in the philosophy conveyed in symbols, as displayed in the so-called sacred characters (τὴν διὰ συμβόλων φιλοσοφίαν, ἣν ἐν τοῖς λεγομένοις ἱεροῖς γράμμασιν ἐπιδείκνυνται), and in the regard paid to animals, to which they even pay divine honours."[69]

Philo's description of Moses' education deploys a fairly stereotypical set of ideas about what might constitute the "wisdom of Egypt," already well established in the classical tradition by the time of his writing. Arithmetic, geometry, and music were all commonly identified as Egyptian specialties, geometry in particular being seen as an Egyptian invention; and the writing of hieroglyphic texts and the worship of sacred animals were, as we have already seen, two of the quintessential hallmarks of Egyptian cultural identity.[70] Clement of Alexandria offers a glimpse of the Egyptian (priestly) curriculum in book 6 of the *Stromateis*, in which he enumerates the "forty-two books of Hermes, indispensably necessary"; the contents of these books range from the "hymns of the gods" to astrology, law, geography, and medicine, among other topics. Hieroglyphic writing is said to be the province of the sacred scribe, or *hierogrammateus*, "and he must be acquainted with what are called hieroglyphics (τὰ [τε] ἱερογλυγικὰ καλούμενα) and know about cosmography and geography, and the position of the sun and the moon, and about the five planets; and also the description of Egypt, and the chart of the Nile; and the description of the equipment of the priests and of the places consecrated to them, and about the measures and the things used in the sacred rites."[71] Philo's characterization of Moses' course of study under the tutelage of the "learned Egyptians" is, thus, generally consistent with Clement's sketch of the body of knowledge that an individual who had gone through the rigors of an Egyptian priestly education might be expected to master.

Philo's *De vita Mosis* was widely held to be an authoritative source for the life of the great Jewish culture hero, and Philo's description of Moses' education was frequently repeated by later Christian authors.[72] Clement, for example, quotes Philo directly in *Stromateis* 1, noting that Moses' learning included "the philosophy which is conveyed by symbols, which they point out in the hieroglyphic characters (τὴν διὰ συμβόλων φιλοσοφίαν, ἣν ἐν τοῖς ἱερογλυφικοῖς γράμμασιν ἐπιδείκνυνται)." He adds, again following Philo, that Moses "learned, besides, the writing of the Assyrians (τὰ Ἀσσυρίων γράμματα), and the knowledge of the heavenly bodies from the Chaldeans and the Egyptians; whence in the Acts he is said to have been 'instructed in all the wisdom of the Egyptians.'"[73] Other Christian writers offer similar assessments, adding the occasional detail; Origen notes, for example, that Moses obtained his learning from "ancient writings not accessible to the multitude," by which we should probably again understand hieroglyphic or hieratic inscriptions and/or books, and Augustine, quoting Origen, identifies Moses as "the man of God," who, by virtue of his Egyptian education, "loved geometry." Basil specifies that Moses "received a royal education" and "had for his teachers the wise men of Egypt."[74]

If Moses' education in the wisdom of the Egyptians could not be dismissed entirely, given its scriptural pedigree, the nature and benefits of that education could at least be problematized, and the church fathers went about this task with considerable creativity. Augustine lays out the Christian predicament with remarkable candor, observing that "it must . . . be admitted that there existed before Moses—not, indeed, in Greece, but among barbarous nations such as Egypt—*some degree of learning which might be called their 'wisdom.'* Otherwise it would not be written in the holy books that 'Moses was learned in all the wisdom of the Egyptians.'"[75] Augustine goes on to point out, of course, that this so-called Egyptian wisdom, although it might have been earlier than that of the Greeks, could not possibly predate the wisdom of the Hebrew prophets and patriarchs such as Abraham, for "what wisdom could there be in Egypt before the art of letters had been taught by Isis?"

The Egyptians' misplaced pride in the antiquity of their intellectual traditions recurs at a number of points in *De civitate Dei*, as we saw in Chapter 2, and Augustine does not restrict his critique to the chronological position of Egyptian thinkers within the intellectual history of the nations. Rather, he attacks the content of Egyptian teaching as well, referring to the "great evils" transmitted in the "mystic writings of the Egyptians" and emphasizing that what the Egyptians categorize as wisdom at best comprised sciences like astronomy, "which usually serve rather to exercise men's ingenuity than to illuminate their minds with true wisdom."[76] At worst, Egyptian wisdom is tantamount to sacrilege, as Augustine makes clear in his identification of the first-century Alexandrian Stoic philosopher Chaeremon as "a man learned in these sacred—or, rather, sacrilegious—matters." It is worth recalling in this context that Chaeremon was known in late antiquity not only for his tutelage of the young Nero but also as the author of widely cited treatises on the Egyptian priesthood (the *Aegyptiaca*) and on the hieroglyphic writing system (the *Hieroglyphica*). With this one turn of phrase, Augustine thus casts aspersions not only on Chaeremon himself, but on the whole Egyptian intellectual and religious tradition of which Chaeremon was a highly prominent exponent.[77]

Augustine was not alone in condemning the Egyptians' pride in their wisdom tradition as foolish and vainglorious. A number of the other church fathers also took up this theme, simultaneously acknowledging Egyptian claims to primordial wisdom while also stating that those claims were ill founded. Moses is once again central to this line of argumentation, for he is said both to have received an Egyptian priestly education and also to have beaten the Egyptian priests at their own game, as it were, thereby proving the superiority of divine inspiration over human intellectual effort. Origen makes this point clearly in *Contra Celsum*, where, as discussed above, he makes specific reference to Moses having obtained his learning "wholly from ancient writings." In the same passage, Origen goes on to say that because of his intellectual formation, many people suspected that Moses' miracles came about, not from God, but "by means of his Egyptian knowledge, in which he was well versed (κατὰ τὰ Αἰγυπτίων μαθήματα, σοφὸς ὢν ἐν αὐτοῖς)." When Pharaoh summoned the best of his "Egyptian magicians, and wise men, and enchanters," however, their best efforts availed them nothing "against the wisdom of Moses, which proved superior to all the wisdom of the Egyptians (πρὸς τὴν ἐν Μωυσεῖ σοφίαν ὑπὲρ πᾶσαν Αἰγυπτίων σοφίαν)." Having learned all that the Egyptian priests and their hieroglyphic writings could teach him, Moses demonstrates the false nature of those teachings by defeating the Egyptians in the competition set up by Pharaoh, a victory that the church fathers present as a conflict of two opposing intellectual systems.[78]

Augustine likewise returns to this theme in *De civitate Dei*, where he observes that although the Egyptian magicians were "permitted to perform certain marvels only so that they might be vanquished by still greater ones" the competition was lopsided at best, insofar as Moses was in the right, had greater power, and had angels on his side. Similarly, in a letter to Volusianus, Augustine draws a sharp contrast between Pharaoh's Egyptian magicians, who were "working wonderfully by impious enchantments," and Moses himself, who "by simply calling upon God in prayer, overthrew all their machinations."[79] The message is consistent across all these sources: the venerable tradition of Egyptian wisdom, which is closely associated with both hieroglyphic inscriptions and magical practices, is shown to be inadequate *by one of its own erstwhile practitioners*, and the Egyptians' proud claims of superior knowledge are thereby shown to be empty boasting.

Hieroglyphs, Corruption, and Heresy

In addition to their claims that Egyptian wisdom is fundamentally false, and therefore not to be seen as a source of pride, some of the church fathers also assert that Egyptian priestly traditions are suspect because of their connection to material wealth. The Egyptian temples were widely recognized as sumptuous spaces, where "the halls are surrounded with many pillars; and the walls gleam with foreign stones, and there is no want of artistic painting; and the temples gleam with gold, and silver, and amber, and glitter with particoloured gems from India and Ethiopia; and the shrines are veiled with gold-embroidered hangings," but where the object of worship was revealed to be a "beast, unworthy of the temple, but quite worthy of a den, a hole, or the dirt."[80] In much the same way, the Egyptian mysteries are shown to be false, with outward display and solemn ceremonial concealing a spiritual vacancy within. Moreover, the priests who preside over these luxurious spaces, and who are thus seen as gatekeepers of the Egyptians' mystical traditions, are said to be corruptible. Origen, for example, refers to "the feats performed by those who have been taught by Egyptians, who in the middle of the market-place, in return for a few obols, will impart the knowledge of their most venerated arts," including the expulsion of demons, the summoning of souls, and the animation of material objects—all activities that were commonly identified, in both the classical and Christian traditions, as falling under the purview of Egyptian ritual specialists. Ps.-Clement of Rome similarly refers to purchasing the secrets of the Egyptian mysteries, writing, "I shall go into Egypt, and I shall become friendly with the hierophants of the shrines, and with the prophets; and I shall seek and find a magician, and persuade him with large bribes to effect the calling up of a soul, which is called necromancy, as if I were going to inquire of it concerning some business. And the inquiry shall be for the purpose of learning whether the soul is immortal."[81] The implication underlying both passages is that a wisdom tradition that has been commodified is necessarily suspect. This perceived connection between Egyptian temples, their priests, and material wealth will prove to be a tenacious one, as we shall see in Chapter 5.

Another useful tool in the patristic arsenal that could be directed against the valorization of Egyptian wisdom was the claim that an Egyptian education could lead to heresy or even to that most quintessentially Egyptian of sins, idolatry. Merely residing in Egypt, it would seem, had the potential to corrupt one's thinking; in his *Historia Ecclesiastica*, Socrates relates the story of a "Saracen" who married a woman from the Thebaid and settled with her in Egypt. "Having versed himself in the learning of the Egyptians (τὴν Αἰγυπτίων παιδείαν)," Socrates writes, "he subtly introduced the theory of Empedocles and Pythagoras among the doctrines of the Christian faith (τὴν Ἐμπεδοκλέους καὶ Πυθαγόρου δόξαν εἰς τὸν Χριστιανισμὸν παρεισήγαγεν)."[82] These corrupt Egyptian doctrines, Socrates claims, lie at the root of Manichaeism. The author of the *Refutatio omnium haeresium* likewise notes that a number of movements deemed heretical had their roots in specifically Egyptian modes of thought. He singles out in particular what he calls the "heresy of Valentinus," claiming that Valentinus' teachings derive ultimately from ancient Egyptian traditions by way of Plato and Pythagoras. Another suspect movement, the "heresy of Basileides," is likewise said to be the strange and undesirable fruit of an Egyptian education: "these are the myths of Basileides, who studied in Egypt (σχολάσας κατὰ τὴν Αἴγυπτον). From the Egyptians, then, he was taught so great a 'wisdom' and produced a like harvest" (καὶ παρ' αὐτῶν τὴν τοσαύτην σοφίαν διδαχθείς, ἐκαρποφόρησε τοιούτους καρπούς).[83]

The connection between heresy and Egyptian wisdom, particularly as articulated in hieroglyphic temple inscriptions, is expressed in somewhat greater detail in a fascinating passage from the twelfth book of Gregory of Nyssa's treatise *Contra Eunomium*. Gregory claims that, in trying to comprehend where the Arian Eunomius came by his understanding of the nature of the Trinity, "the thought struck me, whether it could be that he was an admirer of the speculations of the Egyptians on the subject of the Divine, and had mixed up their fancies with his views concerning the Only-begotten." Drawing an analogy between the Egyptians' composite human-animal divine images, which he says are an "enigmatic symbol" of the "mixed nature" of daemons, and Eunomius' Arian understanding of the "mixed" nature of Christ, Gregory writes,

> our sage theologian seems to us to be importing into the Christian creed an Anubis, Isis, or Osiris from the Egyptian shrines (ἐκ τῶν Αἰγυπτίων ἀδύτων), all but the acknowledgment of their names: but there is no difference in profanity between him who openly makes profession of the names of idols, and him who, while holding the belief about them in his heart, is yet chary of their names. If, then, it is impossible to get out of Holy Scripture any support for this impiety, while their theory draws all its strength from the riddles of the hieroglyphics (ἐκ δὲ τῶν ἱερογλυφικῶν αἰνιγμάτων), assuredly there can be no doubt what right-minded persons ought to think of this.[84]

It is unlikely that Gregory actually believed Eunomius had derived his Arian Christology from the study of Egyptian temple inscriptions; rather, in *Contra Eunomium*, alluding to Egyptian wisdom traditions is a way of establishing Eunomius' guilt by association. Comparing his teaching to Egyptian idolatry—which, many of the church fathers agreed, represented the absolute nadir of polytheistic religious practice—is effectively a shorthand way of demonstrating how utterly irredeemable it is.[85]

Even such a seemingly banal subject as geometry—widely viewed in antiquity as an Egyptian specialty, as we have already seen, and closely associated in the classical tradition with the hieroglyphic teachings of the Egyptian priesthood—was imbued with dangerous potential. Thus Ambrose asks, "what shows such darkness as to discuss subjects connected with geometry and astronomy . . . to measure the depths of space, to shut up heaven and earth within the limits of fixed numbers, to leave aside the grounds of salvation and to seek for error?" He goes on to state that Moses, "learned as he was in all the wisdom of the Egyptians," turned away from the study of these subjects as "both harmful and foolish" and instead "sought God with all the desire of his heart, and thus saw, questioned, heard Him when He spoke. Who is more wise than he whom God taught, and who brought to naught all the wisdom of the Egyptians, and all the powers of their craft by the might of his works?"[86]

In Ambrose's assessment, the wisdom attained through the study and practice of empirical disciplines like astronomy and geometry, which he identifies as specifically Egyptian intellectual traditions, cannot possibly stand against the spiritual teachings of God. This type of argumentation is characteristic of Ambrose's larger agenda in *De officiis*, throughout which, as Ivor Davidson notes, "Ambrose again and again sets up antitheses between classical thought and exemplars and the teaching and characters of the Bible," aiming thereby to supplant Cicero's original text with a Christianized version suitable for the intellectual culture of the late fourth century.[87]

Ambrose's remarks in *De officiis* concerning Moses' repudiation of his Egyptian education point to one of the church fathers' most consequential arguments against the Egyptian wisdom tradition—namely, the claim that all human wisdom, including but by no means limited to that wisdom expressed in hieroglyphic texts, has been rendered obsolete by the coming of Christ. This line of argumentation is grounded in a reading of 1 Corinthians 2:6–16, which outlines a distinction between worldly wisdom ("a wisdom of this age or of the rulers of this age") and "God's wisdom, secret and hidden, which God decreed before the ages for our glory." In their commentaries on this passage, the church fathers frequently state that the worldly wisdom to which Paul refers can be identified with the intellectual traditions of various peoples, including the Egyptians. Origen, for example, writes that the "wisdom of the rulers of this age" is exemplified by "the secret and occult philosophy, as they call it, of the Egyptians, and the astrology of the Chaldeans and Indians," as well as "that manifold variety of opinion which prevails among the Greeks regarding divine things."[88]

Moreover, just as Paul writes in 1 Corinthians that the Christian community is distinguished by its privileging of spiritual over worldly wisdom, the church fathers at times privilege the knowledge of God over the achievements of science. Eusebius claims, for example, that the Egyptians, "who through their excess of knowledge boast of the discovery of geometry and astronomy and mathematics," nonetheless failed to "recognize or understand how to weigh in their hearts and calculate the measure of the power of God and its superiority to mortal, irrational nature." (This failing, Eusebius goes on to say, ultimately led the Egyptians to the sin of animal worship.) Similarly, John Chrysostom writes of the distinction between education and faith, noting that the apostles, through their faith, "were victorious over Plato and Pythagoras, in short, over all that had gone astray; and they surpass those whose lives had been worn out in astrology and geometry, mathematics and arithmetic, and who had been thoroughly instructed in every sort of learning."[89] Although John Chrysostom does not speak explicitly about the Egyptians in this passage—which he prefaces with the wearily rhetorical question "why have not the Greeks been able to find out anything?"—Egyptian wisdom traditions are nevertheless a plausible subtext, given the widespread belief that Plato and Pythagoras had studied in Egypt and the oft-repeated statement that the fields of geometry and mathematics were peculiarly Egyptian specialties.

Conclusion

Other Christian writers take the problematization of traditional sources of wisdom even further than the examples cited above. Clement of Alexandria, for example, writes that "since the Word Himself has come to us from heaven, we need not, I reckon, go any more in search of human learning to Athens and the rest of Greece, and to Ionia," and Origen inverts classical notions of paideia by identifying the uneducated not with those who are untrained "in the branches of Greek learning," as he puts it, but with idolaters, "who are not ashamed to address (supplications) to inanimate objects, and to call upon those for health that have no strength, and to ask the dead for life, and to entreat the helpless for assistance." In the same passage, Origen goes on to claim that Christian wisdom, which comes from God, is accessible to the most ignorant and the most educated alike, for "all human wisdom is folly in comparison with the divine."[90] This argument anticipates claims that would be made in later hagiographic literature, in which desert monks are lauded for their spiritual discernment even as they proclaim their lack of formal education. One is reminded, for example, of Athanasius' characterization of Antony as illiterate yet wise, and of Antony's own claim that a sound mind obviates the need for literacy.[91] This point should not be carried too far, of course; Antony is now thought to have been literate in Coptic, at least, and Gregory of Nazianzus' passionate invectives protesting Emperor Julian's edict forbidding Christians from teaching the Greek classics show that many of the church fathers, themselves highly educated, continued to see great value in the traditions of classical paideia, even if they rejected the religious content of the classical literary canon.[92] What the remarks of Origen, Clement, and the other authors discussed above suggest, however, is that alternative sources of intellectual authority were emerging in the late antique Christian worldview, and that the locus of "wisdom" was to some extent shifting away from the learned philosophers and priests of the Greek and Egyptian traditions toward the divinely inspired ascetics and mystics who populate the late antique literary landscape. This notion will be explored further in Chapter 5 below, which deals with Christian attempts to "translate" hieroglyphic inscriptions; in certain of the late antique sources, as we shall see, divine inspiration essentially supplants actual literacy in the hieroglyphic script as the necessary prerequisite for successful hermeneutic activity.

Chapter 4

Laws for Murdering Men's Souls

Between 1738 and 1741, William Warburton, then Lord Bishop of the city of Gloucester, published a wide-ranging theological work entitled *The Divine Legation of Moses Demonstrated*; he continued to revise and expand the text through the fourth edition of 1765. Intended as a vindication of revealed religion in the face of an increasingly prominent and vocal community of deists or "Free-thinkers," to whom Warburton pointedly dedicated the second edition, *The Divine Legation* draws on the full breadth of Enlightenment historical and philological scholarship to prove the truth of the Mosaic dispensation. Egypt, not unexpectedly, plays a central role in Warburton's exposition; what is somewhat surprising, however, is the amount of space the author devotes to an extended discussion of the origins, nature, and development, as he understood them, of the ancient Egyptian writing system. One of the most striking claims that Warburton puts forth in *The Divine Legation* is that hieroglyphs were the ultimate source of Egyptian idolatry. The use of animal hieroglyphs to designate the various Egyptian gods, he argues, led initially to the worship of the hieroglyphic signs themselves; this "symbolic worship" once established, it was no great leap to the worship of actual animals. It was for this reason, he claims, that "all Hieroglyphic Writing was absolutely forbidden by the Second Commandment."[1]

In this extraordinary argument, Warburton echoes, all unknowingly, the longest and most detailed discussion of Egyptian hieroglyphs to survive in the Coptic language. The text in question is preserved among the writings of the fourth/fifth-century abbot Shenoute of Atripe (ca. 347–465), whose monastic federation was situated on the west bank of the Nile across from the city of Panopolis (ancient Shmin, modern Akhmim) and who is known for his adversarial relationship with certain polytheistic residents of the town he punningly referred to as "Sin City" (ΠⲀⲚⲞⲘⲞⲤ ΠⲞⲖⲓⲤ).[2] The Panopolite nome was the birthplace of several prominent members of the late antique Egyptian intelligentsia, including that master of hieroglyphic speculation Horapollo, and the city of Panopolis itself has long been viewed as one of the last redoubts of a particularly "intellectual" strain of traditional polytheism, where the traditions of classical paideia seem to have flourished in some form well into the fifth century.[3]

A major theme of Shenoute's written work is his effort—perhaps more rhetorical than real, as Stephen Emmel has recently shown—to extirpate all vestiges of traditional religion in the region of Panopolis.[4] This larger agenda underlies the sermon dealing with hieroglyphs, in which Shenoute applies a reductionist and confrontational mode of interpretation to the inscriptions on the walls of a local temple. He identifies the hieroglyphs as foolish and misleading images and denies any possibility that they could be "read" in a Christian light, calling rather for their wholesale replacement with Christian images and scriptural quotations. By emphasizing the many animal hieroglyphs used in the temple inscriptions, Shenoute situates hieroglyphic writing within the broader Judeo-Christian discourse on Egyptian idolatry, which condemns the worship of cult images and the veneration of sacred animals, both key features of traditional Egyptian religious practice. This link between hieroglyphs and idolatry provides Shenoute with a strong theological justification for his ultimate goal of transforming the temple into a Christian church, and his reluctance to try and "read" meaning into the hieroglyphs serves as a clear refutation of the allegorical mode of interpretation promoted by his Neoplatonist contemporaries.

Shenoute in Context

Within the historiography of late antique Egypt, and more particularly that of the relationship between Christianity and traditional Egyptian religion, the figure of Shenoute of Atripe looms larger than life. In fact, he appears to have cultivated that stature during his lifetime; recent scholarship indicates that Shenoute carefully constructed his public persona and curated the extensive corpus of his own writings so as to shape his postmortem legacy as well.[5] Despite the survival of numerous volumes of his written work, the precise details of Shenoute's life, and especially his chronology, remain a matter of some debate; the problem is only exacerbated by the lack of external attestations for his life and activities. Traditionally credited with a preternaturally long lifespan of some one hundred and eighteen years, Shenoute is said to have been born in the Panopolite village of Shenalolet in the mid-fourth century, circa 347. His uncle, Pcol, served as the founding head of a monastery located a few kilometers north of the village of Atripe (modern Sohag), across the Nile from Panopolis, and Shenoute entered the monastery as a young man, by the year 372. By around 386, Shenoute had risen to the leadership of the monastic community, a position he enjoyed until his death in the mid-fifth century, likely around 465.[6]

During Shenoute's time as archimandrite, the monastery consisted of a federation comprising three communities: the main (male) community, referred to today as the Monastery of Father Shenoute (*Deir Anba Shinuda*) or the White Monastery (*Deir el-Abiad*), a smaller male community located a short distance away at the site now known as the Red Monastery (*Deir el-Ahmar*), and a female community housed in the village of Atripe, in and around the repurposed temple of the goddess Repit/Triphis. Estimates of the total size of the White Monastery federation vary—the Arabic *Life of Shenoute* proposes a total population of twenty-two hundred monks and eighteen hundred nuns, although this has been challenged as an unrealistically high number—but in any case it is clear that through his leadership of the federation, Shenoute occupied a position of considerable local power.[7] As a "rural patron," to borrow a term used by Ariel López in his recent study of Shenoute's social activism, Shenoute maintained close ties to both the patriarch in Alexandria and to the Roman provincial authorities active in the Thebaid, and he was in a position to exert his influence in the immediate environs of the White Monastery, including nearby Atripe and the larger city of Panopolis on the east bank of the Nile.[8]

Early twentieth-century scholarship on Shenoute presented him as the leader of a populist and nationalist Egyptian Christian movement that was said to have grown up in the fourth and fifth centuries in opposition to both the "intellectual paganism" espoused by certain members of the local elite and (later) the Chalcedonian orthodoxy of the Byzantine leadership. To be a Copt, according to this model, meant to be poor, rural, Egyptian speaking, uneducated in the traditions of classical paideia, and staunchly miaphysite in theological orientation. This indigenous Egyptian identity was thought to exist in polar opposition to that of the era's wealthy, urban, Greek-speaking, classically educated, and pro-Chalcedonian elite.[9]

Both the dichotomy between "pagan elite" and "Christian peasantry" and the existence of any sort of late antique Egyptian "nationalism" have been called into question by more recent scholarship, however, and over the past few decades the focus of attention has shifted to Shenoute's pastoral leadership, his social activism, and, most relevant to the concerns of the present study, his belligerent attitude toward traditional cult practices and beliefs.[10] Shenoute's uncompromising stance vis-à-vis traditional Egyptian religion and the fiery rhetoric he leveled at its local practitioners have made him an emblem of monastic antipagan violence, a living caricature of the type of fanaticism described in Libanius of Antioch's oration *Pro templis*. His name has been associated with zealotry, religious hatred, and terrorism; a statement he made when defending himself against allegations of misconduct, "there is no crime for those who have Christ," even serves as the title of a recent book on religious violence in late antiquity.[11] As Ariel López has argued, this reputation for extremism—specifically, extremism in support of a Christian cause—is not simply an artifact of scholarship but something that Shenoute himself actively cultivated through his sermons and written works.[12]

But how much faith can we put in Shenoute's propagandistic representation of the local religious landscape and his own actions there? To take Shenoute at his word would be to see Panopolis as the site of unusually tenacious and long-lived temple cults (notably those of the local patron deity Min/Pan and his consort Repit/Triphis) and the home of committed pagan intellectuals who, in the words of Roger Rémondon, "recruited from among the aristocracy of Panopolis . . . the leisured classes who could study and learn Greek." In his influential article on resistance to Christianization in late antique Egypt, Rémondon posited that fifth-century Panopolis was "a pagan center where the temples still drew crowds."[13] More recently, Panopolis appears as a case study in the work of David Frankfurter, who uses the writings of Shenoute and his successor, Besa, to argue for the existence of a "resilient and well-supported native religiosity" in the city and its immediate environs. Set against this backdrop of recusant polytheism, Shenoute himself appears in high relief as the defender of the Christian faith, a heroic figure cast self-consciously in the mold of Old Testament prophets like Elijah. He advocated on behalf of Christians who had destroyed a temple in a nearby village, claimed to have burned a temple in the village of Atripe himself, and carried out nocturnal raids to remove "idols" from the home of a prominent local landowner.[14]

This picture of an embattled pagan stronghold deep in the Upper Egyptian countryside is not without its detractors, however, and the notion that traditional cults were thriving in the city into the fifth century has received significant criticism in recent years. Alan Cameron, whose classic article on the "wandering poets" from fifth-century Upper Egypt presented those individuals as "unrepentant and militant adherents of the old gods," has since returned to the subject with a significantly altered viewpoint. Cameron now argues that the poets' work represents not a pious attachment to the old ways but rather a kind of cultural Hellenism, completely disconnected from polytheistic cult practice and espoused by the classically educated *Christian* elites of late antique Egypt.[15] The 2002 volume *Perspectives on Panopolis* likewise deals with the issue of religious and cultural continuity in that region, and several of the contributors caution against reading too much into Shenoute's antipagan rhetoric. This theme emerges clearly in Peter van Minnen's chapter on the archive of the fourth-century *scholastikos* Ammon, where the author notes that "Shenute unmasked a single pagan in Panopolis, Gessios, a big landowner, and the quarrel with him was over social and economic matters. . . . If it had not been for Gessios, there might not have been another pagan at Panopolis for Shenoute to unmask, and even in this case there was no pagan cult left to fight over."[16] In a similar vein, Mark Smith's contribution highlights the fact that Shenoute's descriptions of the cult practices that he claimed were being maintained by certain Panopolites are often generic, reflecting little actual knowledge of traditional religion (whether Egyptian or Greek) as it had been practiced in Panopolis during the Hellenistic and Roman periods.[17] This issue of Shenoute's knowledge (or lack thereof) of the particulars of local cultic practice will be addressed further below insofar as it relates to his portrayal of hieroglyphs; for the moment, suffice it to say that the purported vitality of traditional cults in fourth- and fifth-century Panopolis must be treated with some caution, and Shenoute's claims about those cults (and his own actions in regard to them) must be considered in light of their rhetorical function within his own literary oeuvre.

Just as the conventional understanding of Panopolis and its "pagan resistance" has been challenged of late, so too has Shenoute's portrayal of his own actions in the region. As the aforementioned remarks of van Minnen suggest, the scope and scale of Shenoute's antipagan activities may have been somewhat more restricted in scope than the man himself would have us believe. This has been highlighted in recent work on Shenoute's interactions with his archnemesis, a wealthy local landowner named Gesios, who is probably to be identified with Flavius Aelius Gessius, governor of the Thebaid in the late 370s who subsequently retired to Panopolis. Gesios has long been seen as the leader of local resistance to Christianity, against whom many of Shenoute's attacks were directed.[18] However, on the basis of a newly published work of Shenoute's, the "open letter" *Let Our Eyes*, Stephen Emmel has persuasively argued that Gesios was more likely a "crypto-pagan" who had publicly agreed to accept Christian baptism but privately maintained his adherence to traditional cults.[19] If Shenoute's ultimate enemy—the figure whose actions in support of traditional cult practice were deemed so heinous that his name was not even to be spoken publicly—can be reduced to the status of a quondam Christian with a questionable art collection, how much more might we doubt the strength of the "pagan resistance" in the fifth-century Panopolite?[20] In fact, it has been suggested that Shenoute's actions, particularly his midnight invasion of Gesios' home, were likely met with disapproval even by the Christian residents of the city, who valued law and order over militant Christianization: "religious intolerance was a luxury that most Christians could simply not afford, and a lesser priority in comparison to issues like taxation or the maintenance of public order. When pursued beyond the control of the local elites and beyond the realm of temple desecration, it was downright intolerable."[21]

Panopolis in the Hellenistic and Roman periods was a multicultural city, with a religious landscape shared between exponents of traditional Egyptian religion, cultural Hellenism, and, by the time of Shenoute, a particularly militant and uncompromising brand of monastic Christianity. In the fourth and fifth centuries, all these groups seem to have been looking back and considering what role the past should play in their changing world. Cameron's wandering poets offer one possible answer: continued reverence for ancient (classical) mythology, divorced from any cultic context and accommodated within an elite Christian culture founded on classical paideia. Depending on how one chooses to characterize his religiosity, Gesios may offer a second answer: either cultural Hellenism in the tradition of the poets, or limited continuity with earlier cultic practices, now carried out under much reduced and distinctly private circumstances. Shenoute, for his part, represents a third way: the total rejection of earlier traditions, whether Hellenic or Egyptian, and an outright refusal to see any value in the cultural output of the pre-Christian past. As we shall see in the following pages, this attitude underlies Shenoute's discussion of hieroglyphic temple inscriptions and shapes his argument for their erasure.

The "Monastic Invective Against Egyptian Hieroglyphs"

A substantial corpus of Shenoute's written work has survived to the present day; this material includes nine volumes of *Canons*, comprising letters from Shenoute to the monastic communities under his leadership, rules for the monks, and sermons or treatises; eight volumes of *Discourses*, primarily public sermons; and assorted *Letters*.[22] At least some of these texts were apparently collected and edited by Shenoute himself, and many of the surviving manuscripts come from the library of the White Monastery, albeit from a period several centuries after Shenoute's own lifetime. These manuscripts did not survive unscathed, however; many of the codices containing Shenoute's works were dismembered in modern times and the resulting fragments scattered throughout library and museum collections worldwide. Thus it is unsurprising that the text that concerns us here is incomplete; as the incipit is lacking, the work is designated *Acephalous work A6* (hereafter *A6*) in Stephen Emmel's codicological reconstruction of Shenoute's literary corpus. The text is attested by fragments in the Bibliothèque Nationale de France, the University of Michigan Papyrology Collection, and the British Library. The Michigan fragments, the first of which contains the description of hieroglyphs, were published in 1981 by Dwight Young under the title "A Monastic Invective Against Egyptian Hieroglyphs," and this portion of the text is commonly used to identify the work overall as "a sermon preached on an occasion when a pagan temple was converted into a Christian church."[23] The other extant portions of the text do not treat either hieroglyphs or the conversion of the temple directly, although the possible thematic links between those sections and the discussion of hieroglyphs will be addressed in more detail below.

The text of Michigan MS 158.13a/b picks up in the midst of a description of the process by which a temple, surely dedicated to an Egyptian deity given the subsequent description of its décor, is to be transformed into a Christian church. Shenoute states: "Thus, then, at the place of a shrine of an unclean spirit (ⲡⲘⲀ ⲚⲦⲟⲡⲟⲥ ⲘⲡⲚⲀ ⲚⲀⲕⲀⲐⲀⲢⲦⲟⲛ), it shall be a shrine of the Holy Spirit (Ⲧⲟⲡⲟⲥ ⲘⲡⲚⲀ ⲉϤⲟⲨⲀⲀⲂ) from this day forth. And at the place of making sacrifice to Satan (ⲡⲘⲀ ⲚⲢⲐⲨⲤⲒⲀ ⲘⲡⲤⲀⲦⲀⲚⲀⲤ) and worshipping and fearing him, Christ shall henceforth be served therein, and he will be worshipped and bowed down to and feared. And at the place of blasphemies (ⲡⲘⲀ ⲚⲢⲈⲚⲘⲚⲦⲢⲉϤϪⲒⲟⲨⲀ), it is blessings which will be in it henceforth, together with hymns."[24] Mark Smith has argued that Shenoute's comments on local polytheistic practices often leave "no trace . . . of the very distinctive features of Egyptian cult and worship which characterised Akhmim and the surrounding area in earlier periods." The same would appear to hold true in this instance as well; the deity to which the temple was dedicated is not named, beyond the rather generic references to a "shrine of an unclean spirit" and "the place of making sacrifice to Satan," nor is any indication given of the temple's geographic location, although such information might have been provided in a portion of the sermon now lost.[25] Moreover, Ariel López has noted the existence of a very close parallel to this passage in an inscription from the martyrium of St. George in Zorava, Syria, dating to the year 515. In that text, the process of temple conversion is described in the following terms: "The abode of demons has become the house of God (θεοῦ γέγονεν οἶκος τὸ τῶν δαιμόνων καταγώγιον). The light of salvation shines where darkness caused concealment (φῶς σωτήριον ἔλαμψεν ὅπου σκότος ἐκάλυπτεν). Where sacrifices to idols occurred, now there are choirs of angels (ὅπου θυσίαι εἰδώλων, νῦν χοροὶ ἀγγέλων). Where God was provoked, now he is propitiated (ὅπου θεὸς παρωργίζετο, νῦν θεὸς ἐξευμενίζεται)."[26] The strong similarities between the two texts suggests that there existed something of a stock repertoire of images and phrases used to speak about the phenomenon of temple conversion, regardless of the particular local circumstances. Indeed, recent research has shown that temple conversion was as much a rhetorical construct as an archaeologically attested historical phenomenon, so the notion that Shenoute was recycling standard motifs and imagery in his sermon is not altogether surprising.[27]

Shenoute does pass from the generic to the particular as the sermon goes on, however. The passage that follows clearly reflects the décor of an Egyptian-style temple, its walls covered with relief carvings and hieroglyphic inscriptions:

> And if before today it was laws for murdering men's souls
> (ϨⲈⲚⲚⲞⲘⲞⲤ ⲘⲘⲚⲦⲢⲈϤϨⲈⲦⲂⲨⲨⲬⲎ ⲚⲢⲰⲘⲈ) which were in it,
> written in blood and not in black ink alone (ⲈⲨⲤⲎϨ ϨⲚⲞⲨⲤⲚⲞϤ
> ⲀⲨⲰ ϨⲚⲞⲨⲘⲈⲖⲀ ⲀⲚ ⲘⲀⲨⲀⲀϤ), there is nothing else written
> with respect to them except the likeness (ⲠⲒⲚⲈ) of the snakes and
> the scorpions, and the dogs and the cats, and the crocodiles and
> the frogs, the foxes, the other reptiles, the wild beasts and the birds
> and the domestic animals and the rest; moreover, (there is) also
> the likeness (ⲠⲒⲚⲈ) of the sun and the moon and all the rest, all of
> their works (ⲚⲈⲨϨBⲎⲨⲈ ⲦⲎⲢⲞⲨ) being laughable and false things
> (ϨⲈⲚϨⲰⲂ ⲚⲤⲰBⲈ ϨⲒⲂⲞⲖ).[28]

The continuation of the sermon makes it clear that Shenoute envisions nothing less than the wholesale renovation of the temple, including the concealment or erasure of the hieroglyphic signs and their replacement with scriptural quotations: "And in the place of these (things) (ⲈⲠⲘⲀ ⲚⲚⲀⲒ), it is the soul-saving Scriptures of life (ⲚⲈⲄⲢⲀⲪⲎ Ⲛ̄ⲰⲚⲎ Ⲛ̄ⲢⲈϤⲦⲀⲚⲎⲈⲨⲨⲬⲎ) which will henceforth be in it, fulfilling the word of God, his name being written for them, together with his son Jesus Christ and all of his angels and righteous men and saints. And in every place (Ⲉ ⲘⲀ ⲚⲒⲘ), the things which are therein teach concerning every good work, especially purity. And how will it [i.e., the temple] not become pure (Ⲛ̄ ⲀⲰ Ⲛ̄ⲎⲈ Ⲛ̄ϤⲚⲀⲰⲰⲠⲈ ⲀⲚ ⲈϤⲞⲨⲀⲀⲂ)?"[29] The remainder of the first Michigan fragment is structured around an extended metaphor in which the fate of the temple is compared with that of a man or woman who converts to Christianity. The fragment breaks off midsentence, and a lacuna of some nine pages separates it from the second fragment (Michigan MS 158.13c/d), which deals with the spiritual rewards of charity toward the church. Pious women who make donations to the name of God are favorably contrasted with "defiled women" who adorn themselves instead of ransoming their souls with their possessions.[30] The thematic link between this section of the sermon and the first is nowhere made explicit in the text; it is possible that in the second portion of the sermon Shenoute was appealing for funds to carry out the program of conversion he had already described so vividly, but this is purely conjectural.

Laws for Murdering Men's Souls

In some respects, *A6* offers a fairly realistic representation of the types of signs that make up the hieroglyphic writing system. Although it is extremely unlikely that anyone in Shenoute's audience as he delivered this sermon would have been able to read hieroglyphs, monumental inscriptions of the type he describes would still have been visually familiar, if illegible, to the members of his congregation. However, the apparent realism of Shenoute's description is sharply undercut by his characterization of the inscriptions as "laws for murdering men's souls" and his assertion that they are "written in blood and not in black ink alone." With this short passage, Shenoute establishes the notion that the temple is a locus of spiritual danger, an idea already suggested by earlier references to the "shrine to an unclean spirit" and the "place of making sacrifice to Satan," and he emphasizes that the inscriptions carved on the walls represent a particular threat to those who view them.

The striking phrase "laws (ⲎⲈⲚⲚⲞⲘⲞⳞ) for murdering men's souls" makes Shenoute's rhetorical agenda clear from the outset. The terminology is reminiscent of Paul's reference to the "law (νόμος) of sin and death," which is said in Romans 8:2 to have been supplanted by the Christian message; such a subtext would be in keeping with Shenoute's overall assertion that these soul-killing inscriptions are to be supplanted by the "soul-saving Scriptures of life." Elsewhere in Shenoute's corpus, the phrase ΡΕϤϨΕΤΒϮΥΧΗ ͞ΝΡШΜΕ is used in reference to those who would mislead Christians into neglecting the precepts laid down for them in the Scriptures.[31] It may be that Shenoute is here highlighting the potential of the hieroglyphic texts to mislead viewers into the error of idolatry, a common late antique concern about the use of religious images in general, as we shall see below. Insofar as Egyptian temples, particularly of the later periods, may be seen as "vessel[s] of cultural memory," where inscriptions and reliefs were intended to codify and preserve the Egyptians' corpus of religious texts and ritual knowledge, this fear of Shenoute's may be seen as having some legitimate foundation, even if his allegation that the texts are "murderous" cannot be taken literally.[32]

The claim that the inscriptions on the temple walls are "written in blood" reflects the widespread pharaonic practice of accentuating the carved figures of temple reliefs and inscriptions with paint of various colors, including red. Paint is still visible on some of the inscribed pharaonic *spolia* used in the construction of the White Monastery church, and there is every reason to assume that Shenoute was familiar with this long-standing decorative convention.[33] By intimating that the inscriptions owed their hue to blood rather than paint, however, Shenoute was likely also making an oblique reference to the allegations of blood sacrifice that played a large role in what has been called a "standard vocabulary of denigration"—stock charges of atrocity bandied about by religious groups attempting to discredit one another.[34] Accusations of human sacrifice were a key component of both antipagan and anti-Christian polemic in late antiquity; David Frankfurter has argued that such stories were circulated in an effort to construct an image of the barbaric Other, and perhaps also to justify the persecution of that Other. A classic example from Upper Egypt comes from the sixth- or seventh-century *Panegyric on Macarius of Tkôw*, in which the worshippers of a local deity called "Kothos" are charged with sacrificing Christian children in order to make harp strings with their guts. Shenoute's sermon fits neatly within this broader pattern; not only are the temple inscriptions hazardous to the souls of those who view them, he tells his listeners, but in their very coloring they bear witness to the atrocious practices carried out within the temple. All the more reason, then, to erase them by any means necessary.[35]

In addition to establishing that the temple is a dangerous locale, the opening phrase of the passage on hieroglyphs also echoes the language of

2 Corinthians 3:3, where the Christian community is likened to "a letter (ἐπιστολή) of Christ . . . written not with ink but with the Spirit of the living God (ἐγγεγραμμένη οὐ μέλανι ἀλλὰ πνεύματι θεοῦ ζῶντος / ⲈⲤⲤⲎϨ ⲘⲘⲈⲖⲀ ⲀⲚ ⲀⲖⲖⲀ ϨⲘ̄ⲠⲈⲠⲚⲀ ⲘⲠⲚⲞⲨⲦⲈ ⲈⲦⲞⲚϨ), not on tablets of stone but on tablets of human hearts."[36] Shenoute inverts this Pauline imagery in his sermon, emphasizing the total contrast between the temple and the church that will replace it. This motif is developed throughout the first fragment of the sermon, where Shenoute uses the language of substitution and replacement to speak of the temple's transformation.

Likeness and Representation: Shenoute's Theory of Images

As Shenoute moves into a more detailed description of the hieroglyphic inscriptions in the temple, he uses the word "likeness" (Coptic ⲈⲒⲚⲈ, commonly used to translate the Greek ὁμοίωμα) to describe the individual signs. This is almost certainly a deliberate echo of the phrasing of the second commandment: "you shall not make for yourself an idol whether in the form of anything (εἴδωλον οὐδὲ παντὸς ὁμοίωμα / ⲞⲨⲈⲒⲆⲰⲖⲞⲚ ⲞⲨⲆⲈ ⲠⲈⲒⲚⲈ Ⲛ̄ⲖⲀⲀⲨ) that is in heaven above, or that is on the earth below, or that is in the waters under the earth," and the proscription of graven images in Exodus 20:4 is a likely subtext for this passage in the sermon.[37] Given the emphasis on the depictions of animals, especially reptiles, among the hieroglyphic signs, it is tempting to also see in Shenoute's phrasing a veiled reference to Ezekiel 8:10, where the décor of a temple is described in similar terms: "there, portrayed on the wall all around, were all kinds of creeping things, and loathsome animals, and all the idols of the house of Israel." The worshippers in the temple that Ezekiel describes are slated for imminent destruction, so this ominous subtext could have helped to heighten the sense of spiritual danger represented by the temple and to provide a biblical precedent for its cleansing at Shenoute's hands. However, the Septuagint omits the reference to animals altogether, as does the Bohairic translation of Ezekiel, so Shenoute is unlikely to have been consciously echoing this passage in his sermon.[38]

The text of Romans 1:23 offers a clearer parallel to support Shenoute's rhetorical agenda. In that passage, Paul describes the ungodly as those who have "exchanged the glory of the immortal God for images resembling a mortal human being or birds or four-footed animals or reptiles (ἐν ὁμοιώματι εἰκόνος φθαρτοῦ ἀνθρώπου καὶ πετεινῶν καὶ τετραπόδων καὶ ἑρπετῶν /

ⲞⲨⲈⲒⲚⲈ ⲚϨⲒⲔⲰⲚ ⲚⲢⲰⲘⲈ ⲈϢⲀϤⲦⲀⲔⲞ ϨⲒϨⲀⲖⲎⲦ ϨⲒⲦⲂⲚⲎ ϨⲒⲬⲀⲦϤⲈ).”[39] This semantic and conceptual link between the hieroglyphic signs and the graven images condemned in both Old and New Testaments provides Shenoute with a clear theological justification for the rejection of the temple's traditional decorative program.

By highlighting the representational quality of the hieroglyphic inscriptions in the temple, Shenoute was inserting himself into a discussion about the value of religious images that was already hundreds of years old by the fourth century. Greek philosophical arguments against religious imagery, which go back to Plato's condemnation of the artist on the grounds that "what he makes isn't the real thing," tended to revolve around three major points: the impossibility of representing the divine, the material quality of man-made images, and the potential danger of such images to turn mankind away from the pure contemplation of the divine and toward the worship of the image as a divinity in its own right.[40] Similar concerns figure prominently in the biblical discussions of graven images and artistic representation more generally. As noted above, an absolute prohibition of images is expressed in the Pentateuch, first in Exodus 20:4 and then, with minor variations, in Leviticus 26:1 and Deuteronomy 4:15–18.

The biblical prohibition of images rests on two key points: the idea that the divine is without form and therefore cannot be represented, and the notion that the existence of images inevitably conduces to idolatry. "Since you saw no form when the Lord spoke to you at Horeb out of the fire," says Moses, "take care and watch yourselves closely, so that you do not act corruptingly by making an idol for yourselves, in the form of any figure."[41] Elsewhere in the Old Testament, prophets and psalmists take this argumentation a step further, highlighting the fact that images are made of insensate, inanimate matter that could just as easily be used for mundane purposes; as Jeremiah says, they are "like scarecrows in a cucumber field, and they cannot speak; they have to be carried, for they cannot walk."[42] This discourse reaches a climax in the deuterocanonical text known as the Wisdom of Solomon, whose author condemns "those who give the name 'gods' to the works of human hands, gold and silver fashioned with skill, and likenesses of animals, or a useless stone, the work of an ancient hand."[43]

The Christian polemicists in whose lineage Shenoute positions himself drew heavily on this traditional Jewish line of argumentation in their efforts to stamp out what they saw as idolatrous ritual practices centered around the veneration of cult images.[44] Shenoute does the same, quite explicitly, in the

opening passages of *Let Our Eyes*, where he quotes the proscription of idolatry in Deuteronomy 4 as a justification for his clandestine entry into Gesios'
home and the removal of the images he found there:

> Not only does the great prophet Moses command, "Be not lawless,"
> and "Make no graven images for yourselves in the likeness of any
> image (ⲘⲠⲢⲦⲀⲘⲒⲈⲔⲀⲨⲠⲦⲞⲚ ⲚⲎⲦⲚ ⲘⲠⲒⲚⲈ Ⲛ̄ⲂⲒⲔⲰⲚ ⲚⲒⲘ), the
> likeness of male or female, the likeness of any beast that is on the
> earth, the likeness of any winged bird that flies under heaven, the
> likeness of any reptile that creeps on the earth, the likeness of any fish
> that moves in the waters under the earth," and "Lift not your eyes
> up to heaven and see the sun and the moon and the stars and all the
> order of heaven and go astray and worship them and serve them," but
> he also ordered, "If they set them up, they shall be killed."
>
> And yet, now someone has made for himself the image of
> Kronos and the images of the other demons, not having contented
> himself with images of effeminate men and lewd and licentious
> women, whose activities are shameful to speak of, just as you saw
> them all, each according to its type, even the images of priests with
> shaven heads and altars in their hands, everything that was in the
> temples back when he whose memory is of good repute, Theodosios
> the righteous emperor, had not yet given orders that they should be
> laid waste.[45]

Later in the same text, Shenoute also draws on the biblical trope of the materiality of cult images, speaking disparagingly of "foolish matter shaped into a
lot of idols (Ⲃ̄ⲨⲖⲎ ⲈⲦ̄ⲰⲞⲨⲈⲒⲦ ⲈⲨⲈⲒⲢⲈ ⲚⲞⲨⲀⲰ̣Ⲏ Ⲛ̄ⲈⲒⲆⲰⲖⲞⲚ) for whom
many lamps had been lit."[46] Although Shenoute is speaking in *Let Our Eyes*
specifically about three-dimensional sculptural representations, we shall see
shortly that the same line of scriptural argumentation informs his rhetorical
approach in the discussion of hieroglyphs as well.

Although the text of *A6* and the excerpts from *Let Our Eyes* quoted above
might give the impression that Shenoute disapproved of *all* religious imagery, this does not seem to have been the case. The archaeological remains
of the great basilica at the White Monastery, which was constructed under
Shenoute's supervision in the mid-fifth century, indicate that the church was
extensively decorated in late antiquity with architectural sculpture and both
figural and nonfigural wall paintings.[47] As Caroline Schroeder has noted,

Shenoute's attitude toward the adornment of the church was not uncompli-
cated; although he praises the construction, he also writes, "it is not the ornamentation of the house and the writings that are inscribed on its edifications
and its beams that will reconcile us to Jesus," and he urges the monks to pay
greater attention to their ascetic practices than to the decoration of the church
space.[48] Nevertheless, even such restrained admiration for the ornamentation
of the church is a far cry from the blanket condemnation of religious imagery
that we read, for example, in Tertullian's assertion that it was the devil who
created artists and that every representation is a potential idol.[49]

Moreover, the triconch funerary chapel discovered at the White Monastery in 2002, identified by archaeologists as the probable tomb of Shenoute
himself, is embellished with an extensive program of figural representations,
including images of crosses, deer, peacocks, and angels.[50] Although the décor
of the funerary monument is most likely a product of the monastic community and not Shenoute's own design, it seems unlikely that the abbot's followers would have chosen to commemorate their leader in such a fashion had he
been a militant iconoclast, rejecting all types of religious imagery. This begs
the question of how Shenoute distinguished "acceptable" images from "unac-
ceptable" ones; in other words, what theory of images underlies his critique
of the inscriptions and relief carvings on the temple walls, or the of statues
removed from the house of Gesios?

In *Let Our Eyes*, Shenoute articulates three principal objections to the
images found in Gesios' home: their subject matter is offensive, representing
as they do demons like Kronos and "effeminate men and lewd and licentious
women"; they are made of "foolish matter"; and they have the potential to
provoke idolatrous actions such as the lighting of lamps and the offering of
incense.[51] Similar concerns are expressed by Shenoute in an intriguing passage
from the sermon *A Beloved Asked Me Years Ago* (D4.3) where he speaks of wall
paintings and decorated tableware, suggesting that the images featured therein
are all representations of the devil: "Rather, there is terror for those who worship his likeness which has been painted on images (ⲡⲉϥⲉⲓⲛⲉ ⲛⲧⲁⲩⲥⲁϩϥ
ⲉϩⲉⲛϩⲓⲕⲱⲛ), and on the walls of their inner rooms, and on their eating and
drinking utensils, and on many things and in many places. Or are they not
all his images (ⲛⲉϥⲉⲓⲛⲉ) and the image of his teeth which instill fear in the
foolish? It is on the idols (ⲉⲓⲇⲱⲗⲟⲛ) which we took from their houses!"[52]
In this passage, as in the excerpt from *Let Our Eyes* quoted above, Shenoute
echoes the views of several prominent theologians, including Clement of Alexandria, Jerome, and John Chrysostom, all of whom weighed in on the dangers

of art and its potential to lead the unwary into idolatry. That this concern extended not only to what we might now consider "fine art," but encompassed the decorative arts as well, is clearly articulated in the *Protrepticus* of Clement, who writes,

> casting off shame and fear, they have their homes decorated with
> pictures representing the unnatural lust of the daemons. In the
> lewdness to which their thoughts are given, they adorn their
> chambers with painted tablets hung on high like votive offerings,
> regarding licentiousness as piety; and, when lying upon the bed,
> while still in the midst of their own embraces, they fix their gaze
> upon that naked Aphrodite, who lies bound in her adultery. Also, to
> show they approve the representation of effeminacy, they engrave in
> the hoops of their rings the amorous bird hovering over Leda, using
> a seal which reflects the licentiousness of Zeus.[53]

Shenoute's description of demonic images painted "on the walls of their inner rooms" clearly parallels Clement's portrayal of bedchambers decorated with "painted tablets" depicting mythological motifs, and both authors condemn such imagery for its depiction of "licentiousness" and "effeminacy."

The use of classical mythological motifs as decorative elements on household furnishings, textiles, and table silver is well documented for fifth-century Upper Egypt, and Alan Cameron has argued that such images were both common and unremarkable in the wealthy and cultured circles of the educated Christian elites in cities like Panopolis. It is probably just such mythologizing motifs that Shenoute is attacking in *A Beloved Asked Me Long Ago*, and Stephen Emmel has proposed that the reference to images of "effeminate men and lewd and licentious women" in *Let Our Eyes* similarly refers to sculptures of deities from classical mythology. That the condemnation extends to sculpture in the Egyptian style as well is evident from the description of "the images of priests with shaven heads and altars in their hands," clearly a reference to the naophorous priestly statues that became popular in Late-Period Egypt.[54] For Shenoute, it seems that the act of representation is not objectionable in itself; rather, it is the subject of representation and the uses to which the resulting images are put that constitute the potential danger. Although Shenoute could not read the inscriptions he describes in *A6*, it is clear from his assertion that they are "laws for murdering men's souls" that he considered their content to be just as damning as the representations of Kronos and Hecate—"through whom people are deceived at the oracles"—and just as liable to lead viewers into the sin of idolatry.[55]

Although it might seem to modern, Western eyes, accustomed to distinguishing between writing and figural representation, that hieroglyphic signs, relief carvings, and three-dimensional cult images are functionally distinct, Shenoute condemns them all in the same terms, and in fact the boundaries between these different categories of representation may have been perceived fairly fluidly by the ancient Egyptians themselves. It has long been argued that in certain contexts (notably Old Kingdom funerary monuments), two- and three-dimensional representations of the human figure might serve as determinatives in the writing of an individual's name, blurring the boundary between script and figural representation. Moreover, the selective mutilation of individual hieroglyphs in tomb and temple inscriptions suggests that the signs making up the writing system were seen as having their own potentially dangerous agency, just as statues and relief carvings were thought to have the potential to become animated or actualized through the power of Heka.[56] Belief in the power of images (of all sorts) persisted well into late antiquity, and although Shenoute could not have known how Egyptians of earlier periods understood the complex interplay of text, relief, and three-dimensional representation, his sense that the hieroglyphs on the temple walls held a power beyond the simple function of rendering speech visible is not out of keeping with earlier Egyptian ways of conceptualizing the hieroglyphic writing system and its relationship to other modes of visual representation.[57]

In suggesting that hieroglyphic signs, as representations, function in a similar manner to relief carvings and sculpture in their potential to incite idolatry, Shenoute anticipates a line of argumentation that would reach its fullest expression more than a thousand years after his death. As described above, in his reconstruction of the development of Egyptian scripts William Warburton argued against the widespread belief that hieroglyphs were first developed to conceal esoteric priestly knowledge from the common man (a view founded on the ancient sources discussed in the previous chapter and notably expounded in the early modern period by Athanasius Kircher). Warburton claimed that the reverse was true, and that hieroglyphic writing shifted over time from being a means of communication to being a means of concealment.[58] An important corollary to this claim was that the Egyptians, as their writing system became more complex, developed a "symbolic" script (cryptography) in which signs no longer represented things, but depended on "metaphor or metonymy" to express complex and abstract concepts. For

Warburton, these "symbolic" hieroglyphs stood at the origin of Egyptian animal worship, and as a consequence of this view, he proposed an exegesis of the second commandment reflecting specifically Egyptian concerns. "All Hieroglyphic Writing was absolutely forbidden by the second Commandment," he writes, "and with a View worthy the Divine Wisdom, Hieroglyphics being . . . the great Source of the most abominable Idolatries and Superstitions."[59] Shenoute's objections to hieroglyphs are not spelled out at such great length as Warburton's extended analysis, but in the end both writers articulate a remarkably similar understanding of the nature of hieroglyphs as images. According to such an understanding, the inscriptions on the temple walls can never be seen as "neutral." Like the statues removed from the inner rooms of Gesios' home, they are inherently problematic by virtue of their potential to incite idolatrous practices. Moreover, as we shall see, the fact that many of the hieroglyphs represent animals makes them all the more suspect in Shenoute's eyes.

Snakes and Scorpions, Dogs and Cats

The core of Shenoute's description of hieroglyphs in *A6* consists of a list of animal signs, ranging from wild beasts and snakes to domesticated cattle, and these animal hieroglyphs play several key roles in Shenoute's overall rhetorical project. On one level, they reflect fairly accurately the range of signs that make up the hieroglyphic script. One need look no further than Gardiner's Sign List to confirm that a significant proportion of the hieroglyphic repertoire represents some form of Egyptian fauna; for an example of such animal hieroglyphs utilized in a monumental context, see Figure 8.[60] Beyond this basic realism, however, by placing such a heavy emphasis on the appearance of the various animal hieroglyphs, Shenoute is also participating in a mode of describing Egyptian monumental inscriptions that was standard among earlier Greek, Roman, and—as the Book of Thoth now demonstrates—Egyptian authors. Emphasizing the animal signs also allows Shenoute to associate the hieroglyphic inscriptions ever more closely with the notions of idolatry and animal worship so strongly condemned in his biblical and patristic proof texts.

A focus on animal hieroglyphs is absolutely characteristic of Greco-Roman speculation on the nature and meaning of the hieroglyphic script, seen in the works of authors from Diodorus to Ammianus and beyond. So, for example, Diodorus writes, "it is found that the forms of their letters take the shape of animals of every kind (Συμβέβηκε τοίνυν τοὺς μὲν τύπους ὑπάρχειν

Figure 8. Fragmentary hieroglyphic inscription, now in the Open-
Air Museum at the temple of Karnak. Photo by author.

αὐτῶν ὁμοίους ζῴοις παντοδαποῖς). . . . For instance, they draw the picture of a hawk, a crocodile, a snake, and of the members of the human body."
Some four centuries later, Shenoute's close contemporary Ammianus Marcellinus similarly describes the Egyptians "engraving many kinds of birds and
beasts, even of another world, in order that the memory of their achievements
might the more widely reach generations of a subsequent age." Indeed, for
Diodorus and his later colleagues, these animal hieroglyphs came to represent
the very essence of the entire Egyptian writing system, a view clearly expressed
in Tacitus' pithy statement that "the Egyptians, in their animal-pictures (*per
figuras animalium*), were the first people to represent thought by symbols."[61]

As discussed in the previous chapter, the most elaborate and influential
explication of hieroglyphic writing to be produced for a Greco-Roman audience was penned by another contemporary of Shenoute's, Horapollo. Animal
hieroglyphs feature prominently in Horapollo's system of allegorical interpretation, which frequently attributes the meaning of individual signs to the
physical or behavioral characteristics of the objects represented by those signs.
This mode of interpretation via observation of the natural world is echoed

throughout the *Hieroglyphica*, and as many commentators on the text have noted, in this respect Horapollo's work represents a kind of compendium of late antique natural-historical knowledge. In fact, Horapollo's claims about the nature of animals often parallel the information found in the highly influential compilation of animal allegories known as *Physiologus*, itself probably a product of third- or fourth-century Alexandria.[62] Insofar as the natural world was seen by the Neoplatonists as a reflection of divine archetypes, animal hieroglyphs could be understood as a sort of double encoding of those mysteries—the first in the "book of nature," and the second in the "language of nature" that hieroglyphs were thought to represent.[63]

Incorrect as Horapollo and his Greco-Roman colleagues undoubtedly were in their understanding of how the hieroglyphic script actually functioned, the focus on animal hieroglyphs that we see in the classical sources nonetheless rings true in light of the large number of animal signs present in the hieroglyphic repertoire. This way of talking about hieroglyphs also echoes the ways in which Egyptian priestly scribes of the Hellenistic and Roman periods described their own writing system. As discussed in Chapter 3, Egyptian scribes appear to have used the names of birds to identify the different consonant sounds in the Egyptian language, and it has been suggested that this practice may have been maintained even after the widespread adoption of the Coptic script in Egypt. The Book of Thoth is also replete with bird imagery, as in lines 242–44, where hieroglyphs are described as "the Ba-souls of Re" that fly up to Thoth and nest within documents; as Jasnow has noted, this imagery extends to the work of the scribe as well, with netting and trapping serving as an extended metaphor for the act of writing.[64] Nor are birds the only fauna to be cited by Egyptian scribes in conjunction with hieroglyphs. In the Book of Thoth, hieroglyphs are equated with various types of animals, including dogs and reptiles.[65] Read in this light, Tacitus' characterization of hieroglyphs as "animal-pictures" seems less a declaration of ignorance than a genuine reflection of the way Egyptian scribes of his day were speaking about the ancient hieroglyphic script.

Having established that Shenoute's focus on animal hieroglyphs shares certain common features with the broader contemporary discourse on hieroglyphic writing, it remains to be seen how he exploits that discourse to serve his own particular religious agenda. Unlike Horapollo and his classical forebears, Shenoute does not "read" supplemental (allegorical) meaning into the hieroglyphic signs, nor does he comment on the significance of the individual animals depicted in the hieroglyphs. The categories of living things represented in the list, which include reptiles (snakes, crocodiles), mammals (dogs, cats, foxes, wild beasts, and cattle), and birds, correspond broadly to the categorization of forbidden images in Deuteronomy 4:17–18, which prohibits "the likeness of any animal that is on the earth, the likeness of any winged bird that flies in the air, the likeness of anything that creeps on the ground, the likeness of any fish that is in the water under the earth."[66] As we have already seen, the text of Romans 1:23 is a likely model as well, condemning as it does the worship of "likenesses resembling a mortal human being or birds or four-footed animals or reptiles." What seems to be most significant for Shenoute's understanding of the animal hieroglyphs is the close connection, outlined in these biblical texts, between animal imagery and animal worship—a form of devotion that many late antique commentators characterized as a particularly Egyptian (and particularly troubling) form of idolatry.[67]

The Greek and Roman authors who discussed hieroglyphs with such great interest were no less fascinated by Egyptian animal cults, but their attitudes toward the latter were typically less than admiring. Roman visitors to Tebtunis may have enjoyed offering the customary "tidbits for Petesouchos and the crocodiles," as a letter from 112 B.C.E. attests, but they could nonetheless see the humor in Juvenal's vicious Satire 15, in which the poet famously asks his audience, "is there anyone who doesn't know the kind of monsters crazy Egypt worships?"[68] Distaste for this quintessential aspect of Late-Period Egyptian religious practice was shared across religious and cultural divides, and it is even more marked within the Judeo-Christian tradition than in the context of Greek and Roman literature. A fine example of this attitude is found in *De vita contemplativa*, where Philo writes scathingly of the Egyptian cults that it is "hardly decent even to mention them. The Egyptians have promoted to divine honours irrational animals, not only of the tame sort but also beasts of the utmost savagery, drawn from each of the kinds found below the moon."[69] The late antique church fathers, for their part, built on the Hellenistic Jewish discourse on idolatry and used Egyptian animal worship as a key example of the dangers of idolatry and, conversely, the power of Christianity to put an end to idolatrous practices. Thus Cyril of Jerusalem writes that it is "the cross that has given the Egyptians knowledge of God instead of (the worship of) cats, dogs, and the manifold error."[70] It is precisely this type of project—replacing the likenesses of the cats and dogs with the sign of the cross, and the darkness of Egyptian idolatry with the new light of Christian teaching—that Shenoute advocates in his sermon dealing with hieroglyphs.

Laughing at Lies

Having enumerated the many animal and cosmological signs present in the hieroglyphic repertoire, Shenoute concludes with a disparaging circumstantial clause, "all of their works being laughable and false" (Є2ЄΝ2ШВ Ν̄ϹШВЄ ΝЄ ΝЄϒ2ВНϒЄ ТНРОϒ 2ІϬОλ). This is less of a throwaway comment than it might at first appear, for ridicule was a powerful tool of late antique rhetorical practice. As Susanna Elm has shown, derision could be used for political ends. It was also a valuable tool of religious polemicists of all varieties; in an era when religious leaders claimed exclusive access to universal truths, "truth emerged in trials where the enemy was publicly battled to the ground through derisive laughter, exposed to all as the twitching, stumbling object of mockery."[71] Far from idle laughter, by evoking derision in his sermon, Shenoute is seeking to expose the inherent weakness of the images he had previously identified as dangerous and threatening.

The repeated use of the noun 2ШВ (plural 2ВНϒЄ) in this context is no idle choice, echoing as it does the claim of Psalm 115:4, "The idols of the nations are silver and gold, the work of human hands" (τὰ εἴδωλα τῶν ἐθνῶν, ἀργύριον καὶ χρυσίον, ἔργα χειρῶν ἀνθρώπων / ΝЄІΔШλΟΝ Ν̄Ν2ЄΘΝΟϹ 2ЄΝ 2ΑТ ΝЄ 2ІΝΟϒВ 2ЄΝ2ВНϒЄ Ν̄ЄΝϬІΧ Ν̄РШМЄ).[72] That text, together with Jeremiah 10:1–15 and Isaiah 44:9–20, was frequently cited by Christian polemicists in their refutation of polytheistic ritual practices directed toward cult images; in these biblical passages, the material quality of such cult images is derided, as is the fact that they have been produced by human artisans.[73] So, for example, Clement of Alexandria begins his extended criticism of cult images, and particularly representations of the gods of classical mythology, by urging the reader to inspect statues and thereby "find how truly silly is the custom in which you have been reared, of worshipping the senseless works of men's hands (ἔργα χειρῶν ἀνθρώπων ἀναίσθητα)."[74] Similarly, Cyril of Alexandria speaks out condemning the worship of hybrid deities and suggesting that the latter are so ludicrous as to not be worth even discussing: "In the first place, they (i.e., pagans) attribute life to a crowd of deities who are unknown even to their worshipers, and for some of whom they do not reserve even this common form of humanity; combining it with part of a pig or dog, they present us with what amounts to an adulterous nature, and break apart the fairest image of the things upon earth with their spurious modifications of its features. But why should I extend my remarks about things which are so laughable?"[75] By characterizing the "works" in the temple as "laughable"

(2ⲰⲂ ⲚⲤⲰⲂⲈ) and "false" (ϬⲞⲖ), Shenoute further echoes these scriptural and patristic precedents, particularly the derisive tone of Jeremiah's claim that "They (i.e., idols) are vain works, full of mockery (2ⲀⲚ2ⲂⲎⲞⲨⲒ ⲚⲈⲪⲖⲎⲞⲨ ⲚⲈ ⲈⲨⲘⲈ2 ⲚⲤⲰⲂⲒ); they shall perish on the day of their visitation."[76] If they can be seen as works of human hands, worthy of ridicule, then the threat represented by the inscriptions formerly characterized as "laws for murdering men's souls" can be effectively diminished.

The Christian mockery of cult images (and cult practices and temple personnel) at times moved beyond the realm of rhetoric and into that of action. As Béatrice Caseau has observed, the paradigm for such activity was established by Eusebius in his *De vita Constantini*, where the bronze cult statues publicly exhibited by the emperor are characterized as "toys for the laughter and amusement of the spectators," the display of which was undertaken in an effort to confute "the superstitious error of the heathen in all their ways." Caseau notes that although this may not have been the emperor's true (or only) motive, "Eusebius would not have deliberately written something absurd. It must therefore be the case that the act of subjecting the pagan statues to derision could have seemed plausible to his Christian readers."[77]

Inspired, no doubt, by the Constantinian model, later accounts of confrontations between Christians and polytheists often highlighted the aspect of ritual humiliation that the pagans and their cult images faced. This can be seen, for example, in Sozomen's report of the looting and public exposure of cult items from an abandoned Mithraeum in the vicinity of Alexandria. The historian writes, "while George [the archbishop of Alexandria] was clearing the ground, in order to erect a house of prayer, an *adytum* was discovered. In it were found idols and certain instruments of initiation or perfection which seemed ludicrous and strange to the beholders. The Christians caused them to be publicly exhibited, and made a procession in order to nettle the pagans." In the parallel account of Socrates, the "abominations" are said to have been carried "throughout the city, in a kind of triumphal procession, for the inspection of the people."[78] Shenoute's own ambitions may have been more restricted in scope and scale than those of the archbishop, but his rhetoric suggests that he was well aware of the possibilities afforded by public shaming. After the clandestine raid on Gesios' home recounted in *Let Our Eyes*, Shenoute reports that through the grace of God he and his brethren have "exposed them (the idols) openly so as for everyone to recognize his (Gesios') contempt and his shame, for them to recognize that he is a liar for having said, 'There are no idols in my house.'"[79] If Emmel is correct in proposing that Shenoute's main objective in this affair was to unmask Gesios as a "crypto-pagan," then the very public nature of the idols' exposure would have been of critical importance.

No such mocking parade of cult images is indicated in the surviving text of *A6* (and indeed, as we shall see below, the temple in question had probably long since been stripped of its cultic accoutrements before Shenoute ever took an interest in it). However, the language of derision that Shenoute employs in the sermon clearly resonates with the contemporary discourse on the public humiliation of idolaters and the objects of their devotion. As David Frankfurter has argued, rhetoric itself could be a potent weapon used to neutralize a potentially threatening idol, and denunciations of idols as mere images could function as "speech acts" whereby those same idols are stripped of their power: "the words themselves transform the objects."[80] Reading Shenoute's remarks in *A6* as just this sort of performative speech, we can see the abbot actively working to strip the potentially dangerous hieroglyphs of their power to lead viewers astray into the sin of idolatry. By his claim that the signs on the walls are "ridiculous and false," Shenoute has the power to actually make it so, thereby defusing the sense of threat and danger he had built up so carefully in the earlier part of the sermon.

Cleansing the Temple

Having described the temple's hieroglyphic inscriptions in mocking detail, Shenoute continues to lay out his vision for the conversion of the space: "in the place of these (things)," he says, "it is the soul-saving Scriptures of life which will henceforth be in it." The use of the phrase "in the place of" (ЄПМА Ṅ) at this juncture signals the continuation of the series of thought couplets that opens the first fragment of the sermon. In this carefully balanced composition, for each attribute of the temple, Shenoute provides a corresponding Christian replacement: the Holy Spirit for the unclean one, Christ for Satan, blessings and hymns for blasphemies, and the soul-saving Scriptures of life for the soul-murdering hieroglyphic inscriptions. Shenoute notes further that this wholesale transformation of the temple will fulfill the word of God, with the Scriptures and the names of Christ and the angels and saints "teaching about every good thing, especially purity."

Purity is a critical concept in Shenoute's works, encompassing not only the bodily practices of *askesis* but also obedience to the monastic rule and to the head of the monastery; its converse, impurity, could arise in the context of

numerous different sins, including sexual transgressions, disobedience, theological heterodoxy, and idolatry.[81] The connection between impurity and idolatry has deep biblical roots, expressed for example in Galatians 5:19–21, where
the "works of the flesh" are identified as "fornication, impurity, licentiousness,
idolatry, sorcery, enmities, strife, jealousy, anger, quarrels, dissensions, factions,
envy, drunkenness, carousing, and things like these." That Shenoute himself
associated the two concepts is indicated in the opening lines of *Let Our Eyes*,
where he writes, "Let our eyes—in accordance with the Scriptures—look at
what is right, and let our eyelids gaze at just things, and we will recognize how
great is the impurity of the soul of every pestilential person who is inimical
toward the faith of the universal Church."[82] This injunction is immediately
followed by the quotation from Deuteronomy 4:16–19 discussed above, allowing us to identify the "pestilential person(s)" inimical to the church with the
creators and worshippers of graven images, notably Shenoute's chief antagonist in the text, Gesios. If idolatry and impurity go hand in hand, then by
cleansing the temple of the graven images conducive to idolatry, Shenoute sets
out the necessary preconditions for the purification of that space. He closes
this portion of the sermon with a rhetorical question: "how will it (i.e., the
temple) not become pure?"; and indeed, his rhetoric leaves little room for an
alternative outcome.[83]

As noted above, it is widely believed that Shenoute was speaking in *A6*
about a real temple, likely in the vicinity of Panopolis, that he intended to
transform into a church. This raises the question of whether or not his remarks
can be correlated with any documented archaeological site in the area. There is
considerable debate, as we have seen, concerning the scope and precise nature
of Shenoute's antipagan activities in Atripe and its environs, and this controversy extends to the question of precisely which cult place(s) may have been the
focus of those activities. A principal locus of cultic activity in Atripe itself was
the Greco-Roman temple of the goddess Repit/Triphis; Petrie worked briefly at
the site in 1907 and concluded on the basis of his findings that the temple had
been repurposed as a church. He went on to observe that "the figures of gods
in relief on the inside were chopped away, and the whole whitewashed. Then it
was attacked for stone; and as some inscribed stones, apparently from here, are
in the Deir Amba Shenudeh, it is probable that this temple was quarried for
this monastery."[84] Subsequent discussions of the site have tended to uphold the
connection between the fire damage observed in the temple of Triphis with Shenoute's claim to have "burned the pagan temple in Atripe," and David Klotz's
recent epigraphic survey of the inscribed spolia from the White Monastery

church indicates that a group of roofing slabs used in the construction of the church came from a temple of Repit/Triphis, very likely the one in Atripe.[85] Whether or not Shenoute may be said to have "destroyed" the temple is far less certain, however. It has been argued that the "burning" of the temple should be seen as an act of purification rather than destruction and that it represents the "first step toward the transformation of the temple into a site that could be used by fifth-century Christians."[86] Moreover, as Klotz acknowledges in his study of the spolia found at the White Monastery, "the destruction may have been largely symbolic. . . . The Atripe blocks derive almost exclusively from the ceiling of the Repyt temple, and the builders probably removed them specifically for reuse in the White Monastery staircase."[87]

Excavations at the temple of Repit/Triphis in Atripe are ongoing, but the findings published to date have the potential to shed some light on the various phases of the site's reuse during the time of Shenoute. Although Petrie claimed rather broadly that the temple was turned into a church, recent discoveries—notably communal dining facilities located on the east side of the temple—suggest more specifically that the temple precinct came to house a monastic community in late antiquity. Further modifications to the site include a dyeing workshop installed in the naos and a triconch church constructed in the forecourt.[88] It is thought that this monastery should be identified with the women's community that formed the third constituent part of the White Monastery federation According to el-Sayed's reconstruction of the site's chronology, the women's monastery, which already existed in the time of Shenoute's predecessor Pcol, was originally situated outside the temple temenos. The expansion of the community led Shenoute to appropriate space within the precinct, where there is evidence for continuous use and redevelopment from the early fifth century into at least the seventh.[89]

If this interpretation of the temple's later history is accurate, it is extremely tempting to associate Shenoute's appropriation of the Repit/Triphis temple precinct with the program of purification and reuse outlined in the text of A6. Such an association has been proposed by Ariel López, who suggests that the reuse of the temple "would be an important step in Shenoute's attempt to carve out a sphere of religious and economic influence around his monastery. Indeed, the temple's conversion could have amounted to nothing less than making the town of Atripe his own."[90] It is worth noting that the later modifications to the temple include the selective mutilation of wall reliefs, targeting in particular figures of the king and of anthropomorphic deities. There are also indications that subsequent to this damage, walls throughout the temple were plastered over and then whitewashed, and traces of Coptic *dipinti* are found in some areas.[91] Such actions would be wholly consistent with Shenoute's expressed desire to replace the temple's original epigraphic program with Christian imagery and texts. It is to be hoped that continued work at the Triphis precinct will further elucidate the site's complex development in the late antique period; until additional evidence is brought to light, any connection between that site and the unnamed temple of *A6* must remain speculative.

Conclusion

In the text of *A6*, Shenoute offers a mode of interpreting Egyptian hieroglyphs starkly at odds with that of his Neoplatonist contemporaries, who advocated an allegorical mode of "reading" the ancient script. Ultimately, I would suggest that much of the rhetorical power of Shenoute's remarks actually comes from his refusal to engage with the hieroglyphs as readable text. Having provided the inscriptions with a pithy caption in the phrase "laws for murdering men's souls," he makes no further attempt to ascribe meaning to them, referring to them not as words or texts but rather as "likenesses," which stand in sharp contrast to the Christian "Scriptures" that will take their place. Although the Neoplatonists similarly emphasized the figural quality of the individual signs, Shenoute effectively turns their interpretive strategy on its head. Whereas Plotinus and his followers believed that the hieroglyphs were symbolic expressions of philosophical truths, which could be interpreted allegorically, by characterizing the signs as "likenesses," Shenoute essentially denies them their proper linguistic function and any possibility of deeper meaning. As likenesses, the hieroglyphs are semantically linked with the graven images condemned in both Old and New Testaments; they are "works of human hands" which, in the words of the psalmist, "have mouths, but do not speak."[92] This negation of meaning (and thereby, of power to harm the Christian viewer), is drawn out further when Shenoute dismisses the images he has just described as "laughable and false" and thus subject to erasure and replacement with Christian texts.

By focusing attention on the fact that the hieroglyphs are graven images, especially images of animals, Shenoute is able to draw on an extensive Judeo-Christian discourse of Egyptian idolatry in order to drive his point home. In the Hebrew Bible, Egypt appears as the quintessential land of idolatry, a view echoed both by Hellenistic Jewish authors such as Philo and also by the early church fathers. For Shenoute, the hieroglyphic inscriptions on the temple walls are of a piece with the cult images he removed from the home of Gesios, described in similar terms and condemned by the same biblical proof texts. In the end, *A6* offers not so much a mode of reading hieroglyphs as an unequivocally negative commentary on the value of pharaonic Egyptian culture. Like the statues he describes in *Let Our Eyes*, the hieroglyphic inscriptions in the unnamed temple are not—cannot ever be—ideologically neutral remnants of a bygone era. Nor are they to be read or even reinterpreted in a Christian context, as we will see Christian authors doing in the next chapter. In Shenoute's uncompromising worldview, the temple and the history it enshrines have no place or value in the present, except perhaps as the dark pole marking the starting point of Egypt's journey into the spiritual light of Christianity.[93]

Shenoute's rhetoric in *A6* is so striking that it would be easy to overstate the importance of this text and to take it as representing a kind of "normative" Egyptian Christian view of the hieroglyphic script. Indeed, Shenoute fits neatly into the mold of John Ray's "nervous monk," anxiously covering up hieroglyphic inscriptions lest they steal away his soul.[94] However, it is important to stress that the text of *A6* is, to the best of my knowledge, unique in the corpus of surviving Coptic literature; if other Coptic authors shared Shenoute's stern views on hieroglyphs, their comments on the subject have not come down to us. In the material remains from late antique Egypt, it may be possible to see some echoes of Shenoute's position—as, for example, in the erasure of the hieroglyphic inscription on the front face of the Ptolemaic altar that was reused in the church that was constructed inside the temple of Isis at Philae. Elsewhere, however, the record is more equivocal; at the temple of Dendera, for example, where the systematic mutilation of relief images has been widely documented and is typically attributed to Christian agency, the hieroglyphic inscriptions accompanying those reliefs have not suffered similar iconoclastic damage. At other sites, Christians dipinti peacefully share wall space with hieroglyphic inscriptions, and, as we shall see in the following chapter, Christian authors ultimately ventured to offer their own new readings of these already-ancient texts.[95]

Chapter 5

Translating Hieroglyphs,
Constructing Authority

The complex linguistic situation that prevailed in Egypt from the Hellenistic period onward necessarily resulted in extensive translation activity as the country's various language communities sought to communicate with one another and with the state. Over the course of the millennium separating the Ptolemies from the early caliphs, legal, financial, and administrative documents were translated into and from Egyptian (in various scripts), Greek, Latin, Aramaic, Pahlavi, and Arabic, among other languages. The sources occasionally refer to this process explicitly, as in the case of a sixth-century decree issued by the dux of the Thebaid, which includes instructions for the document's translation "into the vernacular language," that is, from Greek into Coptic (τῇ ἐπιχωρίῳ μεθερμηνε[υ]θῆναι διαλέκτῳ). More commonly, however, the translation of such texts seems to have passed largely unremarked as a necessary and unexceptional aspect of daily life in a multilingual environment.[1]

Documentary sources were not alone in receiving such treatment; literary and religious texts were also the object of translation activity during this time period. The most famous example is probably the production of the Septuagint, purportedly carried out at the behest of Ptolemy II for the benefit of the Alexandrian Library, but the Septuagint represents only one example of a much larger corpus of religious and literary translations produced in the Hellenistic and Roman periods.[2] These range from Greek translations of Egyptian cultic texts such as the Book of the Temple to the Coptic translation of a portion of Plato's *Republic*, and from the Greek translation of the Demotic Myth of the Sun's Eye to the Coptic translations of the Old and New Testaments.

In the midst of all this interpretive activity, the translation of Egyptian *hieroglyphic* texts into Greek, Latin, or other languages always remained something of a special case. Although such translations are known, as are translations in the opposite direction, from Greek or Latin into hieroglyphs, they are relatively uncommon, their production and consumption constrained by the increasingly restricted use of the hieroglyphic script and by the small number of individuals who would have been capable of engaging with that script in any meaningful way.[3] Somewhat more common are claims that a text in Greek or Latin represents the translation of a hieroglyphic or Demotic Egyptian original. As discussed briefly in Chapter 2, these have often been interpreted as a kind of marketing ploy, whereby the author of a Greek or, less commonly, Latin text sought to lend his work additional gravitas by providing it with a pedigree tied to the ancient and highly respected Egyptian scribal and priestly traditions. At the same time that such claims were in circulation, however, there also developed a kind of counterdiscourse that proposed that hieroglyphs were fundamentally untranslatable—or rather, as some authors argued, that they *should not be translated*, lest they lose their intrinsic magical efficacy. Such is the view expressed, for example, in treatise 16 of the *Corpus Hermeticum* and echoed in the work of Iamblichus, who argues (*De mysteriis* 7.4–5) that the Egyptian language possesses unique properties that would be vitiated by the act of translation.

The translation of hieroglyphic texts thus became, in late antiquity, a kind of contested space, where claims to authority—both the authority *to* translate a text or inscription and the authority gained *from* the act of translation— were constantly being negotiated. This chapter examines three late antique cases where such a negotiation can be closely observed: the presentation of a Greek translation of the Piazza del Popolo obelisk inscriptions in Ammianus Marcellinus' *Res Gestae*; the legend of the discovery and interpretation of mysterious "cross-shaped" hieroglyphs following the destruction of the Serapeum in Alexandria, as related in the ecclesiastical histories of Rufinus, Socrates, and Sozomen; and finally the story of the patriarch Theophilus' discovery and miraculous translation of hieroglyphic temple inscriptions, recounted in a cycle of late Coptic homilies.

Although the authors of these various accounts came from different linguistic, cultural, and religious backgrounds, a similar pattern can be discerned in all three cases. Despite the widespread belief that hieroglyphs were by nature untranslatable, attempts were nonetheless made in late antiquity to translate them, and the resulting translations (or "translations") served the authority-building agendas of various constituencies. Ammianus' obelisk translation speaks to the establishment of Roman imperial authority over Egypt; the interpretation of the cross-shaped hieroglyphs at the Serapeum lends strength to the Christian Church's claims to superiority over the cult of Serapis; and Theophilus' divinely inspired reading of the temple inscriptions allows him access to the riches of the temple treasury, giving him the means to cement his reputation as a prolific builder of new churches. Spurious though the majority of these "translations" undoubtedly were, they were nevertheless powerful tools that might be used in shaping both imperial and ecclesiastical authority. The works of the Christian authors under consideration here also signal a sea change in the location of hermeneutic agency. Whereas Ammianus appeals to an outside expert, the scholar Hermapion, to provide the translation for the obelisk inscription he quotes in the *Res Gestae*, the ecclesiastical historians and the author(s) of the homilies on Theophilus present the ability to read hieroglyphs as the result, not of a traditional Egyptian education in the House of Life, but of inspiration by the Holy Spirit.

The (Im)possibility of Translation in Classical and Christian Sources

P.Berol.inv. 21243, a magical text from Abusir el-Melek dating to the reign of Augustus, opens with a prologue stating the document's pedigree: "Excerpt from spells in the sacred book (ἱερὸς βύβλος) called 'of Hermes,' found in Heliopolis in the sanctuary (ἄδυτον), written in Egyptian characters (Αἰγυπτίοις γράμμασιν) and translated (διερμηνεύειν) into Greek."[4] Such a claim is hardly unprecedented, particularly in the genre of magical texts. Hermes was, as we have already seen, widely reputed as a master magician, and Heliopolis was viewed, particularly among classical authors, as one of the preeminent centers of Egyptian priestly learning. Nor is the statement that the Greek-language text represents the translation of an Egyptian original particularly unusual. The editor proposes that this should be regarded as an attempt to provide the text, which was probably composed in Greek, with "a hint of authenticity, age, and sacredness," and similar claims appear in other magical texts as well, probably for much the same reason.[5] *PGM* IV 885–86 offers a particularly striking parallel; in this text, written in Greek, the practitioner bids the spirits come to him "since I speak your names which thrice-greatest Hermes wrote in Heliopolis with hieroglyphic letters." A string of *voces magicae* follows in

which the name of the Egyptian deity Osiris features prominently.⁶ At roughly
the same time as the translation claims of texts like *P.Berol.inv.* 21243 and
PGM IV.885–86 were being articulated, however, a countervailing discourse
was emerging that problematized the very possibility of translation, especially
of theological and ritual texts. A forceful statement of this issue is expressed
in the opening lines of treatise 16 of the *Corpus Hermeticum*, which famously
begins with a meditation on the differences between the Greek and Egyptian
languages and an injunction against the act of translation from Egyptian to
Greek. The speaker, Asclepius, claims that he had been told by his teacher,
Hermes, that his writing "is unclear and keeps the meaning of its words concealed." Although a modern reader might take this as a criticism, both Hermes
and Asclepius see it as a good thing, and Asclepius goes on to relate the rest of
Hermes' remarks: "furthermore, it will be entirely unclear (ἀσαφής) (he said)
when the Greeks eventually desire to translate (μεθερμηνεύειν) our language
(διάλεκτος) to their own and thus produce in writing the greatest distortion
and unclarity. But this discourse (λόγος), expressed in our paternal language
(τῇ πατρῴᾳ διαλέκτῳ), keeps clear the meaning of its words. The very
quality of the speech and the <sound> of Egyptian words have in themselves
the energy of the objects they speak of (καὶ γὰρ αὐτὸ τὸ τῆς φωνῆς ποιὸν
καὶ ἡ τῶν Αἰγυπτίων ⟨ἠχὼ⟩ ὀνομάτων ἐν ἑαυτῇ τὴν ἐνέργειαν τῶν
λεγομένων)." Asclepius then makes a request of "King Ammon," to whom
the treatise is addressed. He says,

> Therefore, my king, in so far as you have the power (who are all
> powerful), keep the discourse uninterpreted (ἀνερμήνευτος), lest
> mysteries (μυστήριον) of such greatness come to the Greeks, lest the
> extravagant, flaccid, and (as it were) dandified Greek idiom extinguish
> the gravity, the solidity, and the efficacious quality (ἐνεργητικός) of
> the words (ὄνομα) of (our) speech (φράσις). For the Greeks have
> empty discourses (λόγος), O king, that are energetic only in what
> they demonstrate, and this is the philosophy of the Greeks, an inane
> foolosophy of speeches. We, by contrast, use not discourses (λόγος)
> but sounds (φωνή) that are full of action (ἔργων).⁷

In this introduction, Asclepius lays out a series of contrasts between Greek
and Egyptian: Greek, characterized by the production of empty philosophical
discourses, is weak and overly ornamented, while Egyptian is serious, solid,
and above all *efficacious*. Translating a text from Egyptian into Greek risks not

only the loss of clarity but also, more important, the loss of a fundamentally energetic quality that is intrinsic to the very sounds of the Egyptian language but wholly absent from the Greek.[8]

The supreme irony of *CH* 16 is, of course, that the text survives only in Greek and was almost certainly composed in that language. The tension between the linguistic attitude expressed by the author and the language in which the text is preserved presents the reader with a striking paradox, which scholars have been at some pains to resolve over the course of the last several decades.[9] In a seminal article on the subject, Claire Préaux argues that, within the Hermetic corpus in particular, the arguments for and against translation reflect two distinct Greek modes of thinking about both language and religion. In the first mode, articulated most forcefully in *CH* 16, the refusal to translate stems from a desire to both preserve the efficacy of the words in which divine knowledge was first revealed to mankind and also to restrict access to that knowledge.[10] The second mode of thought, expressed in treatise 12 of the *Corpus Hermeticum*, proposes that although languages differ from one nation to another, "humanity is one; therefore, speech is also one, and when translated it is found to be the same in Egypt and Persia as in Greece."[11] Préaux characterizes this as a quintessentially rationalistic and Hellenistic outlook, consistent with the extensive translation activity carried out under the Ptolemies and reflecting an "egalitarian" understanding of the communicability of religious revelation.[12]

Also focusing his attention primarily on the *Corpus Hermeticum*, Garth Fowden has argued that the authors of the Hermetic treatises themselves recognized the tension between their claims to linguistic exclusivity and the existence of Greek-language Hermetica, and that they attempted to resolve this tension by appealing to the tradition articulated in the *Book of Sothis*. In that text, discussed above in Chapter 3, hieroglyphic stelae carved before the Flood by "Thoth, the first Hermes" were said to have been subsequently translated into Greek "by the second Hermes, the son of Agathodaimon and the father of Tat." In Fowden's estimation, this tradition offers a tidy resolution to the paradox of translation; moving from one language to another may be problematic, but who better to meet that challenge than the god who invented language in the first place?[13]

More recently, Jacco Dieleman has examined the "paradox of translation" in his study of linguistic and cultural interactions in the milieu of the so-called Theban Magical Library. Reflecting on the attitudes expressed in *CH* 16, which he sees as originating in an Egyptian priestly milieu, he argues that the author of this text was self-consciously playing with the classical discourse

on Egypt, on Egyptian hieroglyphs, and on the famously secretive and exclusive Egyptian priesthood, essentially giving his Greek-speaking audience what
they wanted and expected to hear.[14] Similarly, in a discussion of the concept
of "mysteries" in the Hermetic corpus, Christian Bull suggests that language
choice, and the decision to translate or not to translate, offers a measure of
control over the material encoded in the hieroglyphic text: "the loss of meaning which occurs when translating the sacred books of the Egyptians into
Greek, as seen in *CH* 16.1–2, is thus a way to keep the appearance of possessing
an inviolate secret while divulging it only piecemeal."[15]

The concepts expressed in *CH* 16, in particular the uniquely efficacious
quality of the Egyptian language and the impossibility of translating from
Egyptian into Greek, were shared to some degree by the later Neoplatonists
who dealt with the subject of Egyptian hieroglyphs. As discussed above in
Chapter 3, Plotinus and Iamblichus both present the hieroglyphic script as a
unique means of communication. Plotinus, for his part, emphasizes the difference between Egyptian hieroglyphs, which he claims manifest "the non-
discursiveness of the intelligible world" according to a system by which "every
image is a kind of knowledge and wisdom," and other writing systems, which
"use the forms of letters which follow the order of words and propositions
and imitate sounds and the enunciations of philosophical statements." Egyptian, he stresses, is not a matter of "discourse or deliberation."[16] Plotinus does
not explicitly state that his primary comparison is between the Egyptian and
Greek languages, but his emphasis on the notions of rational discourse and
"the enunciations of philosophical statements" that characterize the language
or languages that he sets in opposition to the Egyptian hieroglyphic script
echoes the phrasing of *CH* 16, which similarly insists on philosophical discourse as particularly characteristic of the Greek language in contrast to the
Egyptian. Unlike the author of *CH* 16, however, Plotinus appears to reject
the idea that associates Egyptian with efficacious *speech*; if the hieroglyphs are
purely images, then no sounds can be associated with them. Translation is
nonetheless problematized, for how could one hope to move between a system
that offers a direct representation of reality via symbols and a system that relies
instead on the imitation of sounds and the linkage of those sounds into words
and then into discourses?

Writing a generation or so after Plotinus, Iamblichus' view of hieroglyphs
and the issue of translation echoes the theories articulated in both Plotinus'
Enneads and in the *Corpus Hermeticum*. As discussed above in Chapter 3, Iamblichus, like Plotinus, understood hieroglyphs as a fundamentally symbolic

system whereby the Egyptians "display certain signs (εἰκών) of mystical, arcane and invisible intellections by means of symbols (διὰ συμβόλων)."[17] However, he was also concerned with spoken Egyptian and its use in ritual practice, and here his comments align very closely with the views expressed in *CH* 16. Because the meaning of divine names in the "barbarian" languages of Egyptian and Assyrian is not dictated by convention but directly reflects reality, he argues that "the names (ὄνομα) do not exactly preserve the same meaning when they are translated (μεθερμηνεύειν); rather, there are certain idioms in every nation that are impossible to express in the language (φωνή) of another. Moreover, even if one were to translate them, this would not pre-serve their same power (δύναμις). For the barbarian names possess weightiness (ἔμφασις) and great precision (συντομία), participating in less ambiguity, variability, and multiplicity of expression. For all these reasons, then, they are adapted to the superior beings."[18] In other words, for Iamblichus as for the author of *CH* 16, Egyptian is uniquely appropriate to ritual contexts by virtue of its very nature; unlike Greek, which is innovative and experimental, Egyp-tian is eternal, pleasing to the gods, and "wholly suitable for sacred rituals."

Christian authors shared many of the same concerns about the possibility of translation, particularly in the realm of ritual practice. This is exemplified by a section of Origen's *Contra Celsum* in which the apologist discusses the use of sacred names. Origen was responding to Celsus' claims that, on the one hand, Christians obtain supernatural power by "the names of certain demons, and by the use of incantations" and, on the other hand, to the syncretistic proposition that "it makes no difference whether the God who is over all things be called by the name of Zeus, which is current among the Greeks, or by that, e.g., which is in use among the Indians or Egyptians."[19] In his reply to the first of these allegations, Origen argues that Christians do indeed produce miracles by speaking the name of Jesus. He takes issue, however, with the notion that sacred names are interchangeable. Rather, following the Platonist and Stoic position that saw the development of language and the assignment of names to things and beings as a function of nature rather than conven-tion, Origen argues strongly against the possibility of translation, especially of sacred names and ritual formulae: "those who are skilled in the use of incanta-tions, relate that the utterance of the same incantation in its proper language can accomplish what the spell professes to do; but when translated into any other tongue, it is observed to become inefficacious and feeble. And thus it is not the things signified, but the qualities and peculiarities of words, which possess a certain power for this or that purpose."[20] As John Dillon points out in his analysis of these passages from *Contra Celsum*, Origen's understanding of the nature of language, the power of sacred names, and the difficulty of translation is wholly in line with the attitudes expressed in contemporary Hermetic and Neoplatonic sources.[21] Indeed, these attitudes seem to have been fairly common currency in late antique intellectual circles; as such, they form the cultural backdrop against which the translation activity surveyed in this chapter must be evaluated.

In Ammianus' *Res Gestae*, the translation of the Piazza del Popolo obelisk inscription occasions no particular anxiety, although Ammianus otherwise adheres to the norms of the classical discourse on hieroglyphs and might have been expected to share the common belief that the translation of hieroglyphs was intrinsically problematic. Such an anxiety over the possibility of translation *does* appear in the ecclesiastical histories, however, where viewers of different religious backgrounds dispute each other's interpretation of the cross-shaped hieroglyphs discovered at the Serapeum. And finally, in the homilies on Theophilus and his church-building activities, the translation of a hieroglyphic inscription becomes the mystical key that opens a sealed temple doorway, in a clear echo of contemporary discussions of the magical efficacy of the Egyptian language.

Translation and Quotation in Classical and Early Christian Historiography

Despite Greco-Roman authors' well-documented fascination with the hieroglyphic script, discussed in Chapters 2 and 3 above, the translation of extended passages from Egyptian hieroglyphic texts into Greek or Latin is relatively rare in classical sources. When hieroglyphic translations are presented, they are normally restricted to individual words and short phrases, often related to the etymology of sacred names and toponyms. For example, Plutarch quotes Manetho as stating that the name of the god Amun "means 'what is concealed' and that concealment is signified by this word." In a similar vein, Josephus comments unfavorably on Manetho's explication of the name Moses, arguing that "his real name means 'saved out of the water,' for the Egyptians call water '*mōy*.'"[22] In both cases, the writers are aware of the meaning of individual Egyptian words—the name Amun does reflect the notion of concealment, and *mw* is the Egyptian word for water—but they stop short of offering translations of continuous text. Elsewhere, Greek and Roman authors may correctly transmit the general sense of inscriptions without attempting a literal translation. A good example of this is Tacitus' account of the tribute lists seen by Germanicus at Thebes, discussed above in Chapter 2; although the historian accurately represents the kind of information conveyed in Theban temple inscriptions like the annals of Thutmose III at Karnak, he does not purport to actually translate those texts.

It is noteworthy that even those writers who visited Egypt at a time when hieroglyphic inscriptions were still being produced, and could presumably have been translated for them by native interlocutors, make little use of translated sources in their work. This has sometimes been put down to a simple lack of curiosity or intellectual rigor. Iversen, for example, observes that among the Greek writers who discuss hieroglyphs, "none of them had taken the trouble to get acquainted with the practical and theoretical problems of the system, and, irrespective of their insufficiency, certain conceptions were generally accepted and acknowledged and uncritically handed over from one author to another."[23] This view was echoed more recently in the introduction to an important survey of the reception history of pharaonic Egypt, where Timothy Champion and Peter Ucko argue that despite the prominence of hieroglyphs in the classical discourse on Egypt, few authors "showed any interest in how this writing system actually worked." This phenomenon is, for Champion and Ucko, an indicator of "how intellectually incurious the various writers seem to have been," and on this basis they are led to question how genuine classical interest in Egypt really was.[24] Such a view is not universally accepted, however. John Winkler, for example, has argued strongly against judging what he claims is the primarily "theosophical" interest of most Greek and Roman commentators on hieroglyphs against the modern study of Egyptian philology, and he also notes that the "rather fanciful allegorical etymologies" so prevalent in sources like Plutarch and Horapollo actually reflect genuine Egyptian ways of speaking about their own writing system.[25] This latter point has been echoed more recently by Jean Winand in his work on the history of decipherment; although Winand, like Iversen, remarks on the classical writers' seeming lack of curiosity in the inner workings of the hieroglyphic system, he demonstrates that, in many cases, the accounts of the classical authors do directly reflect the reality of late hieroglyphic inscriptions, produced at a time when hieroglyphic writing "had taken on, in some of its manifestations, a particularly concise form which accentuated the symbolic aspect."[26]

Leaving aside for a moment the question of curiosity (or lack thereof) on the part of the classical authors who address hieroglyphs, what other factors might have prevented them from incorporating more translated hieroglyphic inscriptions into their work? The phenomenon may be due in part to a simple question of access, which was constrained by the high degree of specialization within the ranks of the Egyptian priestly elite in the Hellenistic and Roman periods. As discussed above in Chapter 1, even within the priesthood, literacy in hieroglyphs was a highly specialized skill that few individuals would have possessed, and Greek and Roman visitors could not necessarily guarantee that their tour guides and informants came from that most highly educated population. Given the widespread Greco-Roman belief in the wisdom of the Egyptian priesthood, it may also be the case that the Egyptian interlocutors cited as authorities by Herodotus and his later colleagues were, in some cases at least, simply trying to live up to the prevailing model of priestly wisdom, regardless of whether or not they actually possessed the requisite educational background. It is not hard to imagine a priest who, tasked with showing a visitor around the temple, offered a creative reading of inscriptions he could not really translate rather than confessing his ignorance of what was, after all, his own cultural heritage.[27]

The generic conventions of classical geography and historiography probably also contributed to the relatively infrequent appearance of translated Egyptian sources in texts belonging to those genres. As Momigliano has argued, the direct quotation or transcription of primary sources in any language was uncommon in the work of classical historians, who preferred to utilize "a maximum of invented speeches and a minimum of authentic documents." If they declined to make use of primary sources in their own native tongues, how much less may we fault the classical authors for failing to incorporate source material translated from other languages? The norms of historiography began to change with Eusebius' heavy reliance on primary sources in the *Ecclesiastical History*. However, his focus, and that of later Christian historians, was on those documents that illuminated the larger narrative of the church triumphant, a story in which hieroglyphic inscriptions could not be expected to play a large role—although they do occasionally appear in this context, as we shall see shortly.[28]

Symbols of Empire

One place where we *can* observe some kind of translation activity at work is in Ammianus Marcellinus' account of the Egyptian obelisks that were transported to Rome and reerected on the spina of the Circus Maximus, the first by

Augustus in 10 B.C.E. and the second by Constantius II in 357 C.E.[29] Ammianus begins this section of the *Res Gestae* with a general description of the Egyptian city of Thebes and its monuments, particularly its obelisks, "which kings of long ago, when they had subdued foreign nations in war or were proud of the prosperous condition of their realms, hewed out of the veins of the mountains which they sought for even among the remotest dwellers on the globe, set up, and in their religious devotion dedicated to the gods of heaven."[30] Noting that obelisks were often furnished with inscriptions, Ammianus continues with a brief précis of the hieroglyphic writing system, which betrays all the traditional misconceptions discussed in Chapters 2 and 3 above:

> Now the infinite carvings of characters called hieroglyphics
> (*formarum autem innumeras notas, hieroglyphicas appellatas*),
> which we see cut into it on every side, have been made known
> by an ancient authority of primeval wisdom (*initialis sapientiae*
> *vetus insignivit auctoritas*). For by engraving many kinds of birds
> and beasts, even of another world, in order that the memory of
> their achievements might the more widely reach generations of a
> subsequent age, they registered the vows of kings, either promised
> or performed. For not as nowadays, when a fixed and easy series of
> letters (*litterarum numerus praestitutus et facilis*) expresses whatever
> the mind of man may conceive, did the ancient Egyptian also write;
> but individual characters stood for individual nouns and verbs
> (*sed singulae litterae singulis nominibus serviebant et verbis*); and
> sometimes they meant whole phrases (*non numquam significabant*
> *integros sensus*). The principle of this thing for the time it will suffice
> to illustrate with these two examples: by a vulture they represented
> the word "nature," because, as natural history records, no males can
> be found among these birds; and under the figure of the bee making
> honey they designate "a king," showing by this imagery that in a
> ruler sweetness should be combined with a sting as well; and there
> are many similar instances.[31]

Like his earlier Greek and Roman counterparts, Ammianus sees a close connection between the use of hieroglyphs and the institution of Egyptian kingship; he also emphasizes the widely noted fact that many hieroglyphic signs take the form of animals. But how exactly should we understand the transmission of knowledge that Ammianus speaks of here? The implied indirect object of *insignivit* is ambiguous: to whom were the hieroglyphs made known—the Egyptians themselves, or classical viewers of hieroglyphs, including Ammianus? The sense of *vetus auctoritas* is also somewhat ambiguous. It might refer to the accumulated body of traditional knowledge about hieroglyphs that was passed down within the Egyptian priesthood, but it could also refer to the works of the earlier classical authors who had investigated the "primeval wisdom" of the Egyptians and whose earlier discussions of hieroglyphs so clearly influenced Ammianus' own. Elsewhere in the *Res Gestae, auctoritas* is used in both senses; in 22.14.7, for example, Ammianus describes the lifespan of the Apis bull as having been "prescribed by the secret authority of the mystic books" (*quam secreta librorum praescribit auctoritas mysticorum*), while in 15.9.8 he refers to the authority of a specific author, in this case Pythagoras (*auctoritas Pythagorae*). Whichever meaning is intended here, in this passage Ammianus situates the hieroglyphic obelisk inscriptions squarely within the prevailing classical paradigm of the ancient wisdom of Egypt and suggests that he has drawn on a body of preexisting information in his presentation of this material.

Ammianus goes on to offer a profoundly unoriginal assessment of the purportedly analphabetic nature of the hieroglyphic script, emphasizing the contrast between the ancient Egyptian writing system and the "fixed and easy series of letters" that characterizes Greek and Latin. As Iversen notes, Ammianus' account of hieroglyphs is "couched in conventional terms."[32] Although he is not entirely incorrect in stating that individual hieroglyphic signs could signify entire nouns and verbs, Ammianus' claim that single signs could represent entire sentences clearly derives from the prevailing late classical view of hieroglyphs as a symbolic, rather than phonetic, system. Nor is Ammianus particularly original in the examples he selects to illustrate the nature and interpretation of hieroglyphs, namely the vulture and bee signs. Both hieroglyphs are discussed by Horapollo, and it is likely that Ammianus and Horapollo relied on a common source for these shared examples; the *Hieroglyphica* of Chaeremon is a possible candidate, for the vulture and bee signs both appear as examples in the fragment of Chaeremon preserved in John Tzetzes' *Exegesis in Iliadem* 1.97.[33]

In the case of both hieroglyphs, however, the information provided by Ammianus, Horapollo, and Chaeremon diverges somewhat. Whereas Ammianus notes that the vulture sign is used to signify the word "nature," Horapollo identifies a different set of words that can be written with that hieroglyph ("mother," "sight," "limit," "prescience," "year," "heaven," "merciful," "Athena," "Hera," or "two drachmas").[34] Charemon, for his part, aligns more closely with Horapollo: "for '[a woman] who generates females' and for 'mother' and 'time' and 'heaven,' a vulture."[35] Like Ammianus, Horapollo also explains the use of the vulture sign with reference to the purported nonexistence of male vultures, but he also adduces an extended natural-historical excursus on the reproductive habits of the species. Similarly, although Ammianus, Horapollo, and Chaeremon all report that the bee hieroglyph is used to denote the concept of kingship, and both Ammianus and Horapollo explain this connection with reference to the combination of sweetness and sting that is seen as desirable in a ruler, Horapollo again provides a lengthier and more detailed exegesis of the sign, connecting his explanation to the observed behavior of bees.[36] Breaking no new ground here, Ammianus seems content to reiterate what was, essentially, the common "knowledge" of his day, as one might expect from a historian with a passing familiarity with the earlier Greek and Latin sources on hieroglyphic writing.

Although his overall assessment of the nature of hieroglyphic writing is wholly conventional and substantially incorrect in its emphasis on the symbolic nature of the script, Ammianus differs greatly from his earlier counterparts by providing readers with a lengthy example of a hieroglyphic text in translation. Having described in some detail the transportation of Constantius' obelisk from Egypt to Rome and its reerection in the Circus Maximus, and having spoken in general terms about the nature of hieroglyphs, he inserts into his narrative a Greek translation of "the text of the characters cut upon the ancient obelisk which we see in the Circus (*notarum textus obelisco incisus est veteri, quem videmus in Circo*)"—that is, the Heliopolitan obelisk of Ramesses II that had been removed to Rome and placed on the spina of the Circus Maximus by Augustus and that now stands in the Piazza del Popolo (Figure 9).[37] This translation, which Ammianus ascribes to an individual referred to only as "Hermapion," is essentially unparalleled in the surviving classical and late classical sources on hieroglyphs, and it offers a remarkable opportunity to observe Egyptian-to-Greek translation activity in practice.[38]

Hermapion's translation has suffered greatly over the centuries at the hands of Latin-speaking copyists who struggled to faithfully reproduce the interpolated Greek text. In one of the earliest surviving manuscripts of the *Res Gestae*, the ninth-century *codex Fuldensis*, the scribe appears to have given up in despair, copying only ninety-seven Greek characters and leaving the following thirty-eight lines blank, evidently with the intention of returning to complete the burdensome task at a later point in time. The version of the text that has survived to the present day is based on Sigismond Gelenius' 1574 edition

Figure 9. View of the Piazza del Popolo (Flaminian) obelisk. Photo by author.

of the now-lost ninth-century *codex Hersfeldensis*.[39] There exist two major modern studies of Hermapion's translation and its relationship to the text of the Flaminian obelisk—Adolf Erman's seminal 1914 article and a detailed analysis by Bérénice Lambrecht from 2001. Whereas Erman concluded that Hermapion's work represented a rather fluid and casual translation, not of the

Flaminian obelisk, but of another obelisk since lost, Lambrecht convincingly demonstrates that Hermapion's text is certainly a translation of the hieroglyphic inscriptions on the Flaminian obelisk.[40]

Hermapion's translation, as it has come down to us through this troubled process of transmission, presents three lines of text (στίχοι, corresponding to columns of hieroglyphic signs) from the south face of the obelisk, three lines from a face whose orientation is not specified, and one line from the east face. The present orientation of the obelisk in the Piazza del Popolo represents a 180-degree rotation from its position at the time when Hermapion had access to it (perhaps when it stood in the Circus Maximus, or even in Heliopolis prior to its removal to Rome). As a result, Hermapion's "south face" is now oriented to the north, his unidentified face is identifiable as the actual south face, and his "east face" corresponds to the present west face. According to Lambrecht's calculation of the number of characters that could have fit into the long lacuna of *codex Fuldensis*, the original text of Hermapion probably included the translation of all four faces of the obelisk.[41]

Lambrecht's parallel analysis of the obelisk inscription and the text of Hermapion enables us to see the process by which an Egyptian text was presented to a Greek-speaking audience. For example, the left-hand column of text on the (present) south face of the obelisk reads as follows in Egyptian: *Ḥr kȝ-nḫt mry-mȝ*ᶜ*t nb ḥb.w-sd mi it≠f Ptḥ Tnn nsw.t bity Wsr-Mȝ*ᶜ*t-R*ᶜ *stp.n-R*ᶜ *s R*ᶜ *R*ᶜ*-ms-sw ms-nṯr.w ḳd ḥw.t≠sn nb ȝ.wy Wsr-Mȝ*ᶜ*t-R*ᶜ *stp.n-R*ᶜ *s R*ᶜ *R*ᶜ*-ms-sw di* ᶜ*nḫ mi R*ᶜ, "Horus: mighty bull, beloved of Maat, lord of jubilees like his father Ptah-Tenen, king of Upper and Lower Egypt, Usirmaatre Setepenre, son of Re, Ramesses, who engenders the gods, who builds their temples, Lord of the Two Lands, Usirmaatre Setepenre, son of Re, Ramesses, given life like Re."[42] Hermapion renders this as follows: Ἥλιος θεὸς δεσπότης οὐρανοῦ Ῥαμέστῃ βασιλεῖ· δεδώρημαι τὸ κράτος καὶ τὴν κατὰ πάντων ἐξουσίαν, ὃν Ἀπόλλων φιλαλήθης δεσπότης χρόνων καὶ Ἥφαιστος ὁ τῶν θεῶν πατὴρ προέκρινεν διὰ τὸν Ἄρεα βασιλεύς παγχαρής, Ἡλίου παῖς, καὶ ὑπὸ Ἡλίου φιλούμενος, "Helios the god, lord of heaven, to King Ramestes (Ramesses): I have given you strength and power over everything, you whom Apollo, lover of truth and master of time, with Hephaistos the father of the gods, has chosen, through Ares the king, full of joy, son of Helios, and beloved of Helios."[43] In Lambrecht's analysis, the phrase Ἥλιος θεὸς . . . πάντων ἐξουσίαν represents the interpolation of a passage that corresponds roughly to the legend accompanying the scene carved on the south face of the pyramidion, which reads *R*ᶜ*-Ḥr-ȝḫty nṯr* ᶜȝ, *nb pt. Dd mdw <in>: di.n.i n≠k* ꜥnḫ ḏd wꜣs nb, "Re-Harakhty, great god, lord of heaven. Words spoken: I have given you all life and all stability."[44] Hermapion then proceeds with the translation of the text from the shaft of the obelisk itself, beginning with the equation of Horus and Apollo.

Although Lambrecht emphasizes the overall fidelity of Hermapion's translation, noting in particular that there are only a few instances where the Greek text cannot be matched to any Egyptian expression appearing on the obelisk, she acknowledges that the translation is not fully literal and that in several instances Hermapion elected to leave certain names and epithets untranslated. This is evident from the example quoted above, where the epithets ḳd ḥw.t⸗sn and nb tꜣ.wy are omitted from the translation, as is the second iteration of Ramesses' *praenomen*. Lambrecht suggests that at least some of these omissions may have been due to the translator's desire to avoid what he saw as unnecessary repetition, and she argues that Hermapion sought above all to provide his reader, not necessarily with a literal translation, but with a reasonably accurate sense of the text's content. Other omissions, however, may reflect the translator's imperfect command of the hieroglyphic script.[45]

If the text of Hermapion's translation has proven challenging for generations of subsequent copyists and commentators, the identity of the translator himself remains no less mysterious.[46] Ammianus does not refer to Hermapion elsewhere in the surviving books of the *Res Gestae*, nor is such an individual known from other ancient sources, although it has been suggested that Tertullian's reference to one "Hermateles" in *De Spectaculis* could be an error for "Hermapion." Speaking of the Circus Maximus as a space dedicated to the sun, Tertullian writes, "the huge obelisk, as Hermateles maintains, has been set up in honor of the Sun. Its inscription which, like its origin, is Egyptian, contains a superstition."[47] Given the frequent references to Helios in the translation of Hermapion, where that deity is equated with the Egyptian figure of Re-Harakhty, this is certainly suggestive, and it is not inconceivable that both Tertullian and Ammianus had access to the same work on obelisks. However, given that neither "Hermapion" nor "Hermateles" is known from other sources, this can remain only speculative.[48] The circumstances under which the translation was produced also remain unclear, although Lambrecht points out that if the translation had been made in Egypt prior to the obelisk's removal to Rome, Ammianus would have had no clear way of knowing that the obelisk in the Circus Maximus was the same one translated by Hermapion; thus it is more likely that the translation was produced sometime after the obelisk was brought to Rome, or even at the time of its erection in the Circus.[49]

Although much of the existing scholarship on the translation of Hermapion has focused on establishing the text and determining which obelisk inscription was actually being translated, it is also necessary to consider what role the translation plays in Ammianus' larger narrative. What would a reader of the *Res Gestae* have taken away from this lengthy interpolation, with its strings of Egyptian titles and epithets? In his commentary on the text, de Jonge proposes that this excursus offers Ammianus the opportunity to display his "historical erudition," and in fact the presence of lengthy, learned digressions is a well-known feature of Ammianus' work.[50] The translation of the obelisk inscription essentially represents a digression within a digression. Ammianus' larger subject in 17.4 is, ostensibly, Constantius' erection of the second obelisk in the Circus Maximus, which affords the historian the opportunity to speak at length about ancillary matters, including the nature of hieroglyphs and obelisks more generally, and the chapter ends abruptly with the (truncated) conclusion of the translation. However, the inclusion of the translation does more than just demonstrate Ammianus' learning. The text begins with a statement of Ramesses' divine and universal kingship: "This is what We have given to King Ramesses, who reigns with joy over the whole earth, whom Helios loves, and mighty Apollo," and the connection between Ramesses, Helios, and Apollo is reaffirmed throughout the text, as is the notion that the king's dominion was the direct result of divine benefaction.[51] A Roman reader, encountering this text with the knowledge that the obelisk now resided, not in the land of Egypt, but in the city of Rome itself, would have been forcibly reminded of the impact of Roman imperial power throughout the Mediterranean world—power that was capable of appropriating even the greatest of Egyptian kings' monument to his own divine magnificence.

In a recent response to Erik Iversen's classic monograph, *Obelisks in Exile*, Grant Parker has suggested that obelisk inscriptions in Rome, especially those newly carved in hieroglyphs at the behest and in the name of Roman emperors, like the obelisk inscription of Domitian now in the Piazza Navona, may be seen as "performances of power, that is, the very display of writing as a means of exercising power." Completely illegible to the vast majority of Roman viewers, the inscriptions on Domitian's obelisk could have signaled both the alterity of the monument's Egyptian origins and the power of the emperor to master (or to command scholars and artisans who mastered) the notoriously mysterious Egyptian script.[52] I would argue that the translation of the obelisk inscription in the *Res Gestae*, like the presence of the obelisk itself in the Circus Maximus, was similarly intended to function as a demonstration

of power, both imperial and intellectual; it was, after all, the Roman annex-
ation of Egypt that brought the obelisk within the sphere of Roman scholars
like Ammianus. Such a connection between translation and power is also a
feature of the sources to which we shall now turn, the ecclesiastical histories
of Rufinus, Socrates, and Sozomen. In these Christian works, however, the
power to translate is as much spiritual as it is temporal; so too is the power
derived from the act of translation.

Translation and Triumphalism

The destruction of the great Serapeum in Alexandria late in the reign of Theodosius I has frequently been read as a sign of the end of antiquity. As an event
that resonated on a greater than local scale, it was widely reported in the works
of ancient historians and has also been much discussed by modern scholars, who
have sought to establish the exact date of the temple's destruction and to reconstruct the precise sequence of events from the conflicting and often tendentious
sources. Although the demolition of the temple and the subsequent Christian
remodeling of the site has often been presented as a sign of Christian triumph
over polytheism (a view that goes back to the late antique sources themselves),
more recent work has sought rather to situate this dramatic moment within
the broader contexts of the religious policies of Theodosius I, the aggressive
program of urban Christianization promoted by the archbishop Theophilus,
and the underlying tensions that affected the relationships between the various
religious communities of the late antique metropolis.[53] In their accounts of
the destruction of the Serapeum, the three sources that will be the focus of the
following discussion (Rufinus, *HE* 11.29; Socrates, *HE* 5.17; Sozomen, *HE* 7.15)
all preserve variations on a common motif: an attempt at interpretation across
linguistic, cultural, and religious lines. The object of this interpretive activity
is variously understood as an Egyptian hieroglyph and a Christian cross, and
the ecclesiastical historians' commentary on the subject offers a late antique
view on the nature and meaning of hieroglyphs, and the nature of the translation process, which at times contradicts and at times complements that of
Ammianus, discussed above.

 The encounter with hieroglyphs that is the focus of the present discussion
occurs toward the end of what Edward Watts has characterized as a "series of
disturbances" related to the patriarch Theophilus' efforts to "replace the city's
pagan infrastructure with something that better served the needs of its growing

Christian population."[54] As related by Rufinus, the event that precipitated these disturbances was the discovery of an underground shrine during the course of construction work sponsored by Theophilus; Socrates adds the detail that the shrine still contained a variety of cultic objects, which the patriarch decided to parade through the city in a mockery of traditional ritual processions. Whether sparked by the mere uncovering of the shrine or by the further humiliating public display of its cult images, street fighting followed between pagan and Christian factions, whereupon the pagans barricaded themselves in the Serapeum complex, taking with them a group of Christian prisoners.[55] The Roman officials in the city appealed to the emperor for guidance, and Theodosius responded with a letter stipulating that while the Christians killed during the riots were to be accorded the status of martyrs, their pagan opponents were to be granted amnesty. The letter further refers to the elimination of "the cause of the evils and the roots of the discord which had taken up the defense of the idols," which Rufinus seems to understand as an injunction to close down pagan cults throughout the city, lest further conflicts arise in the future.[56] After the emperor's letter had been read out and the protestors had vacated the Serapeum site, an intrepid Christian soldier, "armed with faith rather than weapons" took an axe to the great cult statue of Serapis, which was then chopped into pieces and dragged throughout the city, only to be ceremonially burned in what has been described as "a ritualized purification of the city."[57]

According to Rufinus, the destruction of the Serapeum led to the demolition of temples throughout Egypt and to the exposure of the various stratagems by which pagan priests were wont to deceive their followers, ranging from the use of magnets to levitate the cult image of Serapis to the hollowed-out "speaking" statue of Saturn that allowed a lascivious priest by the name of Tyrannus to seduce pious women in the guise of the deity. Overall, Rufinus presents a picture of the near-immediate and cataclysmic destruction of the physical apparatus of traditional religious practice in Alexandria itself and in the *chora*.[58] "After the death of Serapis," he writes (*HE* 11.28), "who had never been alive, what temples of any other demon could remain standing?" Rufinus goes on to specify that, far from being abandoned or deserted in the wake of these events, the Serapeum site itself was thoroughly transformed: "on the site of Serapis's tomb the unholy sanctuaries were leveled, and on the one side there rose a martyr's shrine, on the other a church."[59] Although Rufinus himself does not directly attribute these transformative actions to Theophilus, the patriarch is accorded a prominent role by Sozomen and Eunapius, and the construction of Christian churches and shrines on the site of former pagan temples in Alexandria has been explained as an effort by Theophilus to "secure the territory he and his allies had just conquered" by means of "a building and resettlement program designed to garrison these formerly pagan sites with strong Christian fighters."[60] As we shall see in the following pages, in the works of the ecclesiastical historians who wrote about the Serapeum, this reconstructive and reinterpretive agenda extended beyond the treatment of the temple complex's physical remains to encompass the rereading and virtual reinscription of the temple walls in light of the newly achieved Christian dominion over the site.

The motif of hieroglyphic interpretation or translation first appears in Rufinus, the earliest of the sources under consideration here. Having discussed the destruction of the Serapeum itself and the subsequent demolition of temples in the chora, Rufinus returns to Alexandria to speak of "another thing" that was done in the city. The widespread destruction of pagan cultic infrastructure also extended to the busts of Serapis that had been a prominent feature in Alexandrian private homes. These statues, he claims, were so thoroughly destroyed that no trace of their presence remained, and "in their place everyone painted the sign of the Lord's cross (*sed pro his crucis dominicae signum unusquisque . . . depingeret*)." He continues,

> It is said that when the pagans who were left (*qui superfuerant ex paganis*) saw this, they were reminded of an important tradition which had come down to them from of old (*rei magne ex traditione sibimet antiquitus*). The Egyptians are said to have this our sign of the Lord's cross (*signum hoc nostrum dominicae crucis*) among the characters which they call "hieratic," or priestly (*inter illas, quas dicunt hieraticas, id est sacerdotales litteras*), as one of the letters making up their script. They state that the meaning of this character or noun (*cuius litterae seu vocabuli*) is "the life to come (*vita ventura*)." Those then who were coming over to the faith out of astonishment at what was happening said that it had been handed down to them from of old that the things now worshiped (*haec, quae nunc coluntur*) would remain until they saw that the sign (*signum*) had come in which was life. Hence it was the temple priests and ministers (*qui erant ex sacerdotibus vel ministris templorum*) who came over to the faith rather than those who enjoyed the tricks of error and devices of deceit.[61]

According to Rufinus, then, the Christian symbol of the cross was present "of old" in the repertoire of the Egyptian script, and the Egyptians themselves knew of a prophecy that said when this sign came to light, their traditional forms of worship would come to an end. Moreover, in speaking of the conversions that resulted from this discovery, Rufinus emphasizes that the converts came, not from among the rank-and-file worshippers who had been so profoundly misled by the priestly stratagems he had just described in such lavish detail, but from among their misleaders, the very same "temple priests and ministers" who had been responsible for keeping their followers "enmeshed for so many centuries in such vile and shameful deceptions."[62] The nature of these cross-shaped "priestly" characters, their interpretation, and the identity of the priests who are thus driven to convert to Christianity will be discussed in more detail below; first, however, it is necessary to consider the later accounts of Socrates and Sozomen and to see how they embellish Rufinus' tale.

Like Rufinus, on whose work he drew heavily, Socrates also undertook to write a continuation of Eusebius' *Historia Ecclesiastica*, bringing the story from the proclamation of Constantine in 305 up to the year 439. Sozomen, writing slightly later in the mid-fifth century and drawing on Socrates as one of his principal sources, covered a slightly shorter span of time, from 323 to 425. Consequently, both texts deal with the same critical period in the early 390s when the cultic landscape of Alexandria was being profoundly reshaped, and both present interesting variations on Rufinus' tale of the cross-shaped hieroglyph and its interpretation by pagan and Christian communities in the city.[63]

Socrates takes the motif of the discovery and interpretation of the cross sign, which Rufinus had presented as a citywide phenomenon, following but not directly caused by the destruction of the Serapeum, and he ties it much more specifically to that famous landmark. He writes,

> When the Temple of Serapis was torn down and laid bare, there were found in it, engraved on stones, certain characters which they call hieroglyphic (ηὕρητο γράμματα ἐγκεχαραγμένα τοῖς λίθοις, τῷ καλουμένῳ ἱερογλυφικῷ), having the forms of crosses (σταυρῶν ἔχοντες τύπους). Both the Christians and pagans ("Ελληνες) on seeing them, appropriated and applied them to their respective religions: for the Christians who affirm that the cross is the sign of Christ's saving passion, claimed this character as peculiarly theirs;

but the pagans alleged that it might appertain to Christ and
Serapis in common; "for," said they, "it symbolizes one thing
to Christians and another to pagans." While this point was debated
among them, some of the pagan converts to Christianity (τινὲς
τῶν Ἑλλήνων τῷ Χριστιανισμῷ προσελθόντες), who were
conversant with these hieroglyphic characters (τὰ ἱερογλυφικά
τε γράμματα ἐπιστάμενοι), interpreted (διερμηνεύοντες)
the form of a cross (τὸν σταυροειδῆ χαρακτῆρα) and said
that it signifies "Life to come" (ἔλεγον σημαίνειν ζωὴν
ἐπερχουμένην). This the Christians exultingly laid hold of, as
decidedly favorable to their religion. But after other hieroglyphs had
been deciphered (ἐδηλοῦτο) containing a prediction that "When
the cross should appear,"—for this was "life to come,"—"the temple
of Serapis would be destroyed," a very great number of the pagans
embraced Christianity, and confessing their sins, were baptized.[64]

Socrates goes on to say that he personally is not entirely convinced that the
sign was meant to represent a Christian cross, remarking, "I cannot imagine
that the Egyptian priests foreknew the things concerning Christ, when they
engraved the figure of a cross." Rather, he sees the situation as analogous to
Paul's interpretation of the Athenian altar inscription "to an unknown God"
recounted in Acts 17:23.[65] This qualification of the story hints at the contours
of a much larger debate over attempts to identify prophecies of Christianity
in a wide range of pre-Christian sources, of which more will be said shortly.

In Socrates' retelling of the story, several key elements have been significantly altered, although the basic narrative structure of the episode mirrors
Rufinus' account.[66] The cross-shaped symbols are located, not in the private
homes of Alexandrian citizens, but in the Serapeum itself, and the inscriptions are not characterized as Christian crosses that merely remind viewers
of an Egyptian symbol, but as actual Egyptian hieroglyphs that are potentially susceptible to a kind of polyvalent reading or interpretive process. As
in Rufinus' account, here the cross-shaped hieroglyphs are associated with a
prophecy foretelling the end of pagan worship, but Socrates adds another level
of complexity to the story. In his version, the prophecy relates not to the
generalized end of pagan ritual practice but specifically to the destruction of
the Serapeum, and it is not simply said to have been "handed down from of
old," as Rufinus would have it, but actually encoded in a secondary hieroglyphic inscription. The end result of Socrates' editorializing is a story that is

at once much more detailed and rather less plausible than the original version of Rufinus; it also affords considerably greater scope for discussing late antique notions of translation and interpretation, as we shall see shortly.

In comparison to Socrates' lengthy discussion of the matter, from which it seems to be derived, Sozomen's account of the cross-shaped hieroglyphs is remarkably laconic. Like Socrates, and unlike Rufinus, Sozomen attaches the story to the sack of the Serapeum, writing, "It is said that when the temple was being demolished, some stones were found, on which were hieroglyphic characters (τῶν καλουμένων ἱερογλυφικῶν χαρακτήρων) in the form of a cross (σταυροῦ σημείῳ ἐμφερεῖς), which on being submitted to the inspection of the learned (ἐπιστημόνων δὲ τὰ τοιάδε), were interpreted (ἑρμηνευθεῖσαν) as signifying the life to come. These characters led to the conversion of several of the pagans, as did likewise other inscriptions (γράμματα ἕτερα) found in the same place, and which contained predictions of the destruction of the temple." This is, in essence, a pared-down version of the story Socrates tells, stripped of any additional narrative detail but retaining all the critical plot points.[67]

Looking at the three accounts side by side, it is apparent that they share the same basic four-part narrative arc, beginning with the destruction of either statues of Serapis (as in Rufinus) or the temple of Serapis itself (as in Socrates and Sozomen), followed by the painting (in Rufinus) or the discovery (in Socrates and Sozomen) of cross-shaped symbols. These symbols are then interpreted as signifying "the life to come" (all three accounts). Thereupon a prophecy is either remembered (Rufinus) or discovered in another inscription (Socrates and Sozomen) that foretells either the end of pagan worship generally (Rufinus) or the sack of the Serapeum specifically (Socrates and Sozomen). All three accounts conclude with the conversion of pagans, or "Hellenes," to Christianity, which is presented as the direct outcome of this process of discovery and interpretation. With this basic narrative schema in mind, we may now turn to some of the larger issues raised by these three accounts, including the nature of the purported hieroglyphic signs, the identity of the so-called "translators," and their interpretive methodology.

The Ankh and the Cross

Although the main concern of the present study is "not with the past as such, but only with the past as it is remembered," to borrow Jan Assmann's formulation, the historical verisimilitude of the church historians' accounts nonetheless needs to be considered.[68] Would a late antique Alexandrian reader of Rufinus, Socrates, and Sozomen have recognized his city, and its preeminent temple, from their depictions? And can there be any historical basis to the claim that cross-shaped hieroglyphs were found in the Serapeum precinct, and that they were interpreted as described above? In confronting these questions, I follow the lead of Françoise Thelamon in seeing Rufinus' narrative of the destruction of the Serapis statues and the ensuing discussion of the painted crosses as the more original and more plausible variation on the theme, even if its historicity cannot be established beyond doubt. As Thelamon observes, the late antique Christian practice of carving or painting crosses on the doorjambs and windows of residences, tomb-chapels, and converted temples is attested in both archaeological and textual sources, as in the example from the temple of Isis at Philae depicted in Figure 10. The notion that non-Christian observers familiar with traditional Egyptian iconography might read their own meaning into these symbols is well within reason.[69]

It has been recognized at least since the work of Jean-Antoine Letronne in the mid-nineteenth century that the "cross-shaped" signs attested in the ecclesiastical histories correspond to a genuine sign in the hieroglyphic repertoire.[70] This hieroglyph, with the phonetic value ꜥnḫ, is continuously attested throughout Egyptian history, from the Early Dynastic (ca. 3000 B.C.E.) through the late Roman period; the primary meaning of the Egyptian word ꜥnḫ, or "life," likewise remains stable across this chronological expanse.[71] In addition to its role as a phonetic sign, which allowed it to be used in writing a wide range of different words, the ankh also appears very frequently as an iconographic element in Egyptian art, where it symbolizes life both in this world and after death. In temple and tomb reliefs, gods and goddesses frequently extend the ankh sign to the nostrils of the king, and the ankh is ubiquitous as a motif in amulets and also in larger three-dimensional figurines. The iconographic use of the ankh sign continued throughout the Ptolemaic and Roman periods, both in temple reliefs and especially on funerary paraphernalia including coffins, mummy cases, and shrouds like the late antique example pictured in Figure 11.[72] In other words, this cross-shaped hieroglyph was a very well-attested iconographic motif in late antiquity as in earlier periods, and it is entirely reasonable to think that there would have been individuals familiar with its meaning present in late fourth-century Alexandria.

It is less clear how seriously we should take the claim that the demolition of the Serapeum resulted in the discovery of hieroglyphic inscriptions. Such inscriptions are, of course, a hallmark of Egyptian-style temple décor, and this

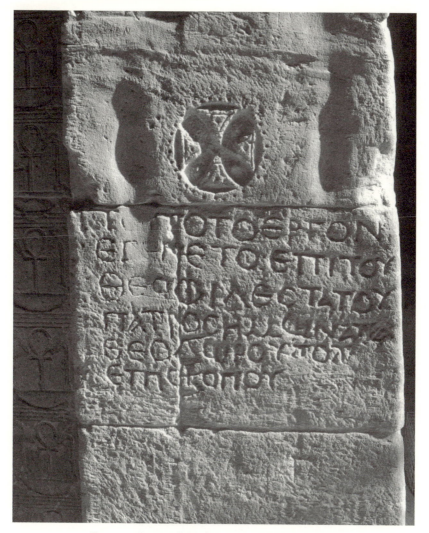

Figure 10. Cross and Greek inscription (*I.Philae* II 204)
from the temple of Isis at Philae. Photo by author.

remained true even in the case of Egyptian temples constructed during the Ptolemaic and Roman periods. Indeed, as discussed in Chapter 1, some of the temple
inscriptions produced during those periods demonstrate a truly virtuosic proficiency with the hieroglyphic script. The Serapeum, however, is not described in
the ancient sources as an Egyptian-style temple, and the recent efforts by Judith
McKenzie and her colleagues to reconstruct the building phases of the temple

Figure 11. Funerary
shroud of a woman,
from the Fayum.
Roman period, third
century C.E. Paris,
Musée du Louvre,
AF 6440. © Musée
du Louvre, Dist.
RMN-Grand Palais/
Georges Poncet/ Art
Resource, New York.

complex from the archaeological evidence indicate that in both its Ptolemaic and Roman incarnations, the architecture and décor of the Serapis temple were thoroughly classical rather than Egyptian. This point should not be pressed too far, however, as McKenzie and her colleagues do cite evidence for the presence of Egyptian-style statuary and inscribed obelisks within the temple complex, and they note that masonry blocks with inscribed hieroglyphs were reused in constructing the base of Diocletian's column, so hieroglyphic inscriptions would not have been altogether foreign to that space.[73] However, given that the discovery of mysterious (and conveniently prophetic) inscriptions is not an uncommon motif in late antique Christian literature, as we shall see shortly, I would argue that the purported hieroglyphic texts from the Serapeum should be seen as a convenient fiction. Introducing this element into his revision of Rufinus' narrative allows Socrates (and Sozomen after him) to fully exploit the long-standing Greco-Roman tradition that presented Egyptian hieroglyphs as one of the most important indicators of Egyptian cultural identity and alterity. In the works of many of the church fathers, traditional Egyptian religion is presented as the very worst kind of idolatry—Augustine, for example, refers to the Romans having "almost descended to the superstition of the Egyptians, who worship beasts and birds"—so emphasizing the identity of the Serapeum as a recognizably *Egyptian* temple makes the story of its overthrow all the more glorious.[74]

It is also possible that the story of the ankh and its interpretation, as presented in the ecclesiastical histories, represents an attempt to explicate—even to legitimize—a process of cultural appropriation that was already well underway. The use of the ankh symbol is attested in securely Christian contexts even before the composition of the histories of Rufinus, Socrates, and Sozomen. A good example of this usage is depicted in Figure 12, which shows the last page of a papyrus codex preserving the book of Proverbs in Akhmimic Coptic; the codex has been dated to the late fourth century and is thought to have come from the library of the White Monastery. Clearly visible in the image, the ornamental panel enclosing the work's title is flanked on either side by the symbol of an ankh.[75] That this symbol was deemed appropriate for use in a biblical manuscript—perhaps even a manuscript from the library of Shenoute's own monastery—suggests that it had already acquired a Christian gloss before the cross-shaped hieroglyphs at the Serapeum were ever "discovered." With this usage in mind, the story presented by the ecclesiastical historians may represent a retrospective effort to justify the Christian adoption of this sign, which was clearly already in progress. The success of this endeavor is demonstrated by the ongoing Christian use of the ankh motif, which, in the fifth and sixth centuries,

Figure 12. Leaf from a papyrus codex preserving the book of Proverbs in Akhmimic Coptic. Staatsbibliothek zu Berlin–Preussischer Kulturbesitz, Orientabteilung, Ms. or. oct. 987, 82r°. Courtesy of the Staatsbibliothek zu Berlin–Preussischer Kulturbesitz, Orientabteilung.

began to move from the margins of manuscripts to textiles, funerary stelae, and other monumental contexts, as depicted in Figures 13 and 14.[76] Coptic usage of the motif continues to the present day; it may be seen, for example, in the logo of the Saint Mark Foundation for Coptic Studies, where its use is explained by reference to the ecclesiastical histories discussed here.[77]

Expertise and Authority

One of the intriguing features of the ecclesiastical historians' accounts is the characterization of the individuals who are called on to interpret the hieroglyphic signs once they are discovered (or, in Rufinus' version, who volunteer

Figure 13. Textile fragment showing ankh signs, crosses, and chi rho monogram, said to be from a tomb at Akhmim. London, Victoria and Albert Museum 258-1890. © Victoria and Albert Museum, London.

their interpretation upon seeing the painted crosses that replace the statues of Serapis). They are identified variously as "the remaining pagans" (Rufinus, *HE* 11.29), "pagan converts to Christianity, who were conversant with these hieroglyphic characters" (Socrates, *HE* 5.17.4), and "the learned" (Sozomen, *HE* 7.15). Who were these individuals, and what was the nature of their hieroglyphic expertise? In her discussion of the ecclesiastical histories, Thelamon asserts that Socrates' recent converts who are "conversant" with hieroglyphs can be none other than the last surviving members of the Egyptian priesthood.[78] The rationale underlying this claim is clear; as discussed in Chapter 1, by late antiquity the priests of Egypt were the sole remaining caretakers of the country's hieroglyphic heritage and the only people who would have been even marginally literate in the use of that script. The sheer ubiquity of the ankh sign meant that it was one of the few hieroglyphs that the majority of Egyptians, literate or illiterate, would have been able to interpret with some accuracy, so it is not absolutely necessary

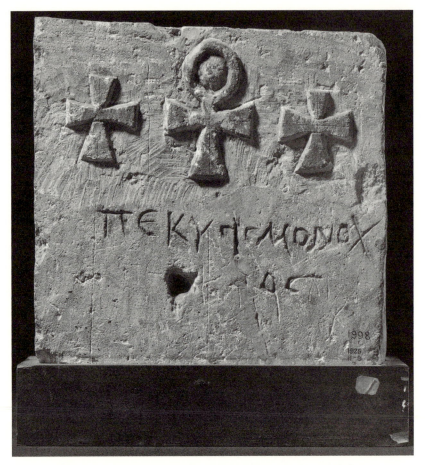

Figure 14. Limestone stela with ankh sign and crosses from el-Badari.
London, British Museum EA 1998. © Trustees of the British Museum.

to see "the learned" individuals in the ecclesiastical histories as members of the
Egyptian priesthood, but this was probably the authors' intended meaning.

As we have already seen, in the classical discourse on Egypt, the figure
of the Egyptian priest was intimately connected to both the general concept
of the "wisdom of Egypt" and to the specific encoding of that wisdom in the
hieroglyphic writing system. Priests also appear very frequently in the classical sources as interpreters par excellence, who explicate Egyptian culture on
behalf of their Greco-Roman interlocutors.[79] In the ecclesiastical histories,
these interlocutors have become the Christian residents of Alexandria, but
the hermeneutic authority of the Egyptian priests is still acknowledged. That

authority has some significant limitations, however, as we see most clearly in the account of Socrates. In that text, the author dramatizes not only the hermeneutic act itself, but also the Christian rejection of certain portions of the resulting interpretation. Although the Christian audience is happy to accept the reading of the ankh sign as signifying "life to come," the interpreters' claim that the same sign might simultaneously signify both Christ and Serapis is rejected. As Socrates says, "the Christians who affirm that the cross is the sign of Christ's saving passion, *claimed this character as peculiarly theirs.*"[80]

The Christians' modification of their pagan interlocutors' interpretation may also bear witness to a developing shift in the locus of spiritual and intellectual authority away from the traditional Egyptian priesthood. The Christian interpreters who "claim" the ankh sign as a symbol of Christ's passion derive their authority to interpret the inscriptions not from any training, and not from any particular hieroglyphic literacy, but from the inspiration of the Holy Spirit. Socrates makes this explicit when he passes from reporting the testimony he has heard to offering his own opinion on the subject. Although he does not approve of the idea that the priests of Serapis could have had foreknowledge of Christ when they carved the ankh sign, he accepts the Christian reading of the sign as correct, and he explicitly associates the interpretive method that identifies the ankh as a sign of Christ with the method by which the apostle Paul interpreted the Athenian altar inscription in Acts 17:23. "For he," Socrates writes, "being made wise by the Divine Spirit, employed a similar method in relation to the Athenians, and brought over many of them to the faith, when on reading the inscription on one of their altars, he accommodated and applied it (προσαρμόζειν) to his own discourse."[81] Such a shift toward spiritually guided hermeneutic practice would seem to correlate with the broader pattern discussed above in Chapter 3, where the concept of Egyptian wisdom passed down through the written traditions of the priesthood was problematized, if not altogether rejected, in favor of divine wisdom conveyed by the Holy Spirit. Similarly, in Socrates' narrative, interpretive authority grounded in the traditional system of Egyptian priestly education is, I would argue, being rejected in favor of a new model of spiritually guided interpretation. This trend is even more clearly in evidence in the cycle of homilies associated with the figure of Theophilus of Alexandria, discussed later in this chapter.

If the "learned" Alexandrian readers of hieroglyphs discussed in the ecclesiastical histories are indeed to be seen as Egyptian priests, the mass conversion that follows the interpretation of the ankh signs in all three accounts takes on added significance. Egyptian religion was commonly presented as the worst possible sort of idolatry in the patristic sources. Egyptian priests, as guardians and promoters of that tradition, were frequently vilified as well, presented as charlatans at best and ministers of the devil at worst.[82] For this reason, the conversion of Egyptian priests and/or their family members is frequently highlighted, even celebrated, in triumphalist accounts of Christianization. For example, both the Coptic *Life of Aaron* and the *Life of Moses*, two texts that deal with the cessation of traditional cult practices at prominent ritual centers, emphasize the conversion of the local priests' children.[83] It is perfectly in keeping with this larger literary trend for the ecclesiastical historians to highlight the conversion of the individuals who interpret the Serapeum inscriptions, whom we should most likely understand as representatives of the indigenous priesthood.

Hieroglyphs and Cultural Translatability

In a 2010 article on the destruction of pagan statuary in late antique Alexandria, Troels Myrup Kristensen represents the interpretive action described in the ecclesiastical histories as a "wishful misunderstanding" on the part of late antique Christians.[84] As we have just seen, however, the ecclesiastical historians actually utilized a carefully considered rhetorical strategy, one that made use of contemporary trends in late antique hieroglyphic speculation and translation theory in order to make the case for the assertion of Christian authority over Alexandria's cultic landscape. The historians' remarks on the Serapeum inscriptions generally echo the widespread view that the hieroglyphic script was symbolic rather than phonetic, and the focus of hermeneutic activity on a single hieroglyphic sign, the ankh, is reminiscent of the approach taken in the classical commentaries on hieroglyphs, which likewise tend to privilege the explication of individual signs over and above that of larger syntactic units. Socrates' account in particular, with its confrontation of Christian and pagan interpretations of the ankh sign, also echoes some of the larger late antique arguments over the nature of language and the possibility of translation between languages and cultures. Origen's comments, discussed above, about the translatability of divine names in *Contra Celsum* are particularly relevant in this context. In response to Celsus' claim that sacred names are essentially interchangeable, so that the name of Zeus, for example, could apply equally well to the Greek deity as to the Christian one, Origen argues strongly against the possibility of translating sacred names and ritual formulae in this fashion, leaning heavily on the Platonist and Stoic position that saw the development of language and the assignment of names to things and beings as a function of nature rather than convention.[85]

In Socrates' account of the Serapeum hieroglyphs, the learned pagans who interpret the hieroglyphs for their Christian interlocutors echo Celsus in their argument that the same symbol could represent both Christ and Serapis, while the Christian viewers, who reject this possibility, take a position much closer to that of Origen himself and arrogate the symbol exclusively to their own tradition. Jan Assmann has argued that a belief in the untranslatability of divine names is often a feature of religions that claim to possess exclusive truth; he writes, "If one religion is wrong and the other is right, there can be no question of translating the gods of the one into those of the other. Obviously they are about different gods."[86] Socrates seems to be making a similar claim about the untranslatability of divine *symbols* in his discussion of the Serapeum hieroglyphs; the validity of the exclusionary Christian reading of these signs over the syncretistic pagan reading is, of course, confirmed by the conversion to Christianity of the pagan interpreters themselves.

If the ecclesiastical historians' presentation of the debate over the meaning of the ankh sign reflects contemporary concerns about hieroglyphs and translation, it also participates in a very significant late antique debate about the existence of pagan prophecies testifying to the Christian message. The belief that certain "wise pagans" had, like the prophets of the Old Testament, foreseen the coming of Christ and left written evidence to that effect was widespread in late antiquity, but the church fathers were divided in their opinions on the subject. Some, like Lactantius and Cyril of Alexandria, embraced the idea and integrated into their theological writings numerous quotations from classical sources that, they claimed, offered evidence for the foreknowledge of Christian truth.[87] Others, like Eusebius and Augustine, displayed a more cautious approach, desiring on the one hand to diminish the significance of the pagan oracular tradition (and particularly that of the anti-Christian oracles included in Porphyry's *Philosophy from Oracles*) while on the other hand making selective use of that same tradition for their own apologetic purposes.[88] By the late fifth century, a compilation of "pagan witnesses" to Christianity, including oracular statements and quotations from classical authors, was available in the form of a Greek text known as the *Tübingen Theosophy*, which formed the appendix to a now-lost anonymous work entitled *On True Belief*.[89] The popularity of the theosophical genre over several centuries is attested by the existence of later Syriac and Coptic translations of similar compendia.[90]

The claim advanced in the ecclesiastical histories of Socrates and Sozomen—that a prophecy had been discovered in the ruins of the Serapeum, written in hieroglyphs and predicting the downfall of the temple and the subsequent conversion of pagans to Christianity—fits seamlessly into this larger theosophical tradition, which included prophecies purporting to foretell the end of polytheistic ritual practice. So, for example, the *Tübingen Theosophy* presents an oracle in which Apollo predicts the future abandonment of his temples, and the Coptic theosophical fragments collected by van den Broek include prophecies attributed to Odysseus and Pythagoras urging an end to the building of temples and the fashioning of cult images on the grounds that both will soon become obsolete.[91] Some of these oracles related specifically to Egypt: the apocalyptic section of the *Asclepius* (§24–26) was cited in late antiquity as a prophecy of the end of traditional Egyptian religion that was being fulfilled by the spread of Christianity in Egypt, and a prophecy concerning the destruction of the Serapeum itself was said to have been uttered (though in Greek, not in hieroglyphs) by the late fourth-century philosopher Antoninus.[92]

Moreover, Socrates' statement—that he personally could not "imagine that the Egyptian priests foreknew the things concerning Christ, when they engraved the figure of a cross. For if 'the advent' of our Savior into the world 'was a mystery hid from ages and from generations,' as the apostle declares; and if the devil himself, the prince of wickedness, knew nothing of it, his ministers, the Egyptian priests, are likely to have been still more ignorant of the matter"—likewise echoes contemporary concerns over whether or not pagan oracles, which Christian commentators typically attributed to the agency of demons, could be seen as truly prophetic.[93] Although Socrates himself comes down on the negative side of the question, the emphatically personal way in which he introduces his opinion—ἐγὼ δὲ οὔ φημι—suggests that he recognizes his own as a minority opinion. Indeed, the *Tübingen Theosophy* and related texts demonstrate that the belief that pagan prophecies could convey Christian messages continued to spread in the centuries after Socrates' writing. The same belief is also foregrounded in the texts to which we shall now turn, a cycle of Coptic homilies in which hieroglyphic inscriptions are likewise said to convey a deeper Christian truth.

Theophilus of Alexandria's "Fantastic Images"

In the reading of the ecclesiastical historians presented above, I argue that the act of interpretation those authors described as taking place in late fourth-century Alexandria represents an assertion of Christian authority over the hieroglyphic texts being translated. By extension, the same authority is also asserted over the polytheistic Egyptian culture from which those texts derive and of which hieroglyphic writing was one of the most ancient and visible identifying markers. This assertion of authority is most clearly expressed in Socrates' rendition of the story, where the possibility that the same sign might represent both Serapis and Christ is explicitly rejected by Christian interpreters, who claim the sign, and the site of the erstwhile temple, as entirely their own. That such an understanding of the power of translation was not unique to the ecclesiastical historians is suggested by a thematically similar episode in a later Coptic text that likewise dramatizes the act of cross-cultural translation (or "translation"). The text in question is an encomium on Ananias, Azarias, and Misael, the three youths in the fiery furnace from the third chapter of the book of Daniel. Pseudonymously attributed to the fifth-century patriarch Cyril of Alexandria but more probably dating from the seventh or the eighth century, the encomium is preserved in two tenth-century Bohairic manuscripts now in the collection of the Vatican Library.[94]

At the start of the encomium, the patriarch Theophilus expresses a desire to build a martyrium for the Three Youths in the city of Alexandria. Although he lacks the funds to carry out the project, in a prophetic dream he hears a voice that tells him, "Theophilus, you will build many churches, and I will arrange these works for you (ⲬⲚⲀⲔⲰⲦ ⲚⲞⲨⲘⲎϢ Ⲛ̅ⲈⲔⲔⲖⲎⲤⲒⲀ ⲞⲨⲞϨ ⲀⲚⲞⲔ ⲈⲐⲚⲀϮⲐⲰϢ ⲚⲀⲔ ⲈⲚⲞⲨϨⲂⲎⲞⲨⲒ)." Sometime thereafter, Theophilus and his nephew Cyril (the narrator of the story, later patriarch of Alexandria himself) are walking in the countryside when they come upon a temple that is identified, later in the text, as "the temple of Alexander (ⲠⲒⲈⲢⲪⲈⲒ Ⲛ̅ⲦⲈ ⲀⲖⲈⲜⲀⲚⲆⲢⲞⲤ)": "And it happened that, as I was walking with my Father, we came upon a temple of the pagans (ⲞⲨⲈⲢⲪⲈⲒ Ⲛ̅ⲦⲈ ⲚⲒϨⲈⲖⲖⲎⲚⲞⲤ), there being some fantastic images and inscriptions on it along with some other pagan inscriptions (ⲈⲞⲨⲞⲚ ϨⲀⲚⲪⲀⲚⲦⲀⲤⲒⲀ ⲚⲈⲘ ϨⲀⲚⲤϦⲀⲒ ⲤϦⲎⲞⲨⲦ ⲈⲢⲞϤ ⲚⲈⲘ ϨⲀⲚⲔⲈⲤϦⲀⲒ ⲚϨⲨⲖⲈⲚⲎⲔⲎ). I examined the lintel of the door (ⲠⲒⲐⲞⲨⲀⲒ Ⲛ̅ⲦⲈ ⲠⲒⲢⲞ), and I saw three large thetas that were carved on it (Ⲅ̅ Ⲛ̅ⲚⲒϢϮ Ⲛ̅ⲐⲎⲦⲀ ⲈⲨⲔⲖⲒⲠⲒ ⲈⲢⲞϤ), and I marveled. I said to my Father, 'My holy Father, do you see the works of the pagans (ⲚⲒϨⲂⲎⲞⲨⲒ Ⲛ̅ⲦⲈ ⲚⲒϨⲈⲖⲖⲎⲚⲞⲤ) and these three thetas, which are so large?'"

Theophilus is then filled with "a holy prophetic spirit (ⲞⲨⲠⲚ̅Ⲁ̅ Ⲙ̅ⲠⲢⲞⲪⲎⲦⲒⲔⲞⲚ ⲈⲐⲞⲨⲀⲂ)." He replies to Cyril, saying, "there is a great mystery (ⲞⲨⲚⲒϢϮ Ⲙ̅ⲘⲨⲤⲦⲎⲢⲒⲞⲚ) in these three thetas," and he proceeds to interpret (ⲈⲢⲘⲎⲚⲈⲨⲒⲚ) the thetas as standing for *theos*, Theodosius, and Theophilus.[95] As the patriarch is speaking, the doors of the temple swing open, and gold comes pouring out. The two men are understandably astonished by this, and the narrator goes on to describe how Theophilus seals up the temple and sends a letter to the emperor asking him what to do. In his reply, Theodosius orders Theophilus to use the money for the construction of new churches, and the episode closes with the patriarch constructing the martyrium for the Three Youths as he had envisioned at the start of the sermon.

In this text, as in the ecclesiastical historians' accounts of the Serapeum and the sermon of Shenoute discussed in Chapter 4, Christian viewers are confronted with a temple covered in mysterious inscriptions. However, Ps.-Cyril's presentation of this space differs from these earlier accounts in several important particulars. Unlike the Serapeum, which was situated in a prominent and well-trafficked location in Alexandria, the temple described in the encomium is explicitly said to lie "outside the city in a desert place which was barren (ⲤⲀⲂⲞⲖ Ⲛ̄ⲦⲂⲀⲔⲒ ⲠⲈ ϩⲈⲚ ⲞⲨⲘⲀ Ⲛ̄ϨⲈⲢⲎⲘⲞⲤ ⲈϤϢⲎϤ)." This emphasis on the temple's rural environs echoes, consciously or not, the language of a law promulgated by Arcadius and Honorius in 399 that permitted the demolition of "any temples in the country districts (*in agris*)."[96] More important, the deserted character of the temple and its surroundings allows Theophilus to make his interpretation of the "thetas" unchallenged by any individuals offering alternate (and perhaps better-informed) readings.

Ps.-Cyril's characterization of the temple also differs significantly from the temple description offered in Shenoute's sermon. Far from being a "place of making sacrifice to Satan and worshipping and fearing him,"[97] the temple in the encomium is described in less colorful terms, first as "a temple of the pagans (ⲞⲨⲈⲢⲫⲈⲒ Ⲛ̄ⲦⲈ ⲚⲒϨⲈⲖⲖⲎⲚⲞⲤ)," and later, in the context of Theophilus' letter to the emperor, as "the temple of Alexander (ⲠⲒⲈⲢⲫⲈⲒ Ⲛ̄ⲦⲈ ⲀⲖⲈⲌⲀⲚⲆⲢⲞⲤ)." And here there are no soul-killing inscriptions dripping with blood; rather, the façade of the temple is covered with "fantastic images (ϨⲀⲚⲫⲀⲚⲦⲀⲤⲒⲀ)," "inscriptions (ϨⲀⲚⲤϦⲀⲒ)," and "some other pagan inscriptions (ϨⲀⲚⲔⲈⲤϦⲀⲒ Ⲛ̄ϨⲨⲖⲈⲚⲎⲔⲎ)."[98] Theophilus' interpretive action is also strikingly different from that of Shenoute; whereas the latter's insistence on the figural qualities of the hieroglyphic inscriptions precludes any attempt to read them, Theophilus offers a detailed exegesis of what he and Cyril observe carved on the façade of the temple.

The focal point of the description, as of the façade itself, are the three so-called thetas carved on the door lintel. Egyptologist László Kákosy, in his discussion of the text, has argued that this may be a reference to the three winged sun disks often carved on the lintels of temple doorways from the Ptolemaic and Roman periods; an example of this motif can be seen in Figure 15.[99]

Figure 15. Granodiorite naos of
Ptolemy VIII and Cleopatra II,
said to be from Philae. London,
British Museum EA 1134. ©
Trustees of the British Museum.

Such a visual association between the Egyptian sun disk and the Greek letter theta is supported by a passage in Eusebius' *Praeparatio evangelica*. Quoting Philo of Byblos' *Phoenician History*, Eusebius writes, "moreover the Egyptians, describing the world from the same idea, engrave the circumference of a circle, of the color of the sky and of fire, and a hawk-shaped serpent stretched across the middle of it, and the whole shape is like our *theta*, representing the circle as the world, and signifying by the serpent which connects it in the middle the good *daemon*."[100] The fire-colored circle can easily be identified as an Egyptian representation of the sun disk, commonly painted in orange or red in relief carvings, and the hawk-shaped serpent may be a reference to the pendant *uraei* that typically accompany the winged sun disk, although these normally flank the disk rather than cutting across it. Taking the "thetas" of Ps.-Cyril's encomium as a reference to this extremely common Egyptian motif, we find that Theophilus' interpretive strategy in the encomium closely parallels that of the Christian interpreters in the ecclesiastical histories, faced with the cross-shaped hieroglyphs from the Serapeum.[101] Like Socrates, Ps.-Cyril shows a Christian reader, in this case Theophilus himself, taking an Egyptian icon, the winged sun disk, and transforming it into a Christian message, which is accessible to him only through the inspiration of the Holy Spirit. The validity of Theophilus' interpretation is immediately (and conveniently) confirmed by the miraculous opening of the temple doors and the shower of gold that spills out of them, just as the validity of the Christian interpretation of the hieroglyphic ankh sign is confirmed by the mass conversion that follows that exegetical act.

This story of the discovery of a mysterious inscription, its translation by means of divine inspiration, and the subsequent recovery of hidden temple treasure that is then used to finance church building, must be regarded as a literary trope, rather than as a reference to any specific historical event. The motif of the "thetas," elaborated to a greater or lesser degree, is one of the most characteristic features of later Coptic literary sources concerned with the ecclesiastical construction projects of Theophilus and Cyril.[102] It appears, for example, in the widely popular apocryphal narrative now known as the Vision of Theophilus, which recounts the tale of the Holy Family's visit to the site of Mount Coscam (or Qosqam, modern al-Qusiya) during their sojourn in Egypt and which was transmitted in Arabic, Syriac, and Ethiopic recensions. A Coptic *Vorlage* to this text was long assumed to have existed, and a manuscript fragment of the Coptic version has indeed recently been identified.[103] The "thetas" also appear in the Arabic recension of a Coptic homily attributed to Cyril, detailing the dedication of an Alexandrian church to the Archangel

Raphael,[104] and they are briefly referenced in the Arabic *History of the Patriarchs of Alexandria* attributed to Severus ibn al-Muqaffa[105] and in the Arabic translation of the Coptic *Synaxarium*, under the entry for the eighteenth of Babeh (the feast of Theophilus).[106] As Coquin has noted, the references in the latter two texts are so cursory that they seem to suppose prior knowledge of the story on the part of the reader; the existence of multiple recensions of the Vision of Theophilus, in particular, suggests that that text may have been especially influential in spreading the motif of Theophilus and his divinely guided interpretive efforts.[107]

A more distant parallel to this group of texts is to be found in the *Vita* of the late fourth-century bishop Epiphanius of Salamis. The Greek text of the *Vita* is thought to have been composed sometime in the fifth century, and a Sahidic Coptic translation is preserved in a codex now in the collection of the Egyptian Museum in Turin. In one episode from the *Vita*, Epiphanius finds himself, like Theophilus, in need of funds, although the need in his case is occasioned by the desire to buy wheat in order to feed the hungry during a famine. He is instructed by God to go into a local temple, where he is told he will find treasure with which he can accomplish his purpose. When Epiphanius approaches the entrance of the temple, the seals magically fall away from the doors, the doors open, and he goes in and gets the money he needs.[108] While it is certainly possible that Ps.-Cyril and the author(s) of the cycle of texts dealing with Theophilus' construction program knew of and drew on this episode from the *Vita* of Epiphanius, it is noteworthy that the Coptic stories about Theophilus invariably insist on the process of textual interpretation as the key that literally opens the door to the temple where Theophilus obtains his treasure. Theophilus is clearly presented in the texts as the legitimate heir of his polytheistic predecessors—indeed, in several cases he is said to have been given the keys to all the temples of Egypt by the emperor himself—but it is his correct reading of the "thetas" that provides him with the authority to take up that charge. This is arguably a late expression of a concept with very deep roots in Egyptian culture, as reading and textuality played a major role in Egyptian ritual and magical practice in all periods.[109] It also relates to the notion expressed in a wide range of late antique sources, including the *Corpus Hermeticum* and Iamblichus' *De mysteriis*, that saw the Egyptian language in general and hieroglyphs in particular as possessing magical efficacy.[110]

Another striking feature of the texts dealing with Theophilus and the "thetas" is the fact that the treasure that Theophilus recovers through his interpretive efforts is explicitly associated with the figure of Alexander the Great.

In the Bohairic encomium on the Three Youths, this connection is not spelled out in any great detail; the site of the discovery is simply identified as "the temple of Alexander." The *Synaxarium* entry for the Feast of Theophilus provides only slightly more information; it states that the treasure, which was found beneath a paving stone engraved with the "thetas," dated to the time of Alexander, the son of Philip the Macedonian.[111] The long Arabic, Ethiopic, and Syriac recensions of the Vision of Theophilus, in contrast, offer a more detailed narrative, as does the Arabic homily on the Archangel Raphael. The Vision of Theophilus locates the treasure in the "Camp of Alexander" and specifies that Alexander himself had sealed the doors with the symbol of the "thetas," in order to protect the space until the coming of Theophilus: "indeed, it had never been opened from the day of Alexander down to this day in which God who opened the eyes of the blind from their mothers' womb opened it."[112] Finally, the homily on the Archangel Raphael preserves two versions of the story of the "thetas," and Alexander figures prominently in both. In the first version, Theophilus and Theodosius go to "the temple in which the treasure was." Theophilus interprets the "thetas" carved on the lintel, and the two men enter the temple; the treasure they discover inside is vast and is said to represent the spoils that Alexander had gathered in the course of his conquests.[113] The second version of the story is considerably more detailed; in this case, the door of the temple is said to have been covered with engraved signs of a magical nature, which Theophilus specifies are not written in his own mother tongue. However, the Holy Spirit enables him to interpret them, and when he does so, the text is revealed to be a dedication written by Alexander the Great himself. In this text, the Macedonian conqueror of Egypt is presented as a kind of Christian *avant la lettre*; he states that the temple contains unimaginable riches, attainable only through the will of God and the correct interpretation of the three "thetas." Theophilus, of course, proceeds to interpret the "thetas" correctly, and the rest of the story unfolds much as before—treasure is revealed, and a church is built using those funds.[114]

The motif of Theophilus as a despoiler of temples (indeed, as the one chosen by the emperor to carry out that destruction) can be traced back to the historical figure of the patriarch and his aggressive campaign to Christianize the Alexandrian landscape.[115] But why should the Christian authors of these late homilies have insisted so strongly on the association with Alexander the Great? Although scholars could, as late as the 1990s, point to the relative paucity of Coptic manuscript witnesses to the Alexander Romance and suggest that Alexander might have been "too much of a Greek to stimulate the imagination of the nationalistic Copts," it is now widely admitted that Alexander was very much alive in the imagination of late antique Egyptian Christians, as indeed he was throughout the Christian and Muslim cultures of the late antique Near East and beyond.[116] Respected as a world conqueror and reimagined as a proto-monotheist, Alexander could, as Faustina Doufikar-Aerts puts it, become "the model of everything one wanted to see in him," from philosopher-king to prophet of the One God, and the authors of the cycle of texts associated with Theophilus make good use of this malleability.[117] The claim that Alexander had set treasure aside for later Christian usage, implicit in the homily on the Three Youths and stated explicitly in the Vision of Theophilus and the homily on the Archangel Raphael, clearly echoes the representation of Alexander as a "pious ruler, seeking world dominion in order to convert all nations to monotheism," which can be seen in the Syriac, Ethiopic, and Arabic Pseudo-Callisthenes traditions.[118] And the protections that Alexander is said to have placed around the site where the treasure is stored—not only the "thetas," which must be properly interpreted, but also the "amulets" or "phylacteries" described in the homily on the archangel, which prevent the unworthy from accessing the site—have a close parallel in the powerful talismans that Alexander is described as fashioning in the Syriac and Arabic tales of Al-Iskander/ Dhū 'l-Qarnayan and his construction of an iron wall to defend against Gog and Magog. In one of the texts discussed by Doufikar-Aerts, a manuscript of the *Sīrat al-Malik Iskandar Dhū 'l-Qarnayan*, we are told that after the construction of the wall was completed, Alexander fashioned a gate in the wall on which he set a wide range of protections:

> Then he made the front and also closed the gate with *yāsūs*, and
> these are *qalfaṭīniyāt* [magic signs] from Greek books, which
> prevent the gate from being opened, except upon God's orders.
> Then he called for iron and copper, had it kneaded and made for
> the gate a key with twelve teeth that had to be carried by several
> men. For that he made a copper lock by which he closed the gate
> and said: "When the promise made by God the Exalted is fulfilled
> and He orders it to be opened, this [key] will open it. We make it
> [so] special that people will be amazed." When he had finished the
> gate and had locked, reinforced and strengthened it and covered it
> with magical signs, against which neither iron, fire, nor any other
> material has any power, he placed an inscription in Greek above the
> gate, like the inscription on the lighthouse in Alexandria.[119]

This inscription, much like the one translated by Theophilus in the homily on the archangel, states that the gate will remain impermeable "until the moment that God orders it."[120]

Given the extraordinary dispersal of Alexander literature across linguistic, cultural, and religious lines during the late antique and early medieval periods, it is not altogether surprising to see motifs from the Alexander legends appearing in Coptic, Syriac, and Christian Arabic homiletic sources, but it remains to be seen why the authors of those homilies felt the need to insert Alexander into the narrative in the first place. Tito Orlandi offers a route to answering this question in his proposal that the texts of the Theophilus cycle were composed in an effort to celebrate the antiquity and importance of certain Alexandrian churches by attributing their construction to the historical figure of Theophilus.[121] The common motif of the "thetas" and the connection to Alexander the Great takes this process of institutional lineage building a step further. By emphasizing that the churches were built using the funds from temple treasuries that had been set under seal by no less an authority than the proto-Christian Alexander, these establishments are able to trace their lineage back into the pre-Christian period and present their construction even more strongly as the fulfillment of divine preordination.

Conclusion

Even more than the case of the cross-shaped hieroglyphs at the Serapeum or Ammianus' translation of the Flaminian obelisk, the story of Theophilus and the "thetas" offers an opportunity to speak about both the act of translation from one language or semiotic system to another and what we might now consider a kind of cultural appropriation. If Kákosy's interpretation of the text is correct and Theophilus really is speaking about iconographic elements of the temple's décor, then the identification of those elements as Greek thetas goes well beyond translation; rather, it represents a redefinition of sorts, whereby the Christian viewer effectively claims the symbols as Greek letters—letters that, moreover, his spiritual authority uniquely qualifies him to interpret.

In all three of the case studies examined in this chapter, the hermeneutic act is closely bound up with notions of power and authority. Ammianus presents Hermapion's translation of the Flaminian obelisk within the larger context of a meditation on imperial power, and it is the quintessentially imperial act of returning to Rome with a trophy that brings the obelisk within the ambit of Roman scholars in the first place. In the ecclesiastical histories, the translation (or appropriation) of an ancient and culturally significant Egyptian symbol directly follows the Christian takeover of the Serapeum complex and serves as a justification or spiritual authorization for that takeover. Finally, Theophilus is authorized to interpret the "thetas" by a "holy prophetic spirit," and his interpretation of the signs grants him entry into the temple and access to the temple treasury.

Moving from the earliest of these texts to the latest, we can also see a significant shift in the identity of the translators carrying out the interpretation of hieroglyphic inscriptions and in the source of their authority to translate. Ammianus, illiterate in hieroglyphs himself, calls on the outside authority of Hermapion to provide a translation of the obelisk inscription; Theophilus, equally illiterate in hieroglyphs but guided by the Holy Spirit, sees no such need. In some respects, the story of Theophilus and the "thetas" can thus be seen as the logical outcome of the shifting attitudes discussed in Chapter 3 above, as the traditional temple-centered study of the Egyptian language and scripts gives way to a spiritually guided hermeneutic process. The image that emerges from the Coptic homilies concerning Theophilus, of the Coptic priest or monk standing before a hieroglyphic inscription and offering an authoritative translation of it, had a remarkably long and tenacious afterlife. In the medieval Arabic sources, Coptic monks are not infrequently presented as possessing the ability to read hieroglyphs; so, for example, the thirteenth-century astrologer Al-Jobry described a monk from Al-Bahnasa as "a brilliant philosopher who knows the secrets of the ancient priests, and uncovered their symbols and understood their sciences."[122]

Conclusion

Hieroglyphs in the Late Antique Imagination

In writing this book, I set out to uncover the "mnemohistory" of Egyptian hieroglyphic writing in the period of late antiquity, an era that has been relatively little studied in prior discussions of the reception of pharaonic Egypt and in histories of hieroglyphic decipherment. Of particular interest was the treatment of hieroglyphs by late antique Christian authors, whom modern scholarship has too often dismissed as indifferent to—or even hostile toward—the hieroglyphic tradition. Three principal questions animated my research: what did late antique Christian writers actually know about hieroglyphs, an utterly foreign writing system to most of them? On what basis did they engage with the classical discourse on hieroglyphs, which was already well established by late antiquity? And finally, what light, if any, do these authors' remarks on hieroglyphs shed on their attitudes toward pharaonic Egyptian culture more broadly conceived? Although the case studies examined in the previous chapters have, in some cases, raised as many questions as they have answered, it is possible to at least begin to sketch a picture of how hieroglyphs appeared in the late antique imagination and to outline some directions for future research.

Piecing together references to hieroglyphs from the works of the late antique church fathers and ecclesiastical historians gives us some idea of what those authors knew about the ancient Egyptian writing system. Numerous late antique sources attest to the close connection between hieroglyphs and the gods, although those deities are often subjected to a euhemeristic treatment and reclassified as human culture heroes. Thoth-Hermes-Mercury is most commonly identified as the inventor of the Egyptian writing system, and sometimes of human language and writing more generally, but Augustine's remarks in *De civitate Dei* demonstrate the persistence of a parallel tradition crediting Isis with the invention of writing. As we saw in Chapter 2, that seems to be the version Augustine preferred as being a better fit for his chronological argumentation. It was also widely acknowledged that the Egyptian writing system was very ancient, certainly older than that of the Greeks, although here, too, this chronological primacy could be challenged if it conflicted with scriptural authorities.

Late antique authors also had some sense of the different ways in which hieroglyphs might be employed. The existence of multiple scripts was sometimes acknowledged, most notably by Clement and Porphyry, although the independent existence of hieratic was often ignored in favor of a broad bipartite division between "sacred" and "common" scripts. Hieroglyphs were known to have been used for historical record keeping, notably in the maintenance of royal annals and chronicles, but more pervasive and arguably more significant was the perceived link between hieroglyphic writing and Egyptian religion and magic. Priests were recognized as the quintessential Egyptian literati and temples as the principal locus of hieroglyphic writing. In this context, hieroglyphs were viewed as the preeminent means of both revealing and concealing the teachings of the Egyptian priesthood. Christian discussions of Moses' education in the "wisdom of Egypt" indicate a certain discomfort with this aspect of the hieroglyphic tradition, however, and the wisdom conveyed in hieroglyphic texts is often problematized or even said to have been supplanted by true Christian wisdom, conveyed by the Holy Spirit.

With the exception of Clement and, later, Horapollo, relatively few late antique authors attempted to delve very deeply into the question of how the hieroglyphic script actually functioned. Most commentators adhered to a well-established line of thinking that represented hieroglyphic signs as purely symbolic; the existence of phonetic signs in the hieroglyphic repertoire was typically elided, and hieroglyphs were generally thought to function allegorically, the meaning of each individual sign tied to the nature of the object it depicted. There are various possible explanations for this. As many modern commentators have stressed, in the Ptolemaic and Roman periods, the hieroglyphic script did develop in such a way as to foreground the symbolic quality of individual hieroglyphs, and the classical and late antique authors' focus on this aspect of the writing system to some extent reflects the way the script was being used in the later periods. Access to accurate information would also have been a limiting factor—Smet of Philae may have had some degree of hieroglyphic literacy, but would he have been able to explain the nature and function of the signs he carved into the stone of Hadrian's Gate? Probably not.

Late antique authors also had to contend with the weight of received tradition, which since at least the time of Diodorus had promoted the symbolic inter-pretation of hieroglyphs.

In thinking about what late antique Christian authors knew about hiero-glyphic writing, it is also necessary to consider where those writers obtained their information. Relatively few of the late antique authors discussed in these pages would have ever seen hieroglyphic inscriptions at first hand; fewer still would have had the opportunity to examine such inscriptions with the assis-tance of a native interlocutor, as some of the earlier classical visitors to Egypt might have done. There are some exceptions, of course, notably in the case of those authors with Egyptian backgrounds; Shenoute was certainly familiar with the appearance of hieroglyphs, and the authors of the Coptic homilies dealing with Theophilus and Cyril would probably have had some exposure to them as well. But for the most part, late antique Christian authors were heavily reliant on the accounts of Egyptian writing provided by earlier classical sources. Indeed, the case studies examined in the previous chapters have shown that it is difficult, if not altogether impossible, to isolate a specifically Christian discourse on hieroglyphs in late antiquity. The Christian authors who discuss Egyptian writing were the direct heirs to the classical discourse on Egypt, and that legacy both enriched and constrained them. Certain ideas about Egyptian writing, first articulated by Herodotus, Plato, and Diodorus, among others, proved nearly impossible to dislodge, even half a millennium later.

This was the case, for example, of the traditions surveyed in Chapters 2 and 3, concerning the divine origins and great antiquity of hieroglyphic writing and its use to record Egyptian history and to transmit the arcane knowledge of the Egyptian priesthood. Consequently, we see authors like Eusebius and Augus-tine, Ambrose and Origen, working within the parameters of this received discourse, adopting and adapting it to suit their theological objectives. Thus, in Augustine's work, for example, the inventor of hieroglyphs becomes, not Thoth-Hermes, the thrice-great god, but Isis-Io, the human queen of Egypt, a transformation that allows Augustine to call into question the Egyptians' much-vaunted claims to an extraordinarily ancient tradition of historical record keeping. Similarly, Origen and Ambrose both challenge the long-standing tra-dition of respect for the "wisdom of Egypt" as encoded in hieroglyphic texts by focusing on the figure of Moses, who repudiated his Egyptian education, which Origen specifies he acquired from ancient and inaccessible writings, but nonetheless managed to best the enchanters of Pharaoh. The themes discussed in Chapters 4 and 5 also reflect the Christian reworking of existing ideas about

Egyptian hieroglyphs. In his tirade against hieroglyphic writing, Shenoute draws on both the classical discourse, with its emphasis on animal hieroglyphs, and on the tradition of Judeo-Christian polemic against Egyptian animal cults in order to make the argument that the inscriptions in the temple he seeks to transform are functionally the same as cult images, and therefore must be destroyed. And the ecclesiastical historians and homilists who tell the story of the discovery of hieroglyphic inscriptions in Alexandria during the episcopate of Theophilus utilize contemporary ideas about the nature of language and the process of translation to make the argument that translating hieroglyphs can, under the right circumstances, produce miraculous results.

In addition to informing us about the contemporary state of hieroglyphic knowledge, late antique Christian authors' comments on hieroglyphs also tell us something about their attitudes toward the pharaonic Egyptian culture that produced that unique mode of written expression. In an article on the connection between monuments, travel, and writing in the ancient world, John (Jaś) Elsner has argued that monuments operate simultaneously as artifacts and as objects of discourse. He writes, "monuments as ideas or ideological constructs always have the added dimension of having been real things. They authorise discourse, and thus act to persuade the reader, by referring with apparent simplicity to artefacts outside language. . . . They exist (as artefacts), and so what they mean (as signs in language) must therefore be true."[1] For the late antique Christian writers surveyed in the previous chapters, hieroglyphic inscriptions from Egypt's pharaonic past served just such a discursive function. As one of the most highly visible markers of Egyptian cultural and religious identity, monumental hieroglyphs were physically present in a variety of late antique contexts—in Egypt itself, of course, but also in imperial centers like Rome and Constantinople in the form of artifacts taken as trophies of empire. As such, they were indisputably "real things," like the monuments Elsner discusses in his article, but they also served to "authorise discourse" on a variety of different subjects. Talking about hieroglyphs, in many of these late antique sources, becomes a way of talking about other things altogether: imperialism, history, identity, and spiritual authority, to name only a few possibilities.

One of the places where we can see this discursive process most clearly is in the late antique Christian approach to "reading" hieroglyphs. For classical authors like Diodorus, the ability to read the hieroglyphic script required long and arduous study; once attained, it afforded membership in an elite intellectual class with unique access to the accumulated wisdom of the ages. This view is echoed by Ammianus, who calls on the outside authority of the translator

Hermapion to provide the hieroglyphic translation he interpolates into the *Res Gestae*. In the works of many of the Christian authors surveyed in these pages, however, the act of "reading" hieroglyphs becomes an exercise in spiritually guided *hermeneusis*, and Christian ascetics like Shenoute and ecclesiastical leaders like Theophilus claim the right to interpret monumental inscriptions despite lacking the traditional educational formation. Translation blends into appropriation, while at the same time, the translations that emerge from this practice of *interpretatio Christiana* are ever more consequential, insofar as they are used to shape arguments over access to and control of the monumental legacy of Egypt's pharaonic past.

* * *

For a variety of reasons, histories of the hieroglyphic tradition and of decipherment have, as discussed above in the Introduction, tended to give short shrift to late antique Christian sources. References to hieroglyphs and Egyptian writing more generally are scattered throughout the enormous corpus of patristic literature, and, with few exceptions, the sources fail to show the level of sustained interest in hieroglyphs that characterizes the classical discourse on Egypt. However, as a chapter in the history of Egyptology, these late antique sources play a key role. Not only do they preserve certain very ancient ideas and traditions about hieroglyphs, but their insistence on the symbolic nature of hieroglyphs, which is consistent across religious and cultural divides, from Horapollo and Ammianus to Clement and Socrates Scholasticus, heavily influenced the hieroglyphic speculation of the Renaissance and early modern periods. Late antique Christian comments on hieroglyphs also fit well within the emerging scholarly consensus that late antique Christian responses to pharaonic monuments (and "pagan" monuments more generally) were not exclusively negative. Far from monolithic in their perspective, the sources examined in these pages exhibit a broad range of responses to hieroglyphs and hieroglyphic inscriptions, which can be seen as anything from tools of the Devil to prophecies of the coming of Christ.

* * *

The case studies explored in this book have begun the process of writing late antique commentators, particularly Christian ones, back into the history of Egyptological speculation, but the story does not end here. Focusing on the late antique sources raises some new and important questions, and two avenues of future exploration are, I think, particularly deserving of attention. I have tried, where possible, to signal links between the late antique Christian texts dealing with hieroglyphs and the rich corpus of early medieval Islamic sources on the same subject, but a truly comparative study would require fluency in premodern Arabic and goes well beyond the scope of this project. Okasha El Daly has argued eloquently for the rehabilitation of what he calls the "missing millennium" of medieval Arabic Egyptological inquiry. Nowhere is the importance and promise of this work more clearly indicated than in his discussion of hieroglyphs as they appear in the work of early medieval Islamic historians and geographers.[2] If Ibn Waḥshiyah's late ninth-/early tenth-century treatise on ancient scripts does indeed demonstrate knowledge of the existence of phonograms and determinatives in the hieroglyphic repertoire, as El Daly has proposed, what additional information about the early medieval understanding of hieroglyphs may be awaiting discovery in as-yet unedited Arabic manuscripts in museums and libraries worldwide? Just as late antique theories about hieroglyphic writing developed in conversation with the classical discourse on the subject, early medieval Islamic discussions of hieroglyphs were in dialogue with both their classical and late antique precursors, and reconstructing that dialogue and the role of hieroglyphs in the medieval Islamic imagination remains a major desideratum.

A second axis of inquiry that would reward future investigation revolves around the materiality of hieroglyphic texts and their treatment in late antiquity. My analysis in this study has focused primarily on hieroglyphs as objects of late antique discourse, but this is only part of the story, as hieroglyphic inscriptions also had an independent existence as physical artifacts and can be considered on that basis as well. One might look, for example, at the treatment of hieroglyphic texts at pharaonic sites that were occupied in late antiquity. Prior discussions of this issue have often been based on the false premise that late antique Christians were necessarily frightened or disgusted by the sight of hieroglyphs, as in the example of John Ray's "nervous" monk Jacob. As a result, damage to inscriptions and reliefs has commonly been attributed to Christian agency on a rather uncritical basis. For this reason, a reexamination of the subject that takes into account the plurality of possible Christian responses to hieroglyphs on a site-by-site basis is still needed. Among the questions that could be posed are the following: Under what circumstances were hieroglyphic inscriptions defaced? Plastered over? Obscured with new construction? What evidence is there for interaction between secondary epigraphic activity and existing hieroglyphic inscriptions and relief carvings? David Frankfurter's recent *Christianizing Egypt* demonstrates the rich rewards of examining religious activity and religious change—even the nature of "religion" itself—by means of the material record.[3] Hieroglyphic inscriptions, as artifacts and as a prominent feature of the physical and visual landscape of late antique Egypt, could profitably be examined in this same light.

* * *

In the quotation that serves as an epigraph to this book, Serge Sauneron suggests the following: "one could write a most agreeable book," he says, "about the legends of Egypt born of men's reanimation of the images of a past they no longer comprehended."[4] Whether this book succeeds in being agreeable, let alone "most agreeable," is for the individual reader to decide. I do hope, however, that I have managed to shed some light on the way that certain late antique authors, confronted with "the images of a past they no longer comprehended" in the form of hieroglyphic inscriptions, reanimated those images with new meanings and, in so doing, added their own chapter to the mnemo-history of pharaonic Egypt.

Notes

1. Ray 2007, 13. For the text of the graffito, *SB Kopt.* II 1058; Delattre 2008, 185.

2. Ray 2007, 11–13.

3. Haarmann 2001, 191; 1996, 606. El Daly (2005) offers an important challenge to the notion that medieval Muslim interpretations of pharaonic Egypt were inherently negative.

4. Badawy 1953, 70. Dijkstra (2011) offers an incisive overview of scholarship in this area, with a discussion of major historiographic trends and suggestions for how to move beyond the dominant paradigm of Christian triumphalism.

5. This attitude can be clearly seen in Baillet's (1926) study of Roman-period graffiti from the Valley of the Kings, in which the author insists on a sharp divide between Greco-Roman "tourists" and Christian "pilgrims." For example, *I.Syring.* 2017 from KV9, the supposed tomb of Memnon and a major tourist destination in the Greco-Roman period, reads, "Isaac, fr[om] Antinoe; I came and marveled (Ἰσὰκ ἀ[πὸ?] Ἀντινό[η]ς ἥκω καὶ ἐθαύμασα)." Although the phrasing of the inscription is identical to that used by numerous non-Christian visitors to the site, a small cross preceding the text suggests that Isaac was himself a Christian, and Baillet (1926, 519–20) takes great pains to explain that he must have approached the site from a very different perspective than his non-Christian counterparts.

6. Christians blamed for the destruction of monuments: e.g., Sauer 2003; Kristensen 2013. Shenoute of Atripe's antagonist Gessios, with his private collection of pharaonic and classicizing sculpture, is sometimes taken as emblematic of the embattled traditionalist seeking to preserve his religious heritage; see the discussion of Shenoute and Gessios in chapter 4 below.

7. This particular developmental arc in the historiography of late antique Egypt, with particular reference to the sources from the region of Syene, is traced by Dijkstra (2011, 389–410). For the rhetorical nature of the literary sources, see Averil Cameron 1991; Hahn, Emmel, and Gotter 2008. Although the title of the latter volume emphasizes the phenomenon of temple conversion, several chapters highlight the multiplicity of fates that might befall any given monument.

8. This local focus has been eloquently championed by Dijkstra (2008; 2011). See also O'Connell 2007a and 2007b, in which a relatively narrow local focus allows for an extremely rich picture of late antique Christian interactions with the pharaonic landscape.

9. Byzantine Christians collecting classical sculpture: Mango 1963; 1994; Dagron 1984; Saradi-Mendelovici 1990; Hjort 1993; Lepelley 1994; Marinescu 1996; Hannestad 1999. A countervailing trend in the scholarship has emphasized the *destruction* of classical sculpture at Christian hands in late antiquity; notably, this body of work draws heavily on Egyptian sources, which are markedly less present in discussions of the Byzantine *preservation* of classical monuments: Stewart 1999; Frankfurter 2008a; 2008b; Kristensen 2009. Both trends in the scholarship

are reviewed in Caseau 2001. Bishops seeking to Christianize the urban topography, notably the example of Cyril of Alexandria: Haas 1997; Hahn 2008. Christian townspeople preserving ancient theophoric toponyms: Westerfeld 2012. Monks seeking out abandoned temples and tombs as venues for spiritual combat: Brakke 2006; 2008; O'Connell 2007a; 2007b.

10. For an introduction to the theory of social (or collective, or cultural) memory, Halbwachs 1992; Lowenthal 1985; Connerton 1989. For examples of how memory studies may productively be integrated into the study of the ancient world, Alcock 2002; Assmann 2006.

11. Assmann (1997, 9) defines mnemohistory as "reception theory applied to history"; as such, it deals not with the historical reality of individuals or events in the past but with the diachronic study of how those individuals or events were remembered and reinterpreted in subsequent eras.

12. See, e.g., Vasunia 2001; Bricault, Versluys, and Meyboom 2007; Moyer 2011.

13. Assmann 1997; Curran 2007; Moser 2006; 2012.

14. Reid 2002; 2015; Colla 2007.

15. Marestaing 1913; Iversen 1993.

16. Hieroglyphs in the Renaissance: Hornung 2001, chapter 10; Curran 2007, chapter 10. Histories of decipherment: Parkinson 1999; Ray 2007; Winand 2014.

17. Horapollo: Thissen 1998; 2001. Book of Thoth: Jasnow and Zauzich 2005; 2014.

18. Iversen 1993, 57–59; Winand 2014, 35 (my translation): "Durant le Moyen Âge, le goût pour l'Égypte est en net recul. . . . Il faut attendre le travail des humanistes à partir du XVe siècle . . . pour voir renaître un intérêt pour l'Égypte ancienne."

19. Ray 2007, 13. This interpretation of the graffito is followed by Kristensen (2013, 167), who states that "a monk named Jacob wrote a graffito commenting on life in the reused tomb and recorded his ignorance of the meaning of the hieroglyphs on the tomb's walls. He also noted how he had covered up parts of the hieroglyphs with a veil."

20. SB Kopt. II 1058, trans. after Delattre 2008, 185.

21. Delattre 2008, 183–86. Delattre's interpretation is in line with that of the inscription's original editor, Walter Crum, who noted that "one might suppose this a reference to the use of a cryptogram, *scarcely to the obliteration of a hieroglyphic text*" (Winlock and Crum 1926, 19, emphasis mine).

22. Baillet 1926, lxxii.

23. Górecki and Kropp 2013, 241. I am grateful to the anonymous second reviewer for the University of Pennsylvania Press for bringing this discovery to my attention.

24. Bowersock, Brown, and Grabar 2001. The notion of a "long" late antiquity (indeed, the very concept of "late antiquity" itself) has been the subject of considerable discussion in recent years; see Averil Cameron 2002; Marcone 2008. The concept of late antiquity (long or short) as applied to Egypt is evaluated in Bagnall 2003.

25. Smelik and Hemelrijk 1984.

26. Hieroglyphs as a defining feature of Egyptian identity: see, e.g., Vasunia 2001, 181: "Egypt appears to be defined programmatically by its relationship to the written word."

27. See, e.g., Remus 2004; Lavan and Mulryan 2011; Frankfurter 2018, 7–15.

28. Remus 2004, 197–201.

29. Frankfurter 2018, 7–9. However, see also van Nuffelen (2011, 91), who argues that "paganism, although it gained its present form in Christian polemic, is essentially a dialectical concept, a construct that incorporates earlier strands of pagan reflection on their own religions."

30. Continued use, with acknowledgement of limitations: e.g., Bremmer 2015. "Polytheist/ism" as a possible alternative: e.g., Remus 2004. Problems with "polytheist/ism": van Nuffelen 2011.

31. For Ἕλλην with the meaning "Gentile, pagan," Lampe 1961, 451b.

CHAPTER I

1. *I.Philae.Dem.* 436. For the dating of the text, Devauchelle 1994, 18. For the reading of the name Smet (*'Is.t-mḏ*), Dijkstra 2008, 175n1. More generally on the priests of Isis at Philae in the fourth and fifth centuries C.E., Dijkstra 2008, chapter 6.

2. Parkinson 1999, 178–79; Ray 2007, 9–12.

3. The use of the term "hieroglyphic" (ἱερογλυφικός) to designate the Egyptian writing system is first attested in Diodorus 3.4.1; however, "sacred" and "common" scripts were being distinguished by Greek writers as early as Herodotus (2.36). The implication inherent in the term "hieroglyphic"—that texts in that script necessarily have religious content—is addressed further in Chapter 3 below.

4. Boylan 1922, 92–97. The mythical origins of Egyptian writing are discussed in Plato, *Phdr.* 274c–275b, and the recently published Demotic Book of Thoth offers a fascinating view of Late-Period Egyptian scribes' attitudes toward their own writing system; see Jasnow 2011; Jasnow and Zauzich 2005; 2014. Both classical and Egyptian accounts of the invention of hieroglyphs are discussed further in chapter 2 below.

5. Wilson 2004, 2–6; MacArthur 2010. The distinction between glottographic writing systems like the hieroglyphic script, which retain a fundamental tie to the spoken word, and semasiographic systems, which represent ideas rather than speech, is outlined in Woods 2010b, 18–19.

6. On the somewhat amorphous distinction between early Egyptian writing and the various alternative "semiotic explorations" that appear to have coevolved with it, Stauder 2010, 137. Stauder notes that rather than seeking "a clear-cut divide between writing and other systems of visual communication that convey messages without reference to speech," we should rather consider the development of Egyptian writing in terms of "gradually increasing representation of language and speech." Further on the coexistence of different notational systems in Predynastic Egypt, Regulski 2016.

7. Cemetery U was initially excavated by Flinders Petrie on behalf of the Egypt Exploration Society; see Petrie 1900; 1901. The reexamination of the site has been ongoing since the 1970s under the aegis of the German Archaeological Institute, and tomb U-j was discovered in 1988; on the excavations, see Dreyer, Hartung, and Pumpenmeier 1998; Hartung 2001.

8. Regulski 2008a; 2016.

9. Stauder 2010, 146.

10. J. Johnson 2010b, 150–51. Further on the early stages of this developmental process, Regulski 2016.

11. Introductions to the hieroglyphic writing system are numerous; good brief overviews may be found in Davies 1987; Zauzich 1992; Wilson 2004. The standard reference grammar for classical Middle Egyptian remains Gardiner 1957; more recent teaching grammars include Hoch 1997; Allen 2010.

12. Assmann 1994, 17.

13. Goldwasser 1995, 78.

14. Goldwasser 1995, 32; see also Goldwasser 2002.

15. M. Williams 2011, chapter 5.

16. Two possible exceptions to this may be noted. The second-century Christian theologian Clement of Alexandria appears to refer to the existence of alphabetic signs in *Strom.* 5 (discussed further in Chapter 3 below), and Okasha El Daly has argued (2005, chapter 5) that some medieval Arabic authors—notably the late ninth-/ early tenth-century Ibn Waḥshiyah, whose work

was known to Athanasius Kircher—recognized that certain hieroglyphs served as phonograms and were able to correctly identify some of them.

17. On the symbological interpretation of hieroglyphs by classical and late antique authors, see chapter 3 below. The popularity of this mode of interpretation during the Italian Renaissance and its promulgation in the early modern period have been discussed in several works; see Dieckmann 1970; Iversen 1993; Hornung 2001; Curran 2007; Giehlow 2015. A good overview of the decipherment of hieroglyphs is provided in Parkinson 1999; Ray 2007.

18. For a general introduction to the hieratic script, Bandy 2010; on the origins of hieratic, Regulski 2009.

19. Vernus (1990, 45) notes that the Greek appellation "hieratic" reflects a pattern of script usage specific to the Late Period, when Demotic had come to predominate in administrative contexts and hieratic was increasingly restricted to religious documents and private copies of literary texts. For the differential use of hieroglyphs and the various "tachygraphic" scripts, see Vernus 1990, 41–42.

20. Baines 1989, 471.

21. For a general introduction to the Demotic script, J. Johnson 2010a.

22. Baines and Eyre 1983. The authors note (68) that "Demotic also brought about the final separation of everyday and monumental scripts, the transformation of hieratic into a purely 'literary' form, and a decline in the knowledge of both hieroglyphs and hieratic."

23. Last dated Demotic inscription from Philae: *I.Philae.Dem.* 377. See further Cruz-Uribe 2002; 2010; Dijkstra 2008.

24. Quaegebeur 1982; 1991a; 1991b; Emmel 1992; Choat 2012, 582–86.

25. For a brief overview of the Coptic script and its uses, Choat 2012.

26. Papaconstantinou 2007; 2012; Richter 2009.

27. A useful overview of the relationship between the Greek and Egyptian languages in Hellenistic and Roman Egypt, with particular reference to the role of language choice in the formation of identity, is to be found in Tovar 2010.

28. Generally on Egypt in the Roman and Byzantine periods, Bowman 1986; Bagnall 1993; Ritner 1998a; Keenan 2000; Bagnall 2007; Riggs 2012.

29. Depauw 2012, 500–501; *pace* Rochette 1994, 316–17.

30. For the complex interplay of Greek, Coptic, and Arabic in the late antique and early medieval periods, Papaconstantinou 2007; 2012; Richter 2009.

31. The Satire on the Trades, Simpson 2003, 431–37.

32. Generally on scribes and their training, R. Williams 1972; Baines 1983; Wente 1995; Piacentini 2001; Imhausen 2012. On the high status of scribes from the earliest stages of Egyptian history, Te Velde 1986; Regulski 2008b.

33. The foundational study of education in pharaonic Egypt remains Brunner 1957. On the particular case of education and literacy at the New Kingdom workmen's village of Deir el-Medina, where many educational texts have been found in the course of excavation, Baines and Eyre 1983, 86–91; McDowell 2000. As Baines and Eyre note (1983, 86), the unique context of the village must be emphasized in any attempt to extrapolate from the material found there to more general observations. However, it appears that although a higher percentage of the population at Deir el-Medina was likely literate than in the Egyptian populace overall, the educational methods employed in the village probably did not differ significantly from the norm.

34. Primary education in hieratic: R. Williams 1972, 219; Vernus 1990, 37; Piacentini 2001, 188. On the use of hieratic in administration from the earliest periods of Egyptian history, Baines

1989, 472. Secondary education in hieroglyphs: Wente 1995, 2216. See also Baines 1983, 581–84; Vernus 1990, 37; Piacentini 2001, 189.

35. For education in Greek and Coptic, as evidenced by the papyrological record, Cribiore 1996; 1999; 2009; Bucking 2011. Demotic education, Devauchelle 1984; Tassier 1992; Tait 1994; 1997; Hoffmann 2012, 545–46.

36. Although not dealing specifically with scribal education, Klotz (2012b) uses the high quality of Roman-period inscriptions at sites including the temple of Hathor at Dendera to argue for the continuity of scribal competence in the hieroglyphic script (and thus, by extension, training in that script) into the third century C.E.

37. Bowman and Woolf 1994b, 2.

38. Baines and Eyre 1983; Baines 1983. On the purportedly rising rate of literacy during the Late Period, Ray 1994b, 64–65.

39. For advanced scribal training as a type of vocational study, Baines 1983, 580. The link between literacy in hieroglyphs and service in the priesthood is widely recognized; see Vernus 1990, 36–37; Frankfurter 1998, chapter 6.

40. The apparent lack of either moral obligation or theological training on the part of candidates to the priesthood prior to the Late Period is noted in Sauneron 2000, 35–43. Criteria for admission to the priesthood became more stringent throughout the Late Period and into the Hellenistic and Roman eras, peaking in the Roman period as part of an overall Roman policy intended to decrease the landholdings and tax exemptions of the temples and their staffs; see Ritner 1998a, 7–8; Frankfurter 1998, chapter 5.

41. Generally on the role of the lector-priest, Sauneron 2000, 61–64; Otto 1975; Ritner 1997, 220–22. For lector-priests in the Roman period, Dieleman 2005, 203–54.

42. For a brief overview of Ptolemaic hieroglyphs, Gaudard 2010; see further Sauneron 1982; Kurth 1983.

43. Sauneron 1962, 55–57.

44. Baines 1983, 581–83; Sauneron 1962, 56.

45. Gardiner 1938; Derchain 1965; Weber 1981; Ritner 1997, 204–5; Frankfurter 1998, 238–64; Sauneron 2000, 132–36; Morenz 2001; Jasnow 2016, 342–47; Stadler 2017, 35–46.

46. A House of Life, identified in the basis of stamped mud bricks, was excavated at Amarna; the structure was situated in close proximity to both the Great and Small Temples to the Aten and adjacent to the so-called Records Office; see Pendlebury 1934, 134; 1951, 115 and 150. On the relationship between the institutions of the library (pr-mḏ3.t) and House of Life (pr-ꜥnḫ) and the archaeological evidence for both, Burkhard 1980; Zinn 2011. The ongoing publication and study of the materials from the Tebtunis temple library offers a remarkable window into the holdings of such an institution during the first two centuries of the Roman period; see, e.g., Ryholt 2005.

47. Gardiner 1938, 170.

48. On the changing role(s) of Egyptian priests in the Roman periods, including their interactions with Greek and Roman tourists, Frankfurter 1998, chapter 5. For Egyptian priests as cultural intermediaries, see also Moyer 2002; 2003; 2011, especially chapters 1 and 4.

49. The term is admittedly rare, appearing twice in the Discourse on the Eighth and Ninth from Nag Hammadi Codex VI (at 61,20 and 62,15); see Dirkse, Brashler, and Parrott 1979, 366–67. On the etymology of the term, Lucchesi 1975.

50. P.Oxy. VII 1029. It should not be assumed that these hieroglyph carvers were actually literate in hieroglyphs. In fact, there is ample evidence from earlier periods to suggest that the

individuals who carved hieroglyphic inscriptions in many cases could not read the texts they were so laboriously producing; see Baines and Eyre 1983, 86–88; Vernus 1990, 39–41. However, the fact that the city could still support such a group of specialists does indicate the continued existence of a market for monumental hieroglyphic inscriptions, as well as the presence of some number of individuals with the requisite expertise to produce such texts (or at least identify them in the temple library). With regard to the graffiti of Smet, it has long been noted that the formulaic hieroglyphic graffito must be interpreted by reference to the more legible Demotic inscription; see, e.g., Griffith's notes to *I.Philae.Dem.* 436.

51. Sternberg el-Hotabi 1994; Houston, Baines, and Cooper 2003; Dieleman 2005, 104–10.

52. Houston, Baines, and Cooper (2003, 433) note that "in theory, script requires but one reader. In practice, its survival presupposes a social investment and relatively broad use." Similarly, Martin Stadler has observed (2008, 174) that in the Roman period, Demotic also shows a trend toward increasing complexity with the growing use of unetymological writings, particularly in religious texts; he concludes that "[Egyptian priests] became culturally and religiously isolated, and supported that development by composing both hieroglyphic and demotic texts encoded in a most difficult system. Texts written in that manner required some effort to be understood and were regarded as obsolete, because they did not respond to the contemporary social environment."

53. For the limited adoption of Greek loanwords into Demotic, Clarysse 1987; 2013; Ray 1994a; Houston, Baines, and Cooper 2003, 443; Dieleman 2005, 106–10.

54. Houston, Baines, and Cooper note (2003, 443) that "Greek had prestige in certain domains but was not perceived as the country's traditional cultural language."

55. Klotz 2012b.

56. Frankfurter 1994, 204–5; 1998, 252–53.

57. Houston, Baines, and Cooper 2003, 444–45.

58. Sternberg el-Hotabi 1994; 1999. Sharp critiques of Sternberg el-Hotabi's work have appeared in a number of subsequent publications; see especially Quack 2002; Stadler 2008, 162–63; von Lieven 2009, 104–5; Klotz 2012b, 568. Although Sternberg el-Hotabi's contention that hieroglyphic literacy began to wane as early as the middle of the Ptolemaic period has been rightly called into question, the existence of various types of pseudohieroglyphic inscriptions from the Hellenistic and Roman periods is not disputed; see, e.g., von Lieven 2009.

59. Houston, Baines, and Cooper 2003, 444–45; von Lieven 2009, 105–9.

60. Klotz 2012b. The suggestion of Houston, Baines, and Cooper (2003, 445) that the gap between the illegible-yet-functional inscriptions on the Horus stelae and the sophistication of Ptolemaic temple inscriptions might be related to "the availability of resources as well as to the perceived efficacy of hieroglyphic inscriptions in temples" is not entirely satisfactory given that both stelae and temple inscriptions operated within the same belief system, which insisted on the magical efficacy of the act of representation.

61. E.g., Badawy 1953.

62. Bagnall 1993; Ritner 1998a. For the impact of the fiscal situation on the hieroglyphic tradition, Houston, Baines, and Cooper 2003, 449–50.

63. Ritner 1998a, 7–8.

64. Klotz 2012a.

65. Grégoire 1940; Ritner 1998a, 25–26.

66. Frankfurter 1998; 2018.

CHAPTER 2

1. Sacred and common scripts: Herodotus 2.36 (trans. Grene 1987): "They use two different kinds of writing, one of which is called sacred and the other common (διφασίοισι δὲ γράμμασι χρέωνται, καὶ τὰ μὲν αὐτῶν ἱρὰ, τὰ δὲ δημοτικὰ καλέεται)." Hoffmann (2012, 543) raises the possibility that Herodotus' "sacred" script should be understood as hieratic, rather than hieroglyphic.

2. Cultural primacy of Egyptians: Herodotus 2.4: "These authorities also say that the Egyptians were the first to use the names of the twelve gods, and that the Greeks took these from them, and that the Egyptians were the first to assign altars and images and temples to the gods and to carve figures on stone (καὶ ζῷα ἐν λίθοισι ἐγγλύψαι)." Although it is tempting to take these figures carved on stones as a reference to monumental hieroglyphs, they are more probably relief carvings; see Lloyd 1976, 32–33.

3. Plato, *Phdr.* 274c–e (trans. Fowler, LCL 36); compare Cicero, *Nat. deor.* 3.22.56; Diodorus 1.16.1; Plutarch, *Quaest. conv.* 9.3.2 (738f); Plutarch, *De Iside* 3 (352b). Scholarship has been divided concerning the origin of the story of Theuth as it is related in the *Phaedrus*, with some seeing it as Plato's own invention and others arguing that it represents the transmission by Plato of earlier traditions. A balanced assessment is provided by Werner, who argues (2012, 191) that in the story of Theuth "we see that Plato is appropriating and reconceptualizing a rich array of traditional myths and lore," both Greek and Egyptian. See also Bull 2018, 38–44. More generally on Plato's knowledge of Egypt, McEvoy 1993 (*Phdr.* 274c–e is discussed on p. 262n32). For the association of the Egyptian Thoth with the Greek Hermes, Boylan 1922; Fowden 1993; Bull 2018, chapter 2.

4. Diodorus 1.16.1 (trans. Oldfather, LCL 279).

5. For Thoth as "Lord of Hieroglyphs," Boylan 1922, 93–94; Volokhine 2004, 134; Klotz 2012a, 217. Generally on the figure of Thoth in Egyptian mythology, especially in the context of mortuary literature, Schott 1963; 1972; Stadler 2009; 2012. Somewhat outdated but nevertheless useful are the overviews provided in Boylan 1922; Bleeker 1973; Kurth 1986.

6. For the epithets of Thoth, including these selected examples, Boylan 1922, 180–200. Specifically for Thoth's epithets in the Greco-Roman period, Derchain-Urtel 1981.

7. Chassinat 1930, 191, lines 3–4. For the Mesopotamian story of the creation of cuneiform, Jacobsen 1987, 275–319.

8. P. Bibliothèque Nationale 149, 1/9–10; trans. Mark Smith 2009, 445.

9. Černy 1948.

10. Pliny the Elder, *HN* 7.56.192–93; Pomponius Mela, *De situ orbis* 1.65 (trans. Romer 1998).

11. Pomponius Mela, *De situ orbis* 1.59.

12. For (Thoth-)Hermes as a "figure of memory," Bull 2018, 15–20.

13. *Editio princeps*: Jasnow and Zauzich 2005; revised English translation in Jasnow and Zauzich 2014.

14. Jasnow and Zauzich 2014, 47. The reconstruction of the Book of Thoth from the various manuscript witnesses is discussed on pp. 10–18, and the text's possible connection to the institution known as the House of Life is outlined on pp. 43–48. Quack (2007, 259) has raised some caveats about the identification of the figure of *Ḥs-rḫ* as Thoth himself.

15. Thoth as "the great, great, great one": Book of Thoth, l. 426, Jasnow and Zauzich 2014, 125. "The signs revealed their forms": Book of Thoth, l. 444–47, Jasnow and Zauzuch 2014, 131.

16. For the use of animal imagery to denote hieroglyphic signs in the Book of Thoth, Jasnow 2011. The quotation is taken from the Book of Thoth, l. 242–44, trans. Jasnow and Zauzich 2014, 77.

17. Jasnow and Zauzich 2014, 49. For the *Corpus Hermeticum*, Nock and Festugière 1972 (critical edition); Copenhaver 1992 (English translation).

18. Mahé 1996, 359. The use of the term "pre-hermetic" is discussed on p. 361.

19. The cultural milieu that produced the *Corpus Hermeticum* has been a matter of considerable scholarly debate over the course of the past century, with opinions divided over the question of Egyptian versus Greek influence. For a detailed analysis, Fowden 1993, 155–95; for a more recent overview of the debate, Bull 2018, 4–12. Festugière's (1944–54) contention that the *Corpus Hermeticum* was the product of a purely Hellenic milieu has come under increasingly harsh scrutiny, not least thanks to the discovery of texts like the Book of Thoth.

20. A useful overview of the relationship between classical and patristic literature, within the context of the development of a distinctly Christian literary corpus, is provided in F. Young, Ayres, and Louth 2004.

21. Eusebius, *Praep. evang.* 2.1.4; Lactantius, *Div. inst.* 1.6.2–4 (trans. Bowen and Garnsey 2003), paraphrasing Cicero, *Nat. deor.* 3.22.56. For Lactantius' relationship with the works of Cicero, Kendeffy 2015.

22. Generally on euhemerism, Winiarczyk 2002; on Lactantius' use of Hermetic sources, Digeser 2000, chapter 3; van den Broek 2000a, 130–36.

23. Lactantius, *Div. inst.* 4.6.3; see van den Broek 2000a, 133–36.

24. Cyril of Alexandria, *C. Juln.* 1.41b.

25. Cyril of Alexandria, *C. Juln.* 1.43b–44d; van den Broek 2000a, 136–39. As Gerard Mussies has argued, in this passage Cyril both echoes and challenges the claim of the Hellenistic Jewish historian Artapanus, preserved in Eusebius' *Praep. evang.* 9.27, that Moses was actually the inventor of hieroglyphs, in recognition whereof he was honored as a god and given the name Hermes. Further on Artapanes' equation of Moses and Hermes, Mussies 1982; Droge 1989, 25–35; Kugler 2005.

26. Arnobius, *Adv. nat.* 4.14 (trans. Bryce and Campbell, ANF 6).

27. For the attempts by Arnobius and Lactantius to critique pagan religiosity using classical source-material, Nicholson 2004; more generally on their use of classical sources, Hagendahl 1958.

28. Aristides, *Apol.* 10.2 (trans. Kay, ANF 2).

29. See, e.g., Tertullian, *Coron.* 8.1; Eusebius, *L.C.* 13.2; compare Hippolytus, *Haer.* 5.2 (Litwa 2015, xxxii–xl on the disputed authorship of this text).

30. Tertullian, *Test. anim.* §5 (trans. Arbesmann, FC 10); Eusebius, *L.C.* 13.2 (trans. Drake 1976).

31. Augustine, *Doctr. Christ.* 2.72 (trans. Green 1995).

32. Augustine on Mercury's power over speech: *Civ.* 17.3; on his divinization in return for his gifts to mankind: *Civ.* 18:8. As van den Broek (2000a, 139–40) notes, Augustine was, like Lactantius, also clearly aware of the Hermetic literary corpus, particularly the *Asclepius*, which he discusses at length in *Civ.* 8.23–26; however, Augustine was considerably less willing than Lactantius to attribute much authority to those sources.

33. Augustine, *Civ.* 18.3 (trans. Dyson 1998; emphasis mine).

34. Augustine, *Civ.* 18.37.

35. Augustine, *Civ.* 18.40.

36. Witt's claim (1966, 139) that Augustine "evidently regards Isis as a great civilising influence, for to her he ascribes the invention of literature" implies a more positive attitude on Augustine's part than the larger context of his remarks in *Civ.* would seem to justify.

37. Herodotus 2.41; see Lloyd 2007, 267. Diodorus 1.24.8; Lucian, *D. Deor.* 7; Juvenal, *Satire* 6.526–30. Compare Clement, *Strom.* 1.21.106 (trans. Wilson, ANF 2).

38. Isis' wisdom and skill in magic are described, for example, in the New Kingdom magical text preserved in *P. Turin* 1993: "Now, Isis was a wise woman. Her heart was more devious than millions among men; she was more selective than millions among the gods; she was more exacting than millions among the blessed dead. There was nothing that she did not know in heaven or earth, like Re, who made the substance of the earth." Trans. Robert Ritner in Hallo 1997–2002, 1:22.

39. Plutarch, *De Iside* 2 (351e) and 3 (352a), trans. Griffiths 1970.

40. Augustine on the authority of Varro: *Civ.* 18.40. For overview of Varro's career and the transmission of his works, Butterfield 2015, 1–15. For Augustine's use of Varro, Hagendahl 1967, 589–630 (the Io/Isis connection is discussed at 598); O'Daly 2004, 236–38.

41. Inscriptions dating between the first and third century c.e. from Kyme, Thessaloniki, and Ios all seem to derive from a common textual tradition, as does Diodorus 1.27.3–6. Two earlier Hellenistic inscriptions from Maroneia and Andros represent a parallel tradition in a different literary style, and Apuleius' *Metamorphoses* also shares some common features with the Greek-language aretalogies, as do certain Hermetic texts, notably the *Korê Kosmou*. For a concise introduction to the genre, with particular reference to its position between the Greek and Egyptian literary traditions, see Dousa 2002; Dieleman and Moyer 2010, 444.

42. Text in Totti 1985, no. 1, §3 (trans. very slightly modified from Žabkar 1988, 140).

43. Text in Totti 1985, no. 1, §2 (trans. Žabkar 1988, 140).

44. The literature on the cultural and linguistic background of the Isis aretalogies is extensive; useful overviews may be found in Dousa 2002; Quack 2003. Middle ground in this debate: Žabkar 1988, 146–60; Dieleman and Moyer 2010, 444.

45. Edfou I, 149 and Edfou I, 151 respectively; see D. Müller 1961, 24; Kockelmann 2008, 36. For Thoth as *nb sš*, see Boylan 1922, 189.

46. Edfou I, 378; see D. Müller 1961, 24–25. The parallel text from Philae (Philae II 35, 24) is noted by Bergman (1968, 235). Bergman argues further that the common depictions of Thoth and Seshat as scribes in Egyptian coronation scenes served as a template for the representation of Thoth and Isis in line 3 of the Kyme aretalogy. For Seshat as the companion of Thoth and goddess of writing in her own right, see Boylan 1922, 210–12.

47. Budde 2000, 163–69. Quack (2003, 339–42) likewise highlights the Egyptian background to the claims made in this passage.

48. Diodorus 1.27.4–5.

49. Diodorus 1.27.6.

50. "I am not unaware": Diodorus 1.27.3.

51. Žabkar 1988, 143–46.

52. Isidore, *Etym.* 8.11.84 (trans. Barney et al. 2007).

53. Giovanni Boccaccio, *De mulieribus claris*, chapter 8.1–4 (trans. V. Brown 2001): "Isis, previously called Io, was an extremely famous queen of the Egyptians who afterwards became a most holy and venerated goddess. . . . Marshalling her intellectual powers, she devised alphabetical characters suitable for teaching the language of the inhabitants and demonstrated how the letters should be placed together." Io also appears as the inventor of letters in Christine de Pizan, *Epistre Othéa*, chapter 29.

54. Chance 2013, 141–42. For the imagery of Io in the scriptorium, as depicted in manuscripts of *Epistre Othéa*, Desmond and Sheingorn 2003, 216–29.

55. Herodotus 2.77; on Herodotus' presentation of Egypt as a "locus of graphic activity and . . . the place where history and time are inextricably bound with the written word," Vasunia 2001, 139.

56. Plato, *Ti.* 23a–b (trans. Bury, LCL 276). For the tradition of Solon's visit to Egypt, e.g., Diodorus 1.98.1.

57. Diodorus, 1.44.4–5; Strabo, *Geog.* 17.1.5 (trans. slightly modified from Jones, LCL 267).

58. Dio Chrysostom, *Or.* 11.37–38 (trans. Cohoon, LCL 257).

59. Josephus, *C. Ap.*, 1.8–9 (trans. Barclay 2007); compare *C. Ap.* 1.23–27 and 2.37.

60. Adler 1989, 21–23; see also Rajak 1982. On the development of "historical apologetic" during the Hellenistic period as a form of "subaltern response" to Greek cultural imperialism in Egypt and the Near East, Burgess and Kulikowski 2013, 99–108.

61. See Chapter 1 above for the royal context of the earliest known hieroglyphs.

62. Tacitus, *Ann.* 11.14 (trans. Jackson, LCL 312). A late antique expression of the same view is found in Ammianus, *Res Gestae* 17.4.10, where it is claimed that hieroglyphic inscriptions were first carved in order to record kingly vows.

63. For the Egyptian tradition of royal annals, Redford 1986; Assmann 2002, 36–39.

64. Hecateus and the priests of Thebes: Herodotus 2.143; in his commentary on this passage, Moyer (2002) notes that the description of the Theban priests' extended genealogy is more than just a literary trope used to demonstrate the great antiquity of the Egyptians in contrast to the Greeks. Rather, he argues, it reflects the historically specific cultural reality of Egypt in the Late Period, a time when the Egyptian priesthoods were actively seeking to make connections with their own distant past. For Manetho's claim to have written his history on the basis of "sacred writings," *FGrHist* 609 F10a (Josephus, *C. Ap.* 1.228); compare *FGrHist* 609 F1 (Josephus, *C. Ap.* 1.73).

65. Herodotus 2.106. The identification of the Karabel reliefs with those described in this passage is widely accepted but not entirely unproblematic. The inconsistencies between Herodotus' account and the appearance of the surviving reliefs has led some scholars to suggest that Herodotus had not seen the inscriptions himself; for a clear assessment, see West 1985. With respect to the content of the inscription, Lloyd (1988, 26–27) suggests that "a Hittite source . . . is out of the question since the script was surely indecipherable in his time" and that Herodotus was drawing rather "on the most obvious Oriental precedents, viz. Achaemenid royal inscriptions." More recently, see Rojas and Sergueenkova 2014.

66. Monuments of Sesostris: Herodotus 2.102–3 and 2.106; Diodorus 1.55.7–9; Strabo, *Geog.* 17.1.5. Further on the legend of Sesostris, see Lloyd 1982, 37–40 (with extensive bibliographic references); 1988, 40. In their discussion of Egyptian literature of the Hellenistic period, Dieleman and Moyer (2010, 441) note that the legends of Sesostris represent an important point of contact between the Greek and Egyptian narrative traditions, as Sesostris appears in both Demotic and Greek sources. See further Widmer 2014.

67. Beth Shan stelae: Hallo 1997–2002, 2:4B and 2:4D. Adulis inscription: Meadows 2012. The practice of setting up boundary stelae during the course of campaigns is noted, e.g., in the Annals of Thutmose III; see Hallo 1997–2002, 2:2B.

68. Steiner 1994, chapter 4 (the quotation is from p. 133); Vasunia 2001, 142–46.

69. Herotodus 2.125; Diodorus 1.64.3. In his discussion of the passage in Herodotus, Lloyd (1988, 69–71) suggests that Herodotus' interpreter may have been referring to either hieroglyphic graffiti carved on the blocks of the Great Pyramid (known to have been visible at least into the twelfth century C.E.), to a stela referring to Ramesside-era restoration work carried out by Prince Khaemwaes, or to an offering stela.

70. Tallet 2014.

71. Tacitus, *Ann.* 2.60 (trans. Moore and Jackson, LCL 249); compare Strabo, Geog. 17.1.46. Further on Germanicus' visit to Egypt, Weingärtner 1969.

72. Annals of Thutmose III (trans. James Hoffmeier in Hallo 1997–2002, 2:2A).

73. This distinction between Greek and Roman attitudes toward the pharaonic Egyptian monarchy and its physical remains is discussed in Elsner 1994.

74. Tatian, *Orat.* §1. For early Christian authors' cooption of earlier (especially Jewish) chronological arguments in defense of the antiquity of their religious tradition, Burgess and Kulikowski 2013, 110–14.

75. Eusebius, *Chron.* 1.1 (trans. Bedrosian 2008).

76. Adler 1989, 67.

77. The extremely problematic manuscript history of the *Chronicle* is discussed at length in Mosshammer 1979, 29–83. For the manuscript history of the *Chronici canones* specifically, see Burgess 1999. Eusebius' innovation in the composition of the *Chronicle* and the layout of the *Chronici canones* is highlighted in Grafton and Williams 2006, chapter 3; his debt to earlier Hellenistic chronography is outlined in Burgess and Kulikowski 2013, 121–23.

78. For Eusebius' reliance on extensive citations of original sources as a characteristic compositional technique, Grafton and Williams 2006, 200–208.

79. Eusebius' sources for the *Chronicle*, particularly those relating to archaic Greek history, are discussed in Mosshammer 1979, 128–68.

80. Eusebius, *Chron.* 1.43, quoting Diodorus 1.44.4.

81. Known fragments of Manetho are collected in *FGrHist* 609; an accessible English translation of the fragments is provided in Verbrugghe and Wickersham 2001. The numbering of the various testimonia and fragments of Manetho differs between these two works; tables outlining the correspondences between the different numbering systems are provided in Verbrugghe and Wickersham 2001, 204–9.

82. For a brief discussion of Manetho's Egyptian source-material, see Verbrugghe and Wickersham 2001, 103–15; a more extensive analysis of Manetho's likely sources is provided in Helck 1956; Dillery 2015. For the reception of Manetho in his own time and thereafter, see Adler 1989, 28–42; Verbrugghe and Wickersham 2001, 115–20.

83. Josephus, *C. Ap.* 1.73.

84. *Expos. mundi* 2 (= T9 in Verbrugghe and Wickersham 2001, 124); Syncellus, *Ecl. chron.* 18.22, trans. Adler and Tuffin 2002, 24. In subsequent references, Syncellus' work is cited by page and line number in Mosshammer's 1984 critical edition; the translation of Adler and Tuffin (2002) is cited by page number.

85. A "Manetho the Sebennyte" is also attested much earlier in Plutarch's *De Iside* 28 (362a), where he appears as one of the individuals who identifies the statue of Pluto brought to Alexandria by Ptolemy I as an image of Serapis; this Manetho is widely assumed to be identical with the Hellenistic historian. Further on Manetho's background, Verbrugghe and Wickersham 2001, 95–97; Dillery 2015.

86. The identity of the "Seriadic land" has been much debated, with suggestions ranging from Reinink's proposal (1975) that Seir should be identified with China to the more recent (and rather more convincing) argument of Bull (2018, 47–48) that the "Seriadic land" is a name for Egypt itself, stemming from a play on the name of the Dog Star, Sothis/Sirius.

87. The phrase "from the sacred language into Greek wording with hieroglyphic characters" has long puzzled commentators, and the text is widely believed to be corrupt; I follow Fowden (1993, 31n108) in taking γράμμασιν ἱερογλυφικοῖς as a doublet to be excluded, its addition to the text perhaps influenced by the presence of ἱερογραφικοῖς γράμμασι in the previous clause.

88. Syncellus, *Ecl. chron.* 40.32–41.7, trans. slightly modified from Adler and Tuffin 2002, 54. I follow Bull's correction to Adler and Tuffin's translation, making the translator of the works the "second Hermes," rather than Agathodaimon; as Bull notes (2018, 48n65), this reading aligns with Syncellus' subsequent remarks, in which reference is explicitly made to the identity of the translator. It also corresponds to the larger Hermetic tradition, which recognizes (at least) two Hermes, grandfather and grandson; see Fowden (1993, 29), with reference to *Ascl.* 37, where reference is made by Hermes Trismegistus to his ancestor, also named Hermes.

89. Syncellus, *Ecl. chron.* 41.12–13, trans. Adler and Tuffin 2002, 54.

90. Herodotus 2.3; Strabo, *Geog.* 17.1.29.

91. Syncellus, *Ecl. chron.* 41.16–22, trans. Adler and Tuffin 2002, 55. The letter of Manetho is widely held to be a pseudepigraph; however, an argument for its authenticity and for an equation between the *Book of Sothis* and the *Aegyptiaca* itself is offered in Bull 2018, 47–87.

92 Josephus, *A. J.* 1.70–71; Ammianus, *Res Gestae* 22.15.30. According to Eusebius, who cites Alexander Polyhistor and Berossos, the preservation of textual sources from the Flood was also a concern in Mesopotamia; see *Chronicle* 1.7 and 1.10. Further on this tradition, see Chapter 3 below.

93. A good example is *P.Berol.inv.* 21243, lines 1–5 = *Suppl.Mag.* II 72; see Brashear 1979. Further on this "marketing technique," particularly as it appears in the magical papyri, see Dieleman 2005, 185–89; Dieleman and Moyer 2010, 433–34. The late antique appropriation of such translation claims is discussed further in Chapter 5 below.

94. Eusebius' description of the *Aegyptiaca*: *Chron.* 1.44; fitting and proper to cite Manetho: *Chron.* 1.43.

95. Eusebius, *Chron.* 1.54–57 = Josephus, *C. Ap.* 1.74–92.

96. Syncellus *Ecl. chron.* 59.27–87.23 (Adler and Tuffin 2002, 76–110). Adler and Tuffin note (2002, 76n2) that "seeded throughout these lists are Synk.'s own editorial comments, mainly aimed at proving the inferiority of Eusebios' list to Africanus', especially as it concerns the dating of Moses and the Exodus."

97. For a discussion of the apologetic/polemic content of Eusebius' chronographic and historical works, including the *Chronicle*, Kofsky 2000, 38–48; Burgess and Kulikowski 2013, chapter 3.

98. Van Nuffelen 2010, 166–67. For the apologetic use of chronography, see also Croke 1983, 120–22; Adler 1992, 469–73; Burgess and Kulikowski 2013, chapter 3.

99. Eusebius' reception of Berossos: Madreiter 2013.

100. Africanus, *Chron.*, quoted by Syncellus, *Ecl. chron.* 17.30–18.10, trans. Adler and Tuffin 2002, 23–24.

101. Grafton and Williams 2006, 151.

102. Eusebius, *Chron.* 1.44.

103. Egyptian regnal years equivalent to lunar months: Diodorus 1.26.3–5; see Adler 1989, 75–78; Grafton and Williams 2006, 162–66.

104. Annianus, as quoted in Syncellus, *Ecl. chron.* 36.21 (Adler and Tuffin 2002, 48). For a detailed analysis of the reception of Eusebius by Panodorus and Annianus, and their grounds for criticizing his *Chronicle*, Adler 1989, 72–105.

105. Syncellus' defense of Eusebius: *Ecl. chron.* 17.19–30 (Adler and Tuffin 2002, 23); Eusebius' mathematical errors: *Ecl. chron.* 36.16–20 (Adler and Tuffin 2002, 48); Eusebius' faulty reasoning and poor choice of sources: *Ecl. chron.* 74.21–76.9 (Adler and Tuffin 2002, 95–98); Africanus "entirely more trustworthy" than Eusebius: *Ecl. chron.* 73.5–6 (Adler and Tuffin 2002, 93).

106. Egyptian historiographic texts as "priestly writings": Josephus, *C. Ap.* 1.73; as coming from "temple archives": Eusebius, *Chron.* 1.43, quoting Diodorus 1.44.4.

107. Croke 1983, 116–22.

108. Adler 1992, 476.

109. Augustine's dependence on Jerome's translation of Eusebius: *Civ.* 18.8. For Augustine's debt to Eusebius on matters of chronology, see Hagendahl 1967, 595; Croke 1982, 198; 1983, 126; O'Daly 2004, 263–64.

110. Augustine, *Civ.* 12.11.

111. Augustine, *Civ.* 12.11. Further on Augustine's understanding of the "fixed and final canon of Sacred Scripture" and its infallibility, compare *Civ.* 18.41; he argues that one of the things setting the authors of the scriptural canon apart from the Greek philosophers is the unanimity of the former: "God forbid that they should disagree with one another in any way!"

112. Augustine, *Civ.* 12.11.

113. Augustine, *Civ.* 8.27.

114. Minucius Felix, *Oct.* 21.3. (trans. Arbesmann, FC 10); Athenagoras, *Leg.* §28; compare Tertullian, *Pall.* 3.5 For the letter itself, as reconstructed from various ancient testimonia, see *FGrH* 659. This text constitutes only a small portion of the substantial corpus of pseudepigraphic letters associated with Alexander which circulated in antiquity. A fundamental resource for the discussion of the Alexander letters, and especially their relationship to the Alexander Romance, remains Merkelbach 1954, although Merkelbach's attempted reconstruction of an original "Briefroman" underlying the Alexander Romance has since been called into question. More recently, see Whitmarsh 2013.

115. Leo as Alexander's interlocutor: Pfister 1964; Leo as the author of the letter: Rusten 1980. More recently, in a monograph on the work and later influence of Euhemerus, Marek Winiarczyk has proposed (2002, 72–73) that Leo should be seen as a genuine Egyptian priest, but not the writer of the letter, whose identity remains unknown.

CHAPTER 3

1. *Strom.* 5.4.21.4.

2. "Great evils": Augustine, *Civ.* 8.27; Moses "instructed in all the wisdom of the Egyptians": Acts 7:22; wisdom "taught by the Spirit": 1 Cor. 2:13.

3. Herodotus 2.36; Diodorus 1.81.1 and 1.81.7.

4. Diodorus 3.3.4–5. Given that the hieroglyphic and hieratic scripts were, by the Late Period, essentially restricted in their usage to religious texts, it has long been argued that the category of "sacred writing" attested in Herodotus, Diodorus, and many of the other classical sources may refer simultaneously to both; Winand 2014, 19. Generally on Egyptian scribal training, see the references given in Chapter 1 above.

5. As Winand (2014, 17–21) has noted, this tripartite distinction can in any case only be used to describe the pattern of script usage in Egypt following the development of the demotic script in the seventh century B.C.E.

6. Porphyry, *Vita Pyth.* 12 (trans. Guthrie 1987).

7. Ibn Fatik, *Mukhtar*, 54, quoted by El Daly (2005, 60). El Daly suggests that Clement of Alexandria may have been the source of this information, as Ibn Fatik presents the three scripts in the same order as Clement and in similar terms.

8. For an introduction to the *Stromateis* and a discussion of its (disputed) relationship to Clement's other works, Osborn 2005, 5–15; see also Heine 2004, 117–19; Ashwin-Siejkowski 2015. For Clement's understanding of allegory, Dawson 1992.

9. Clement, *Strom.* 5.4.20.3 (trans. adapted from Wilson, ANF 2, Vergote 1941, and Le Boulluec 1981).

10. Clement, *Stromateis* 5.4.20.4–21.3 (trans. adapted from Wilson ANF 2:449, Vergote 1941, and Le Boulluec 1981).

11. Warburton (1738–65) 1978, book 4, section 4 (vol. 2 of the 1978 facsimile edition reproduces the text of book 4 in the original 1741 edition; vols. 3–4 reproduce book 4 in the heavily revised 1765 edition); Zoega 1797, 423–28. For the importance of Clement to Zoega's decipherment project, Ciampini 2015.

12. The first major study to consider Clement in light of Champollion's work was Letronne 1828; Letronne's analysis was largely supported by Deiber 1904. Opposing views were articulated by Dulaurier 1833; Marestaing 1911. The irony of the fact that decipherment aided the interpretation of Clement, and not the other way around, was noted already by Letronne 1828.

13. Vergote 1939; the same study was reissued, with minor revisions, in Vergote 1941. All subsequent references to Vergote's work refer to the 1941 version.

14. Clement's inaccuracy: Deiber 1904, 12; Marestaing 1911, 10. Clement's accuracy: Vergote 1941, 37: "Ces observations prouvent par conséquent que Clément d'Alexandrie a parfaitement connu le système hiéroglyphique."

15. Vergote's interpretation of this passage is widely if not universally accepted; Iversen 1993, 45; Winand 2014, 23–26; for some caveats concerning Vergote's reading of πρῶτα στοιχεῖα, which he prefers to render as "primary elements," Le Boulluec 1981, 99–101.

16. Vergote 1941, 37–38; Le Boulluec 1981, 98.

17. Generally on Chaeremon: Wendel 1940; van der Horst 1982b; 1984.

18. A reference in John Tzetzes' *Exegesis in Iliadem* 1.97 (trans. F12 in van der Horst 1984, 24–25) offers the barest hint that Chaeremon might have dealt with the phonetic value of hieroglyphs. Following the precedent set by Diodorus (3.3.4) in referring to hieroglyphs as "symbolic Ethiopian characters," the Byzantine scholiast writes, "At another place, if you want, with the aid of Chaeremon I will speak about the Ethiopian pronunciation of the characters themselves." On the other hand, in the fragment of Manetho preserved in the work of Michael Psellos (trans. F2 in van der Horst 1984, 11), we read that "Egyptian wisdom is to say all things symbolically"!

19. Clement's apparent lack of interest in the phonetic hieroglyphs was signaled already by Vergote (1941, 34–35).

20. Clement, *Strom.* 5.4.21.4.

21. Diodorus 3.4.1–4.

22. Diodorus 3.4.2–3.

23. As Iversen (1993, 44–45) notes, Diodorus' "metaphorical and symbolical conception of the hieroglyphs was unanimously accepted by all subsequent writers on the subject, and it was as a matter of fact their supposed allegorical qualities which henceforward to an ever increasing extent intrigued and fascinated the Greeks."

24. Lucan, *Pharsalia* 3.220–24 (trans. Duff, LCL 220).

25. Lucian, *Hermot.* 44 (trans. Kilburn, LCL 430).

26. Ammianus, *Res Gestae* 17.4.10 (trans. Rolfe, LCL 300).

27. The influence of Diodorus' claims is strongly apparent, for example, in the development of Renaissance *emblemata*; see Curran 2007; Giehlow 2015.

28. Tacitus, *Ann.* 11.14.

29. Plato, *Phlb.* 18b–d; Diodorus 1.16.1.

30. Pliny the Elder, *H. N.* 7.56.193 (trans. Rackham, LCL 352); Plutarch, *De Iside* 56 (374a).

31. Plutarch, *Quaest. conv.* 9.3.2 (738f) (trans. Minar, Sandbach, and Helmbold, LCL 425).

32. Minar, Sandbach, and Helmbold in LCL 425, 235–35 note b.

33. Gaudard 2012, 65; see also H. Smith and Tait 1983, 198–213; Zauzich 2000; Gaudard 2009.

34. Gaudard 2012, 67.

35. Plutarch, *De Iside* 32 (363f–364a).

36. Griffiths 1970, 422–23. Compare Horapollo 1.44 and Clement, *Strom.* 5.7.41.4.

37. Plutarch, *De Iside* 51 (371e); here, Plutarch explains that these particular signs are used to write the name "Osiris" because "the one denotes foresight and the other power." A similar hermeneutic approach is apparent in *De Iside* 10 (355a) and 36 (365b), among other examples.

38. Plotinus, *Enn.* 5.8.6 (trans. Armstrong, LCL 444).

39. E.g., Iversen 1993, 47–49; Eco 1995.

40. For "Nilous" as a signifier of Egyptian identity, Masson and Fournet 1992, 234.

41. Thissen 2001, xii–xv. See also J. Maspero 1914; Masson and Fournet 1992.

42. Thissen 2001, xi–xii.

43. On the structure of the work, Thissen 2001, xvi–xxii.

44. For this pattern, Thissen 2001, xvi.

45. Horapollo 1.26; see van de Walle and Vergote 1943a, 64; Thissen 2001, 20–21; see also Iversen 1993, 48.

46. Thirteen manuscript copies of Horapollo's *Hieroglyphica* are known, dating from the fourteenth to the sixteenth century; see Thissen 2001, xxiii–xxiv. For the Byzantine reception of Chaeremon, van der Horst 1982a, 115–16; 1984. Chaeremon was known to at least some of the earlier church fathers as well; see Jerome, *Adv. Jovin.* 2.13, which refers to Chaeremon's discussion of the Egyptian priesthood.

47. Tzetzes, *Exegesis in Iliadem* 1.97 (trans. F12 in van der Horst 1984, 24–25).

48. Herodotus 2.4.

49. Apuleius, *Met.* 11.22 (text and trans. Griffiths 1975).

50. Egyptian "animal-pictures": Tacitus, *Ann.* 11.14. The identification of the scripts Apuleius describes in this passage has been the subject of some debate. Marestaing, who argues (1913, 59) that Apuleius was referring throughout to hieroglyphs rather than hieratic, summarizes some of the earlier discussions. In his edition and commentary on book 11 of the *Metamorphoses*, Griffiths argues on the basis of the paleography of papyri dating from the Third Intermediate Period to the Roman era that Apuleius' second script, with its curved and knotted letter forms, was hieratic rather than hieroglyphic or demotic; he notes further that "there is every reason to believe that [Apuleius] was acquainted with papyri on which various Egyptian scripts were used" (1975, 285). More recently, David Frankfurter has proposed (1998, 255–56) that the second script described by Apuleius is actually a reference to the *kharaktēres* or "ring letters" that often appear in magical texts.

51. Plutarch on Pythagoras: *De Iside* 10 (354e); compare Clement, *Strom.* 1.15.62; Hippolytus, *Haer.* 1.2.8. The tradition of Pythagoras' sojourn in Egypt and the influence of Egyptian thought on his philosophical development goes back to Isocrates (*Busiris* 28) and was widely attested in classical historiography; see Schorn 2014, 298–300.

52. Lucan, *Pharsalia* 10.176–81; Cassius Dio 76.13 (trans. Cary and Foster, LCL 127).

53. On these texts, Sauneron 1982; Leitz 2001.

54. Cryptography and cypher scripts in the Hellenistic and Roman periods: Dieleman 2005, 80–87 (the quotation is from p. 85); Winand 2014, 21. Secrecy and concealment in earlier Egyptian thought: Assmann 1995.

55. Hornung 2001.

56. Iamblichus, *Myst.* 7.1 (trans. Clarke, Dillon, and Hershbell 2003).

57. Clarke, Dillon, and Hershbell 2003, xxxviii.

58. *Jubilees* 8.3 (trans. Charles 1913). For the significance of *Jubilees* in late antique Christian chronography, see Adler 1989, 84–86.

59. Josephus, *A.J.*, 1.69–71 (trans. Feldman 2000).

60. Iamblichus, *Myst.* 8.5; compare *Korê Kosmou* §5; Zosimos of Panopolis, *On the Letter Omega* 8.1–12, in Jackson 1978.

61. Ammianus, *Res Gestae* 22.15.30.

62. Syncellus, *Ecl. chron.* 40.32–41.7. Nor does the tradition end with Christian chronographers; Thoth-Hermes' hieroglyphic compilations of Egyptian wisdom are also attested in the works of medieval Muslim historians and alchemists. See, e.g., Blochet 1913; Fodor 1970.

63. *Discourse on the Eighth and Ninth*, NHC VI 61,18–62,4 (trans. Dirkse, Brashler, and Parrott 1979, 366–69).

64. Bull 2012, 405–6; 2014, 52–59.

65. Pythagoras' Egyptian education: Clement, *Strom.* 1.15.62. Jesus not a magician: Arnobius, *Adv. nat.* 1.43. Compare Origen, *C. Cels.* 1.38 (trans. Crombie, ANF 4), refuting Celsus' claim that Jesus obtained "a knowledge of certain miraculous powers" during his time in Egypt and used those powers to proclaim himself a god, and Augustine, *Cons. evang.* 1.9.14, refuting the allegation that Jesus wrote books of magic. Further on the figure of Jesus the magician in anti-Christian polemic, see Morton Smith 1978; Wilken 1984, 90–101. Smith goes so far as to argue that the charges that Jesus learned magic in Egypt—which were already circulating in first-century rabbinic literature— may have motivated the story of Jesus' infancy in Egypt recounted in Matthew 2:13–21.

66. Moses "educated in all the wisdom of the Egyptians": Acts 7:22; barbarian arts "inventive and practically useful": Clement, *Strom.* 1.16; wisdom taught by the Holy Spirit: 1 Cor. 2:6–16.

67. Hilhorst 2005, 153.

68. The Septuagint offers a slight variation on this passage (1 Kings 5:10), in which Solomon is said to have exceeded "the wisdom of all the ancients and all the wisdom of Egypt" (ἐπληθύνθη Σαλωμων σφόδρα ὑπὲρ τὴν φρόνησιν πάντων ἀρχαίων ἀνθρώπων καὶ ὑπὲρ πάντας φρονίμους Αἰγύπτου). Further on this parallel, Hilhorst 2005, 156.

69. Philo, *Mos.* 1.23. The translation is that of Colson (LCL 289), but I follow Hilhorst (2005, 163n34) in preferring to render γράμμασιν as "characters" rather than "inscriptions."

70. Egyptians as masters of specific subject matter: see, e.g., Plato, *Phdr.* 274c–d (mathematics and geometry); Strabo, *Geog.* 16.2.24 (geometry); Plutarch, *De Iside* 1 (352b) (music, the invention of which is ascribed to Thoth-Hermes). Hilhorst observes (2005, 159–60) that the long-standing tradition of Greeks visiting Egypt to study in certain fields supports the interpretation of Egyptian wisdom in Acts 7:22 as "a body of divergent skills and disciplines rather than a specific kind of speculative wisdom, without, of course, excluding the latter interpretation." Feldman (2007, 51) suggests that Moses' education, as represented by Philo, reflects the author's own training in the liberal arts.

71. *Strom.* 6.4.35.3–37.3; for this passage as a snapshot of "priestly literary culture" in the time of Clement, see Frankfurter 1998, 239–40.

72. The reception of Philo by late antique Christian authors is discussed in Runia 1993.

73. Clement, *Strom.* 1.23.153.2–3 (trans. slightly modified from Wilson, ANF 2). For Clement's use of Philo in this passage, van den Hoek 1988, 54; Hilhorst 2005, 165–67.

74. Origen, *C. Cels.* 3.46; Augustine, *Civ.* 15.27, quoting Origen, in *Gen. homil.* 2.2; Basil, *Hex.* 1.1 (trans. Jackson NPNF² 8); Basil, *Leg. lib. gent.* §3. Further on patristic readings of Acts 7:22, Hilhorst 2005, 165–72.

75. Augustine, *Civ.* 18.37, my emphasis.

76. "Great evils": Augustine, *Civ.* 8.27; sciences that "exercise men's ingenuity": *Civ.* 18.39.

77. Augustine, *Civ.* 10.11. Chaeremon's discussion of the lifestyle of Egyptian priests was of particular interest for some Christian readers, who saw similarities between the priests' rigorous fasting and abstinence and the practices of Christian ascetics; see, for example, Jerome's *Adv. Jovin.* 2.13, which identifies Chaeremon as an eloquent man and offers an extended quotation from Chaeremon's work on the Egyptian priesthood. Jerome goes on to say, however (2.17), that "true" (read, "Christian") fasting must be distinguished from the sort of abstinence practiced by followers of Isis and Cybele.

78. Origen, *C. Cels.* 3.46; compare Ambrose, *Off.* 1.26.122–23. On the church fathers' use of Moses to exemplify the superiority of true (Christian) wisdom over that attributed to the Egyptians, Hilhorst 2005, 171–72. Hilhorst's conclusion (2005, 174) that Philo, Clement, and many of the later patristic readers of Acts 7:22 "saw no need to conceive of the wisdom of the Egyptians as something specifically Egyptian, something definitely non-Greek," seems to me unsustainable in light of Philo's explicit statement, echoed by Clement, that Moses was instructed in the hieroglyphic script, a highly specific marker of Egyptian culture.

79. Augustine, *Civ.* 10.8; Augustine, *Ep.* 137.4.13 (trans. in NPNF¹ 1).

80. Clement, *Paed.* 3.2 (trans. Wilson, ANF 2); compare Origen, *C. Cels.* 3.17.

81. Origen, *C. Cels.* 1.68; Ps.-Clement, *Homil.* 1.5 (trans. Smith in ANF 8).

82. Socrates, *HE* 1.22.3 (trans. Zenos, NPNF² 2).

83. Egyptian roots of the "heresy of Valentinus": *Haer.* 6.16; of the "heresy of Basileides": *Haer.* 7.27.13. Compare *Haer.* 7.33.1 and Irenaeus, *Adv. Haer.* 1.26.1 on Cerinthus; both note that the latter's teachings stem from his education in the "Egyptian learning" (Αἰγυπτίων παιδεία).

84. Gregory of Nyssa, *Eun.* 12.4 (trans. Moore and Wilson, NPNF² 5). For a brief introduction to the text, Louth 2004, 298–99.

85. On Egyptian religion as the worst of all idolatrous practices, see, e.g., Aristides, *Apol.* 12.1–5; Athanasius, *Gent.* 1.9.3 (with reference to the specifically Egyptian error of worshipping hybrid human-animal gods that combine the rational and irrational); Augustine, *Civ.* 2.22.

86. Ambrose, *Off.* 1.26.122–23 (trans. de Romestin, NPNF² 10).

87. Davidson 1995, 319. Further on Ambrose's *De officiis* as an attempt to "usurp and supersede" Cicero's text of the same name, McLynn 1994, 272. For Christian intellectuals' complicated relationship with the natural sciences, particularly as seen through the lens of Eusebius, Kofsky 2000, 123–30.

88. Origen, *Princ.* 3.3.2 (trans. Crombie, ANF 4).

89. Eusebius, *L. C.* 13.4; John Chrysostom, *Hom. 63 in Jo.* §3 (trans. in NPNF¹ 14).

90. Clement, *Prot.* §11 (trans. Wilson in ANF 2); Origen, *C. Cels.* 6.14.

91. Athanasius, *Vit. Ant.* §72–73.

92. Antony's literacy: Rubenson 1995. On the church fathers' complex and evolving relationship to the traditions of classical *paideia*, see, e.g., Jaeger 1961; P. Brown 1992; van Hoof and van Nuffelen 2015.

CHAPTER 4

1. Warburton's argument about the connection between hieroglyphs and animal worship is developed throughout book 4, section 4 of *The Divine Legation*. The quotation comes from Warburton (1738–65) 1978, 2:140.

2. *Editio princeps*: D. Young 1981. On the attribution of the text to Shenoute (as Acephalous Work A6), see now Emmel 2004, 2:688–89. For Shenoute's pun (ⲦⲠⲞⲖⲒⲤ ⲠⲀⲚⲞⲘⲞⲤ) on the city's name (ⲦⲠⲞⲖⲒⲤ ⲠⲀⲚⲞⲤ), see Emmel 2008, 178n72; the rendering of ⲠⲀⲚⲞⲘⲞⲤ ⲠⲞⲖⲒⲤ as "Sin City" is borrowed from López 2013, 22.

3. Generally on Panopolis: Karig 1975; Timm 1984–2007, 1:80–96; Egberts, Muhs, and van der Vliet 2002. Panopolis as a bastion of "intellectual paganism": Rémondon 1952; on the family of Horapollo and his probable Panopolite origins, J. Maspero 1914. The continuity of classical education in the city is suggested by, among other things, the work of Greek-language poets like Nonnus of Panopolis, on whom see Alan Cameron 1965; Shorrock 2011; Dijkstra 2016. Nonnus and his fellow poets were primarily active in Alexandria, however, so this point should perhaps not be pressed too far. It should also be noted that since the original publication of "Wandering Poets," Cameron has considerably modified his position on the degree of cultural and religious continuity that the evidence from Panopolis supports; see now Alan Cameron 2007, reprinted, with some emendations, in Alan Cameron 2016.

4. Emmel 2002; 2008. For further discussion, see below.

5. For a concise biographical sketch of Shenoute, see Brakke and Crislip 2015, 1–23; on the shaping of Shenoute's public persona, López 2013; on the curation of his literary legacy, Emmel 2004, 2:553–58.

6. For a concise overview of Shenoute's chronology, as reconstructed from internal references in his writings, see Emmel 2002, 95–99; 2004, 1:6–14; 2016. The chronology outlined by Emmel has received fairly wide acceptance among scholars working on Shenoute. The alternative timeline proposed by López (2013, appendix A), which would move Shenoute's date of birth into the 380s and place his floruit from ca. 420–60, has been sharply critiqued as lacking evidence; see, e.g., Timbie 2014; Dijkstra 2015b.

7. On the organization of the White Monastery federation and its three constituent communities, Layton 2014, 11–14. On the overall population of the federation, Amélineau 1888, 331; this estimate is seen as unrealistically high by Wipszycka (2005, 294–99). See also López 2013, 49.

8. Rural patronage: López 2013, chapter 3; Shenoute's relationship with representatives of the Roman state: López 2013, chapter 1.

9. Shenoute and Egyptian nationalism: Leipoldt 1903; Barns 1964.

10. The seminal article debunking the "nationalist" theory is Wipszycka 1992; see also Behlmer 1993. Shenoute's pastoral leadership: Krawiec 2002; Schroeder 2007. Social advocacy: López 2013.

11. Sauer 2003; Gaddis 2005.

12. López (2013, 25) makes this point quite bluntly, stating, "If Shenoute has a bad reputation—and he has one: impulsive violence, intolerance, lack of self-control—it is he who has made it." The extent to which Shenoute's public persona can be seen as a rhetorical construct is a major theme of López's work; see in particular chapters 1 and 4.

13. Pagan intellectuals recruited from among the elites of Upper Egypt, Rémondon 1952, 67 (my translation): "ils se recrutent dans l'aristocratie de Panopolis et de Thèbes, dans les classes aisées qui peuvent apprendre et lire le grec." Crowds drawn to the temples of Panopolis:

Rémondon 1952, 70–71 (my translation): "Panopolis est un centre païen où les temples attirent encore les foules."

14. "Native religiosity": Frankfurter 2000b, 279; see also 1998, 77–82. For Shenoute's self-identification with the biblical prophets: Krawiec 2002, chapter 3. Shenoute's antipagan "*curriculum vitae*": Emmel 2008, 162–66.

15. "Militant adherents of the old gods": Alan Cameron 1965, 477; see now Alan Cameron, 2016.

16. Van Minnen 2002, 181.

17. Mark Smith 2002, 243–44.

18. For the identification of Shenoute's opponent with Flavius Aelius Gessius, Emmel 2002, 99–103. Gesios as pagan leader: van der Vliet 1993, 102–3; Frankfurter 1998, 80. The textual sources detailing Shenoute's conflict with Gesios are collected in Brakke and Crislip 2015, part 4.

19. Gesios as a "crypto-pagan": see Emmel 2002, 108–11; 2008, 172–78. An edition and translation of the text that forms the basis of Emmel's argument, the so-called open letter *Let Our Eyes*, appears in Emmel 2008, 182–97.

20. The question of whether or not the sculptures removed from Gesios' home by Shenoute should be understood as devotional objects or objets d'art remains open; see Emmel 2008, 181. Alan Cameron (2016, 160) argues that Shenoute would not have admitted of such a distinction in any case: "Christian fanatics were not only unable to distinguish between cult statues and mythological art, they would have denied the very existence of such a distinction. In some cases at least they were probably raiding the sculpture gardens of well-to-do Christians." Although I agree with Cameron's assertion that Shenoute saw no distinction between art objects and objects of worship, I argue that this is a position he chose quite deliberately—*not* out of ignorance—and supported through careful rhetorical choices, as we shall see below.

21. López 2013, 120.

22. Division of Shenoute's corpus into *Canons*, *Discourses*, and *Letters*: Emmel 2004, 1:vii; for an overview of the nature and contents of the *Canons*, 2:553–58; for the *Discourses*, 2:606–9.

23. For the codicological reconstruction of A6, see Emmel 2004, 2:688–89; the quotation appears at 2:689. The manuscript witnesses are Michigan MS 158.13 a/b and 158.13 c/d, Bibliothèque Nationale Copte 130⁵ fols. 31–32, and British Library Or. 8664. The Paris manuscript leaves were edited by Leipoldt and Crum (1908, 96–98); a section of the British Library manuscript was edited by Shisha-Halevy (1975a; 1975b).

24. A6, text in D. Young 1981, 349, lines 1–24 (my translation).

25. Mark Smith 2002, 243. Christian authors' application of generic names (often Greek) to Egyptian cults is briefly discussed in Frankfurter 2007, 178. An intriguing parallel appears in an encomium on Theodore Stratelates attributed to Anastasius of Euchaita, where an "unclean spirit" dwelling in an idol is identified with Kronos; given Shenoute's frequent references to the worship of Kronos in the Panopolite, it is tempting to posit a connection. For the text, Depuydt 1993. Further on the identity of "Kronos," Aufrère 2005.

26. CIG 8627, reedited in Prentice 1908, no. 437a; the translation is from Trombley 1993, 2:363. See López 2013, 192n30.

27. On the phenomena of temple destruction and conversion as tropes in late antique Christian literature, Emmel, Gotter, and Hahn 2008; Dijkstra 2011.

28. A6, text in D. Young 1981, 349, lines 25–50 (my translation). Kristensen's contention (2013, 142) that this passage reflects Shenoute's "knowledge of the contemporary use of Horus *cippi* . . . and other forms of healing images covered in hieroglyphs" reads too much into Young's

rendering of ⲚⲞⲘⲞⳞ as "prescriptions" and ignores the larger context of the sermon, which clearly refers to the temple overall.

29. A6, text in D. Young 1981, 349, line 50–350, line 14 (my translation).

30. Compare Clement, *Paed.* 3.3.

31. The term appears in this usage in a passage from *God Who Alone Is True*, from volume 9 of Shenoute's *Canons*; on this text, Emmel 2004, 2:600–601. Shenoute writes, "this is how soul killers (ⲊⲈⲚⲠⲈϤⲊⲈⲦⲂ†ⲨⲬⲎⲚⲢⲰⲘⲈ) are, those who will teach men among us to not guard the precepts set down for us"; Coptic text in Leipoldt and Crum 1913, 90, lines 18–20.

32. Late-Period temples as vessels of cultural memory: Assmann 2008, 99.

33. The connotations of the color red in Egyptian thought are discussed in Ritner 1997, 147–48. On the painted *spolia* from the White Monastery church, Klotz 2010.

34. "Standard vocabulary of denigration": Markus 1990, 48; for stock allegations of blood sacrifice, Henrichs 1970; McGowan 1994; Lanzillotta 2007.

35. For the text and translation of the *Panegyric*, D. Johnson 1980; on Christian "atrocity folklore," as exemplified by the *Panegyric*, Frankfurter 2007.

36. Coptic text in Thompson 1932, 150.

37. For the Sahidic text of Exodus 20:4, G. Maspero 1892, 34.

38. On this passage, Greenberg 1983, 165 and 169–70. Ezekiel is incompletely preserved in Sahidic; the Bohairic text of Ezek. 8:10 reads: ⲀⲓϢⲈ ⲈϧⲞⲨⲚ ⲀⲓⲚⲀⲨ ⲞⲨⲞⲊ ⲊⲎⲡⲡⲈ ⲓⲤ ⲊⲀⲚⲂⲞ† ⲞⲨⲞⲊ ⲚⲓⲒⲆⲰⲖⲞⲚ ⲦⲎⲢⲞⲨ Ⲛ̅ⲦⲈ ⲠⲎⲒ Ⲙ̅ⲠⲒⲤ̅Ⲗ̅ ⲈⲨⳠⲎⲞⲨⲦ ⲊⲈⲚⲠⲔⲰ† Ⲛ̅†ⲬⲞⲒ (Tattam 1852, 2:34).

39. Coptic text: Thompson 1932, 90. The church fathers frequently cited Rom. 1:23 in connection with Egyptian cultic imagery and practice; see for example Athanasius, *Gent.* 1.19.2.

40. Plato, *Rep.* 10.597a. Philosophical critique of images: Besançon 2000, especially chapter 1; Barasch 1992, chapter 3.

41. Deuteronomy 4:15–16.

42. Jeremiah 10:5.

43. Wisdom 13:10; on this text as it relates to the debate over divine images, see Besançon 2000, 68–69.

44. On the development of early Christian arguments against the worship of statues, Bremmer 2015. The "discourse of idol destruction" as it appears in Coptic hagiography is briefly surveyed in Dijkstra 2015a.

45. Shenoute, *Let Our Eyes* fr. 1.2–3; Emmel 2008, 182–83 (translation) and 190 (text).

46. Shenoute, *Let Our Eyes* fr. 1.33; Emmel 2008, 186 (translation) and 195 (text).

47. On the White Monastery church, Grossmann 1984; 1991; 2008b; Severin 1991; Klotz 2010.

48. For Shenoute's rhetorical use of the church building as a symbol of asceticism, Schroeder 2007, chapter 3, especially 109–11; the quotation (from Shenoute's *God Is Holy*, canon 7, XU 94) appears on p. 110.

49. Tertullian, *Idol.* 3–4. Further on Tertullian's understanding of images, see Barasch 1992, chapter 6.

50. Bolman, Davis, and Pyke 2010; Bolman et al. 2014.

51. Subject matter: *Let Our Eyes* fr. 1.2; "foolish matter": *Let Our Eyes* fr. 1.33; risk of idolatry: *Let Our Eyes* fr. 1.21 and 1.33.

52. Shenoute, *A Beloved Asked Me Years Ago* 114, 10–34; Wisse 1991, 135 (text) and 138 (translation).

53. Clement, *Prot.* §4; compare Jerome, *Ep.* 27 (on dinner plates decorated with classical mythological imagery) and John Chrysostom, *Hom. 10 in Phil.* (in which it is suggested that household images have the potential to be used for summoning demons).

54. Alan Cameron 2016, 159–60; Emmel 2008, 169–70.

55. People "deceived at the oracles" by Kronos and Hecate: Shenoute, *Let Our Eyes* fr. 1.10; Emmel 2008, 184 (translation) and 192 (text).

56. Omission of determinatives: Fischer 1973; however, Baines (1989, 474) cautions against seeing in this phenomenon, which he notes is not terribly common, any notion that figural representation and script were liable to be confused with each other. Mutilation of hieroglyphs: Wilson 2005, 115–16; Ritner 1997, 163–67.

57. Power of images: Frankfurter 2008a; 2008b.

58. Warburton (1738–65) 1978, book 4, section 4; for a detailed commentary on Warburton's theory of hieroglyphs, Assmann 1997, 102–15.

59. Warburton (1738–65) 1978, 2:140.

60. Gardiner 1957.

61. Diodorus 3.4.1; Ammianus Marcellinus 17.4.9; Tacitus, *Ann.* 11.14.

62. On the probable Egyptian origin and dating of *Physiologus*, Curley 2009, xvi–xxi. An example of the affinity between the texts can be seen in the way they discuss lions. In *Hieroglyphica* 1.19, Horapollo claims that the concept of being on guard is expressed through drawing a lion; the rationale he cites for this is that lions keep their eyes open while sleeping; similarly, *Physiologus* §1 states that "The second nature of the lion is that, although he has fallen asleep, his eyes keep watch for him, for they remain open." Further on the parallels between Horapollo's knowledge of the natural world and *Physiologus*, see Assmann 1994, 30–31.

63. On the understanding of hieroglyphs as a "Scripture of nature" in early modern commentaries, see Assmann 1997, 102–4.

64. Book of Thoth, lines 242–44 (trans. Jasnow and Zauzich 2014, 77); netting and trapping as metaphors for writing, Jasnow 2011.

65. E.g., Book of Thoth, line 33: "Their offering is dog. Their food is donkey. Their fruit is the reptiles." Jasnow and Zauzich (2014, 62–63) note, "These animals represent the hieroglyphs themselves. The Disciple must live only from the study of the sacred script."

66. Two items on Shenoute's list (frogs and scorpions) defied easy classification in antiquity. According to the seventh-century *Etymologiae* of Isidore of Seville, frogs (12.6.58) were classified together with fish, while scorpions (12.5.4) were considered to belong to the larger category of vermin, or creatures "generated for the most part from flesh or wood or some earthy substance, without any sexual congress." In some traditions, frogs were likewise seen as generated from the earth itself; see Augustine, *Civ.* 16.7. In earlier Egyptian ritual practice, scorpions were frequently grouped together with snakes and as venomous creatures that could be subdued through the magical agency of the god Horus; see Ritner 1989; 1998b.

67. Idolatry and animal worship are explicitly conjoined in a fragmentary work of Shenoute's, *Well Did You Come*; see Dijkstra 2015a, 61–62. For Christian attacks against animal worship as a specifically "Egyptian adaptation of the idol discourse," Dijkstra 2015a, 71.

68. Tidbits for Petesouchos: *P.Tebt.* I 33 (March 5, 112 B.C.E.); Juvenal, *Satire* 15.1–2. Generally on attitudes toward Egyptian animal worship, from the earliest Greek sources through to the writings of the church fathers, Smelik and Hemelrijk 1984.

69. Philo, *Contempl.* 8; further on the representation of Egypt in Philo's work, Pearce 2007, chapter 7.

70. Cyril of Jerusalem, *Catech.* 13, quoted in Smelik and Hemelrijk 1984, 1986.

71. Elm 2012, 8.

72. This is equivalent to Ps. 113:12 in the LXX and Ps. 114:1 in the Sahidic text presented in Budge 1898, 123.

73. Further on the use of biblical citations in Christian polemics against idolatry, see Assmann 2008, 130–38; Besançon 2000, chapters 2 and 3; Barasch 1992, chapter 1.

74. Clement, *Prot.* §4 (trans. Wilson, ANF 2); further on this motif in Christian polemics, see Caseau 2007, 122–29.

75. Cyril of Alexandria, *Hom. pasch.* 6 (trans. Amidon, FC 118).

76. Jer. 10:15; Coptic text in Tattam 1852, 1:322.

77. Eusebius, *V. C.* 3.54.1–3; Caseau 2007, 117: "Eusèbe n'aurait pas délibérément écrit quelque chose d'absurde. Il faut donc que le fait de tourner les statues païennes en derision ait pu résonner comme possible pour ses lecteurs chrétiens."

78. Sozomen, *HE* 5.7; Socrates, *HE* 3.2–4. See further Caseau 2007, 137–41.

79. Shenoute, *Let Our Eyes*, fr. 1.25; Emmel 2008, 185–86 (translation) and 194 (text). Emmel notes that a passage in fr. 1.3 also points to the public display of the statuary removed from Gesios' home; after enumerating the different types of statues he had discovered, Shenoute adds, "just as you (pl.) saw them all, each according to its type."

80. Frankfurter 2008b, 672.

81. On Shenoute's "discourse of purity," see Schroeder 2007.

82. Shenoute, *Let Our Eyes* fr. 1.1; Emmel 2008, 182 (translation) and 190 (text).

83. D. Young (1981, 354) renders the phrase ⲀⲨⲰ ⲚⲀϢ Ⲛ̄ϨⲈ Ⲛ̄ϤⲚⲀϢⲰⲠⲈ ⲀⲚ ⲈϤⲞⲨⲀⲀⲂ as "and how will he not become pure," suggesting (357n21) that the third person masculine singular pronoun refers to "any person who worships in the shrine when it has been refurbished as a properly adorned church." However, given that the temple is consistently referred to in the text in the third-person masculine singular, it seems unnecessary to provide such a hypothetical antecedent and preferable to take this phrase rather as a rhetorical question referring to the condition of the temple itself: "(when all of the aforementioned changes have been accomplished) how will it (the temple) not become pure?"

84. Petrie 1908, 5.

85. On the potential identification of the Triphis temple with the site Shenoute claimed to have burned, see Behlmer 1996, lxi; Emmel 2008, 164. Emmel is careful to qualify this identification, stating that "it seems reasonable to assume" that Shenoute was speaking about the temple of Repit/Triphis but cautioning that little specific information is known. That some of the spolia used in the White Monastery church did indeed come from a temple of Triphis is shown in Klotz 2010 (for dissenting views, however, see Grossmann 2008b, 37n6 and 53n89).

86. El-Sayed 2010, 527: "Die Brandstiftung war kein Akt der Zerstörung, sondern vielmehr der 'Läuterung' und ist als erster Schritt bei der Umwandlung des Tempels in eine für Christen des fünften Jahrhunderts benutzbare Räumlichkeit zu sehen." For a similar view, M. Müller 2015, 187.

87. Klotz 2010, 208.

88. Refectory: el-Masry 2001; M. Müller 2015; for dining facilities as a feature of Egyptian monastic architecture, Grossmann 2002, 286–95. Dyeing workshop and triconch church: el-Sayed 2010, 535–36; M. Müller 2015.

89. El-Sayed 2010, 536–37.

90. López 2013, 107.

91. El-Sayed (2010, 534) notes that although the mutilation of the reliefs is quite extensive in some areas, it appears to be highly unsystematic, varying in intensity from one part of

the temple to another, with some reliefs heavily damaged and others untouched. See also M. Müller 2015, 188. Such a pattern of selective mutilation can also be observed, for example, at the temple of Seti I at Abydos and the Hathor temple at Dendera; Sauer 2003, 89–101; Kristensen 2013, 146–58.

92. Ps. 115:4–7.

93. This attitude is reflected in Shenoute's use of the temple as a metaphor in the second portion of the Michigan fragment of *A6*: "And blessed is an ignorant man, blessed is an ignorant woman, whose end will be like the end of this house [i.e., the temple] when they repent of their evil deeds (ⲁⲩⲱ ⲛⲁⲓⲁ̄ⲧϥ̄ ⲛ̄ⲟⲩⲣⲱⲙⲉ ⲛⲁⲓⲁⲧⲥ ⲛ̄ⲟⲩⲥϩⲓⲙⲉ ⲛ̄ⲁⲧⲥⲟⲟⲩⲛ̄ ⲉⲣⲉⲧⲉⲩϩⲁⲏ ⲛⲁⲣⲑ̄ⲉ ⲛ̄ⲑⲁⲏ ⲙ̄ⲡⲓⲏⲓ ϩⲙ̄ ⲡⲧⲣⲉⲩⲙⲉⲧⲁⲛⲟⲓ ⲉ̄ⲭⲛ̄ⲛⲉⲩⲡⲉⲑⲟⲟⲩ). But woe to a man, woe to a woman who has known Jesus, if their end is like the beginning of this house" (ⲟⲩⲓⲉⲓ ⲁⲉ ⲛ̄ⲟⲩⲣⲱⲙⲉ ⲟⲩⲟⲉⲓ ⲛ̄ⲟⲩⲥϩⲓⲙⲉ ⲉ̄ⲁⲩⲥⲟⲩⲛ̄ ⲓ̄ⲥ̄ ⲉⲣϣⲁⲛⲧⲉⲩϩⲁⲏ ⲉⲣ̄ⲑⲉ ⲛ̄ⲧⲁⲣⲭⲏ ⲙ̄ⲡⲓⲏⲓ).

94. Ray 2007, 13.

95. Erasure of hieroglyphs on repurposed altar at Philae, Griffith 1930, 127–28; Dijkstra 2012, 16. Mutilation of relief images at Dendera, Sauer 2003, 97–98; Frankfurter 2008b. Limited damage to pharaonic inscriptions and decorative features in repurposed structures, Grossmann 2008a, 318. Coexistence of Christian *dipinti* and hieroglyphic inscriptions in the Valley of the Kings, O'Connell 2007a, 121; Reeves and Wilkinson 1996, 31.

CHAPTER 5

1. *P.Cair.Masp.* I 67031, line 16 (Antinoopolis, ca. 543–45 C.E.). Citing this document as an example, Fournet (2009, 445) states that "translation must have played a more important role than our documentation allows us to see." Generally on multilingualism in Egypt, Fournet 2009; Papaconstantinou 2010; Depauw 2012. On the process of translation and the identity of translators in Greco-Roman Egypt, Rochette 1994.

2. The miraculous production of the Septuagint—allegedly the work of seventy-two translators, who independently produced identical Greek translations of the Hebrew Bible— was described in the pseudepigraphic *Letter of Aristeas* and widely reported by both Jewish and Christian authors in antiquity; see, for example, Philo, *Mos.* 2.31–40; Josephus, *A.J.* 12.12–100; Irenaeus, *Adv. Haer.* 3.21.2 (quoted by Eusebius, *HE* 5.8.10–15); Clement, *Strom.* 1.22; Augustine, *Civ.* 18.42 and *Cons. evang.* 2.66.128. The modern bibliography on the Septuagint is vast; for the various traditions concerning the circumstances of the Septuagint's production, see Wasserstein and Wasserstein 2006.

3. Translations from Greek or Latin into hieroglyphs: see for example Grenier 1987; Swetnam-Burland 2015.

4. *P.Berol.inv.* 21243, lines 1–5 = *Suppl.Mag.* II 72; trans. after Brashear 1979.

5. Brashear 1979, 266 (my translation): "Auch wenn dieser Text keine direkte Übersetzung aus dem Ägyptischen ist, wollte der Verfasser auf jedem Fall diesen Eindruck erwecken, und um seinem Werk einen Hauch von Authentizität, Alter und Heiligkeit zu verleihen, schrieb er ihm einen ägyptischen Ursprung zu." Cf. Fowden 1993, 66–67.

6. *PGM* IV 885–86 (trans. Betz 1992, 55).

7. *CH* 16.1–2 (trans. slightly modified from Copenhaver 1992, 58).

8. Compare Iamblichus, *Myst.* 8.4, where it is implied that the translation of Hermetic books into Greek "by men not unversed in philosophy" has resulted in confusion.

9. The notion of a "paradox of translation" comes from Dieleman 2005, 1–10.

10. Although Préaux (1967, 382) characterizes this way of thinking as Greek in origin, she acknowledges that it also reflects traditional Egyptian attitudes toward the concealment of religious knowledge, which may have seemed all the more desirable in light of Egypt's changed political situation in the Hellenistic and Roman periods.

11. *CH* 12.13–14 (trans. Copenhaver 1992, 46).

12. Préaux 1967, 381.

13. Fowden 1993, 29–31.

14. Dieleman 2005, 9–10. In making this argument, Dieleman draws on the notion of "stereotype appropriation" described in Frankfurter 1998, 224–37; 2000a, 168–83. Frankfurter proposes this term as a way to characterize the process by which Egyptian priests, particularly under the social and financial pressures of the Roman period, actively took on the role of "magos" that was so commonly assigned to them in the Hellenistic and Roman literary sources. See also Moyer 2003.

15. Bull 2012, 421.

16. Plotinus, *Enn.* 5.8.6.

17. Iamblichus, *Myst.* 7.1.

18. Iamblichus, *Myst.* 7.5.

19. Celsus' claim that Christians obtain power via the names of daemons, Origen, *C. Cels.* 1.6; no difference what names are used for the gods, *C. Cels.* 1.24. Further the importance of this text for understanding early Christian attitudes toward language and translation, Dillon 1985.

20. Origen's claim that Christians obtain power via the name of Jesus, Origen, *C. Cels.* 1.6; translating spells and ritual formulae weakens their power, *C. Cels.* 1.25; compare *C. Cels.* 5.45.

21. Dillon 1985, 216.

22. Plutarch, *De Iside* 9 (354d); Josephus, *C. Ap.* 1.286. For the derivation of "Moses" from the Egyptian word *mw*, "water," see also Philo, *Mos.* 1.17.

23. Iversen 1993, 41.

24. Champion and Ucko 2003, 11.

25. Winkler 1985, 308–11.

26. Winand 2014, 21 (my translation): "À l'époque ptolémaïque, puis romaine, l'écriture monumentale égyptienne, la seule à laquelle les visiteurs étrangers pouvaient être directement sensibles, avait pris, dans certaines de ses manifestations, une forme particulièrement concise qui en accentuait le côté symbolique."

27. Frankfurter's concept of "stereotype appropriation" is relevant in this context; see above, Chapter 5n14.

28. Lack of quotations in classical geography and historiography, Momigliano 1963, 89; Eusebius' use of primary documents, Momigliano 1963, 89–91; Grafton and Williams 2006, 200–208.

29. On the obelisks of Rome and their complicated afterlives, Iversen 1968; Curran et al. 2009.

30. Ammianus, *Res Gestae* 17.4.6.

31. Ammianus, *Res Gestae* 17.4.8–11.

32. Iversen 1993, 50.

33. In his commentary on book 17, de Jonge (1977, 83–84) suggests that Ammianus' principal source for this section was Horapollo's *Hieroglyphica*. However, if one accepts Thissen's proposed late fifth-century date for the composition of the *Hieroglyphica*, this is clearly impossible.

34. Horapollo 1.11; van de Walle and Vergote 1943a, 50–54; Thissen 2001, 10–13.

35. Chaeremon, F12, preserved in Tzetzes, *Exegesis in Iliadem* 1.97, in van der Horst 1984, 24–25. Van der Horst (1984, 44–45) goes so far as to include *Res Gestae* 17.4.11 among the *Fragmenta dubia* of Chaeremon's work.

36. Horapollo, *Hieroglyphica* 1.62; Chaeremon, F12, preserved in Tzetzes, *Exegesis in Iliadem* 1.97, in van der Horst 1984, 24–25. In contrast to the accounts of Ammianus and Horapollo, the fragment of Chaeremon preserved by Tzetzes does not include an explanation for the bee sign's association with kingship.

37. Ammianus, *Res Gestae* 17.4.17. In his translation of the *Res Gestae*, Rolfe claims (LCL 315, 237n6) that the obelisk to which Ammianus refers here is the same as the one brought to Rome by Constantius, that is, the obelisk of Thutmose III/IV now standing in the Piazza di San Giovanni in Laterano. However, as Iversen (1968, 66–67) notes, Ammianus' reference to the "*ancient* obelisk which we see in the Circus" is almost certainly intended to distinguish between Constantius' recently arrived obelisk and the obelisk anciently erected in Rome by Augustus (the so-called Flaminian obelisk, now in the Piazza del Popolo). This view has more recently been seconded in Lambrecht's meticulous analysis of Hermapion's translation and its relationship to the text of the Flaminian obelisk. Lambrecht (2001, 55–56) observes that, as Ammianus had no means of identifying which obelisk was originally carved first, the adjective *vetus* must refer to the time of the obelisk's arrival in Rome.

38. This highly unusual interpolation into Ammianus' text has been much remarked in the scholarship; early analyses are discussed in Erman (1914) 1986, 134–36. See also Iversen 1968, 66–67; 1993, 49–50.

39. Lambrecht 2001, 56–57.

40. Erman 1914 (1986); Lambrecht 2001.

41. On the reorientation of the obelisk, see Lambrecht 2001, 60–61; on reconstructing the lacuna in *Codex Fuldensis*, Lambrecht 2001, 57.

42. My translation, following the hieroglyphic text reproduced in Lambrecht 2001, 63, pl. 2.

43. Text in Lambrecht 2001, 54, my translation.

44. Lambrecht 2001, 80–81.

45. Lambrecht 2001, 82–83. Although Lambrecht credits Hermapion with somewhat greater skill as a translator than Erman would allow, the latter similarly suggested ([1914] 1986, 160–61) that Hermapion's main concern was with intelligibility, rather than absolute accuracy.

46. The various theories are discussed by Lambrecht (2001, 86–89), who argues, I think rightly, that in the absence of any evidence more compelling than the etymology of the name "Hermapion," we can say little about the translator's origin.

47. Tertullian, *Spect.* 8.5 (trans. Arbresmann et al., FC 40). The translators note that "Hermateles" is otherwise unknown and allude to the possible connection to "Hermapion," but they acknowledge that the latter is equally unknown.

48. More recently, Amin Benaissa has proposed (2013) to amend the text of Ammianus 17.4.17 from "*in Circo Hermapionis*" to "*in Circo Maximo Apionis*," thereby transforming the name of the translator from "Hermapion" to "Apion." This is an attractive possibility because, as Benaissa notes, an Alexandrian scholar of that name is known to have been active in the early first century C.E. and to have written an *Aegyptiaca* that was widely cited in antiquity. Benaissa observes further that the same Apion is known to have lived in Rome during the reigns of Tiberius and Claudius, at which time he would have had access to the obelisk. Moreover, the various testimonia to Apion's work indicate that he may have had some familiarity with the Egyptian language and that he was in contact with Egyptian priests who could have served as resources in producing the translation. This proposal must remain somewhat speculative—Benaissa offers a hypothetical reconstruction of the process of textual corruption that could have transformed Apion into Hermapion but acknowledges (2013, 116) that "an authoritative explanation" is "beyond [his] sphere of competence"—but for the purpose of the present discussion, the identity

of the translator is ultimately less important than the fact that Ammianus vests considerable authority in him and in his work.

49. Lambrecht 2001, 89–91.

50. De Jonge 1977, 69. Further on Ammianus' digressions, Emmett 1981; 1983; Matthews 1989, 389–92; den Hengst 1992; Rohrbacher 2007.

51. Ammianus, *Res Gestae* 17.4.18 (trans. after Lambrecht 2001, 53).

52. Parker 2004, 213. On the composition of the obelisk inscription, see Grenier 1987.

53. See, for example, Schwartz 1966; E. A. Clark 1992, 52–58; Haas 1997; Hahn 2006; 2008; Watts 2010.

54. Watts 2010, 192. The following overview of events draws especially on Watts 2010, 192–97.

55. Rufinus, *HE* 11.22 (trans. Amidon 1997); Socrates, *HE* 5.16. Rufinus himself does not directly identify the temple in which the pagan rioters have taken refuge as the Serapeum, stating that they "took refuge in a temple, using it as a stronghold (*ad templum quasi ad arcem refugiebant*)." Sozomen (*HE* 7.15.3) specifies that the temple in question was, indeed, part of the Serapeum complex, and Rufinus' own account suggests as much when he seems to say (*HE* 11.23) that the emperor's letter was read out to the crowd at the site of the Serapeum.

56. Rufinus, *HE* 11.22.

57. Rufinus, *HE* 11.23. "Ritualized purification": Watts 2010, 195; see also Haas 1997, 87–89; Frankfurter 2008a, 146–47.

58. Rufinus, *HE* 11.23–27.

59. Rufinus, *HE* 11.27–28.

60. Sozomen, *HE* 7.15; Eunapius, *VS* 472. On Theophilus' agenda, Watts 2010, 196.

61. Rufinus, *HE* 11.29.

62. Egyptian priests as the source of "vile deceptions": Rufinus, *HE* 11.24.

63. The literature on Socrates and Sozomen is extensive; a useful introduction to their work is van Nuffelen 2004.

64. Socrates, *HE* 5.17.1–6 (trans. slightly modified from Zenos, NPNF² 2).

65. Socrates, *HE* 5.17.7–11.

66. There is some uncertainty in the secondary literature as to the sources used by Socrates in composing this passage; van Nuffelen (2004, 226) raises the possibility that he may have relied, at least in part, on the eyewitness testimony of the Alexandrian priests Ammonios and Halladios, who fled to Constantinople in the aftermath of the Serapeum's destruction.

67. Sozomen, *HE* 7.15 (trans. Hartranft, NPNF² 2). For Sozomen's use of Rufinus and Socrates as sources for this section, van Nuffelen 2004, 492.

68. Assmann 1997, 9.

69. Thelamon 1981, 267–73. Cramer (1955, 5–7) provides a similar but less detailed assessment.

70. Letronne 1844; 1846; see also Cramer 1955.

71. *WB* I: 193–206.

72. Generally on the ankh sign, Derchain 1975.

73. McKenzie, Gibson, and Reyes 2004.

74. Augustine, *Civ.* 2.22.

75. Staatsbibliothek zu Berlin, Ms. or. oct. 987, 82r°; see Böhlig 1958; Fluck, Helmecke, and O'Connell 2015, 32. Compare Bibliothèque Nationale Ms. Copte 135 A 3r°, another fourth-century Akhmimic biblical text from the White Monastery, in which an elongated ankh sign stands in the left margin (Lacau 1911, pl. 1). Additional examples are noted in Cramer 1955, 45–46; Doresse 1960, 24n63.

76. The usage of the ankh motif in Christian art and material culture from late antique Egypt is traced by Cramer; although she acknowledges (1955, 7) that the chronological parameters of the phenomenon are hard to define given the difficulty of dating textile fragments and stelae of unknown provenance, she notes that after the composition of the ecclesiastical histories the motif can be seen in a wider range of contexts than was previously the case.

77. A discussion of the logo and its origins (with specific reference to the ecclesiastical histories) can be found at http://stmarkfoundation.com/about_main.php?page_id=2.

78. Thelamon 1981, 268.

79. Egyptian priests as interpreters: see, for example, Fowden 1993, 16; Frankfurter 2000a; Moyer 2011, 51–63 and 264–73.

80. Socrates, *HE* 5.17.2–3 (emphasis mine).

81. Socrates, *HE* 5.17.7–11.

82. If Egyptian religion represented the worst of polytheism in the minds of the church fathers, animal cults represented the worst of Egyptian religion; see Smelik and Hemelrijk 1984, 1981–96. Egyptian priests as deceivers: see, e.g., Rufinus, *HE* 11.24–26; Egyptian priests as ministers of the devil, Socrates, *HE* 5.17.8.

83. Conversion of the children of priests in the *Life of Moses*: Amélineau 1895, 687, lines 5–6. In the *Life of Aaron*: British Library, Or. 7029, fols. 15b–18a = Budge 1915, 447–51 (text) and 963–66 (translation). A new edition of the *Life of Aaron* is announced in Dijkstra 2013; further on the interpretation of the *Life*, see Dijkstra 2008, chapters 7 and 8.

84. Kristensen 2010, 166.

85. Origen, *C. Cels.* 1.24.

86. Assmann 1996, 31.

87. Van den Broek 2000a.

88. For Eusebius' "complex" attitude toward oracular prophecy, see Kofsky 2000, chapter 5, especially 138–48. Kofsky notes (2000, 142) that although Eusebius devoted considerable energy to the critique of pagan oracles, he nevertheless made use of them "as proof of the truth of Christianity." Christian responses to Porphyry's oracle collection, Chadwick 1984, 125–26.

89. The text of the *Theosophy* now survives only in a single manuscript fragment, supplemented by a Byzantine epitome now known as the "Tübingen Theosophy." See Mras 1906; Erbse 1995; Beatrice 1995.

90. Van den Broek 1978; Brock 1984.

91. *Tübingen Theosophy* §16; see van den Broek 1978, 121–29.

92. Christian interpretation of the apocalyptic passages from the *Asclepius*: e.g., Augustine, *Civ.* 8.23–26; prophecy of Antoninus concerning the Serapeum: Eunapius, *VS* 473; both are discussed in van den Broek 2000b. Van den Broek emphasizes that the apocalyptic sections of the *Asclepius* were interpreted as a prophecy of the coming of Christianity to Egypt by both pagans and Christians in late antiquity, and that Augustine's analysis of these passages responds not only to the text of the *Asclepius* itself but also to contemporary pagan interpretations of the text.

93. Socrates, *HE* 5.17.7–8. Compare the tension between the affirmation and rejection of pagan oracles articulated in the introduction to book 5 of Eusebius' *Demonstrat. Evang.* This passage and its relationship to Eusebius' overall approach to the question of prophecy is discussed in Kofsky 2000, 144–48.

94. On the cult of the Three Youths (Τρεῖς Παῖδες) in Egypt, see Gascou 1984; Papaconstantinou 2001, 198–200. A short excerpt from the encomium was published in Zoega (1810) 1903, 50–51; the full text appears in De Vis (1922–29) 1990, 2:158–202. De Vis acknowledges the pseudepigraphic nature of the text but does not make any alternative suggestions regarding its

authorship or dating. Tito Orlandi has identified a cycle of seventh- or eighth-century homilies detailing Theophilus' construction of various Alexandrian churches, and, given the clear thematic parallels between the encomium on the Three Youths and the texts making up that cycle, it seems likely that the composition of the text under consideration here is to be dated to the same period. The composition of the present text and its complex relationship to the aforementioned cycle is briefly discussed in Orlandi 1970, 102–4; see also Orlandi 1972, 213–14; 1973; 1985.

95. De Vis (1922–29) 1990, 2:163, line 15–164, line 10 (my translation).

96. *CTh* 16.10.16 (trans. Pharr 1952). The fact that the temple is said to have been deserted would also have validated Theophilus' and Cyril's claim to the treasure under the terms of contemporary Roman law. The patriarch's immediate report to the emperor concerning the discovery of the treasure was mandated by a law of Constantine from 315 (*CTh* 10.18.1), and the fact that the temple was so clearly deserted obviated the need to restore any portion of the treasure to its original owners, as stipulated by later laws of Gratian, Valentinian, and Theodosius (*CTh* 10.18.2–3); see E. C. Clark 1886, 350–52.

97. Shenoute, A6, text in D. Young 1981, 349, lines 8–12 (my translation).

98. Here I follow the reading of De Vis (1922–29) 1990, 2:164, who renders the passage as follows: "il y avait des représentations et des inscriptions écrites, et d'autres écritures païennes." In theory, ϨⲀⲚⲔⲈⲤϨⲀⲒ ⲚϨⲨⲖⲈⲚⲎⲔⲎ could also be taken as "some Greek inscriptions as well," as *hellenikos* can in the Byzantine period be translated as either "Greek" or as "Gentile, pagan"; see Lampe 1961, 451b. However, it seems unlikely that Greek speakers like Theophilus and Cyril would have considered Greek inscriptions particularly noteworthy or something to be classified together with the "fantastic images" mentioned in the same context. In one of the later parallels to the text (an Arabic recension of a Coptic homily on the Archangel Raphael, discussed in more detail below), Theophilus specifies that the temple inscriptions are written in a language other than his own, although he does not explicitly identify them as hieroglyphs.

99. Kákosy 1982; on the sun disk/thetas as discussed in medieval Arabic sources, Haarmann 1996, 616.

100. Eusebius, *Praep. evang.* 1.10 (trans. Gifford 1903).

101. An alternative interpretation, not addressed by Kákosy, would understand the thetas as standing for the word *thanatos*, "death," thereby serving as a warning against unauthorized entry into the temple. This interpretation was first advanced by F. Dölger (1932a) in his discussion of the motif as it appears in a Syriac parallel to the text under discussion here. Dölger supported his argument with reference to the use of the letter theta in Latin military rolls to indicate the names of soldiers who had died in combat and to its appearance on a stamp-seal of possible Egyptian origin; see also Dölger 1929; 1932b. Similarly, J. David Thomas (1977) proposed that scribes in the early fourth century avoided the use of the letter theta in the writing of regnal years out of superstition; however, this theory was disputed by Herbert Youtie (1978). Further on the symbolism of theta in the ancient imagination, see Dornseiff 1925, 22–28. A Christian treatise on the symbolism of the letters of the Greek alphabet is preserved in a fourteenth-century bilingual Coptic-Arabic manuscript now in the collection of the Bodleian Library; see Hebbelynck 1902. In that work, the letter theta represents, variously, the firmament, the baptism of Jesus, and the waters of the universe. Although the ancient association of the letter theta with the idea of death seems reasonably secure—it is mentioned, as Dölger (1929, 48–49) notes, in the works of Martial, Rufinus, and Isidore of Seville—epigraphic evidence is wholly lacking for the use of the theta as a no-trespassing symbol in the manner Dölger posits.

102. Orlandi 1970, 99; 1985, 103–4; Dölger 1932a.

103. The literature on the tradition of the Holy Family's sojourn in Egypt and on the various recensions of the Vision of Theophilus is vast; a useful summary is provided in Suciu 2013. The motif of the thetas appears only in the Syriac and the long Arabic and Ethiopic recensions.

104. Coquin 1997. Fragments of the Coptic *Vorlage* to this work were published independently in Orlandi 1972; Coquin 1994. The Coptic version of the sermon is very incompletely preserved, and the episode of the thetas does not actually appear in any of the extant Coptic fragments, but it is assumed by both Orlandi (1972, 214) and Coquin (1994, 44) to have existed in the original.

105. Evetts 1948, 426 and 429–30.

106. Basset (1907) 1980, 346–47.

107. Coquin 1994, 25n3; on the evident popularity of the Vision of Theophilus, see Suciu 2013, 439–40.

108. *Vita Epiphanii* §53; see Saradi 2008, 116. The Coptic translation is edited in Rossi 1893. For the miraculous opening of doors as a trope in Coptic hagiography, Dijkstra 2015a, 68n35; for this motif in ancient literature more generally, Weinreich (1929) 1968.

109. See Ritner 1997, 35–57. On the impact of language and script on magical practice, see also Dieleman 2005.

110. For hieroglyphs as magical characters, see Frankfurter 1994, 205–11.

111. Basset (1907) 1980, 346–47.

112. Vision of Theophilus (Syriac recension), trans. Mingana 1929, 397; cf. Nau 1910, 130; Rossini 1910, 447.

113. Coquin 1997, 43–44: "nous allâmes là où (se trouvait) le temple à l'intérieur duquel (était) le trésor; alors, nous vîmes écrit sur le linteau de la porte trois 'thêta' . . . nous fûmes très étonnés et glorifîmes Dieu de l'immensité des richesses et cela (était) qu'Alexandre avait réuni tous ces biens à partir de tous les rois de la terre, et les avait amassés en ce lieu, par la volonté de Dieu."

114. Coquin 1997, 45: "Je regardais et je vis que la porte du temple apparaissait alors je l'examinai par en haut et je vis des signes gravés, des noms et des amulettes." Coquin notes that the use of the term "amulets" or "phylacteries" indicates that the inscription was of a magical nature and that the author may have intended a reference to Egyptian hieroglyphs.

115. See, e.g., Davis 2004, 63–65.

116. Alexander potentially too Greek for Coptic tastes, Gero 1993, 4. The literature on the reception of Alexander throughout the Mediterranean world is ever expanding; see, e.g., Stoneman 2008; Zuwiyya 2011; Boardman 2018. On the Coptic recension of the Alexander Romance: von Lemm 1903; Selden 2011a and 2011b; MacCoull 2012; Sidarus 2013. More generally on Alexander in eastern Christian and later Muslim traditions, Doufikar-Aerts 2010; Monferrer-Sala 2011; Sidarus 2011; 2012.

117. Doufikar-Aerts 2010, xix.

118. Doufikar-Aerts 2010, 81.

119. Bibliothèque Nationale de France, MS Arabe 3687, translated in Doufikar-Aerts 2010, 159.

120. One might also compare the story recounted by Al-Maqrizi (*Khiṭaṭ* 2.425–29) about the discovery of ancient inscriptions (some pertaining to Alexander) during the demolition of buildings in Cairo during the time of Sultan Baybars; see El Daly 2005, 69–70.

121. Orlandi 1972, 213.

122. El Daly 2005, 62.

CONCLUSION

1. Elsner 1994, 224–25.
2. El Daly 2005, chapter 5.
3. Frankfurter 2018.
4. Sauneron 1971, 53 (my translation): "On pourrait écrire un livre, et des plus agréables, sur les légendes d'Égypte nées de la réanimation, par les hommes, des images d'un passé qu'ils ne comprenaient plus."

Bibliography

Adler, William. 1989. *Time Immemorial: Archaic History and Its Sources in Christian Chronography from Julius Africanus to George Syncellus*. Washington, D.C.: Dumbarton Oaks Research Library and Collection.

———. 1992. "Eusebius' Chronicle and Its Legacy." In *Eusebius, Christianity, and Judaism*, edited by Harold W. Attridge and Gohei Hata, 467–91. Detroit: Wayne State University Press.

Adler, William, and Paul Tuffin. 2002. *The Chronography of George Synkellos: A Byzantine Chronicle of Universal History from the Creation*. Oxford: Oxford University Press.

Alcock, Susan E. 2002. *Archaeologies of the Greek Past: Landscape, Monuments, and Memories*. Cambridge: Cambridge University Press.

Allen, James P. 2010. *Middle Egyptian: An Introduction to the Language and Culture of Hieroglyphs*. 2nd ed., rev. Cambridge: Cambridge University Press.

Amélineau, Émile. 1888. *Monuments pour servir à l'histoire de l'Égypte chrétienne au IVe et Ve siècles*. MMAF 4:1. Paris: Ernest Leroux.

———. 1895. *Monuments pour servir à l'histoire de l'Égypte chrétienne aux IVe, Ve, VIe et VIIe siècles*. MMAF 4:2. Paris: Ernest Leroux.

Amidon, Philip R., trans. 1997. *The Church History of Rufinus of Aquileia: Books 10 and 11*. New York: Oxford University Press.

Ashwin-Siejkowski, Piotr. 2015. "Clement of Alexandria." In *The Wiley Blackwell Companion to Patristics*, edited by Ken Parry, 84–97. Malden, Mass.: John Wiley and Sons.

Assmann, Jan. 1994. "Ancient Egypt and the Materiality of the Sign." In *Materialities of Communication*, edited by H. U. Gumbrecht and K. L. Pfeiffer, 15–31. Stanford, Calif.: Stanford University Press.

———. 1995. "Unio Liturgica: Die kultische Einstimmung in götterweltlichen Lobpreis als Grundmotiv 'esoterischer' Überlieferung im alten Ägypten." In *Secrecy and Concealment: Studies in the History of Mediterranean and Near Eastern Religions*, edited by Hans G. Kippenberg and Guy G. Stroumsa, 37–60. Leiden: Brill.

———. 1996. "Translating Gods: Religion as a Factor of Cultural (Un)Translatability." In *The Translatability of Cultures: Figurations of the Space Between*, edited by Sanford Budick and Wolfgang Iser, 25–36. Stanford, Calif.: Stanford University Press.

———. 1997. *Moses the Egyptian: The Memory of Egypt in Western Monotheism*. Cambridge, Mass.: Harvard University Press.

———. 2002. *The Mind of Egypt: History and Meaning in the Time of the Pharaohs*. New York: Metropolitan Books.

———. 2006. *Religion and Cultural Memory: Ten Studies*. Translated by Rodney Livingstone. Cultural Memory in the Present. Stanford, Calif.: Stanford University Press.

———. 2008. *Of God and Gods: Egypt, Israel, and the Rise of Monotheism*. Madison: University of Wisconsin Press.

Atiya, Aziz S., ed. 1991. *The Coptic Encyclopedia*. 8 vols. New York: Macmillan.

Aufrère, Sydney. 2005. "KRONOS, un crocodile justicier des marécages de la rive occidentale du Panopolite au temps de Chénouté?" *Encyclopédie religieuse de l'univers végétal: Croyances phytoreligieuses de l'Égypte ancienne (ERUV)* 3:77–93.

Badawy, Alexandre. 1953. "Les premiers établissements chrétiens dans les anciennes tombes d'Egypte." In *Tome commémoratif du millénaire de la Bibliothèque patriarcale d'Alexandrie*, 67–89. Alexandria: Patriarchal Library of Alexandria.

Bagnall, Roger S. 1993. *Egypt in Late Antiquity*. Princeton, N.J.: Princeton University Press.

———. 2003. "Periodizing When You Don't Have To: The Concept of Late Antiquity in Egypt." In *Gab es eine Spätantike? Vier Vorträge, gehalten auf der Tagung des Graduiertenkollegs für Antike und Europäische Rechtsgeschichte am 21. Juni 2002*, 39–49. Frankfurt am Main: Graduiertenkolleg für Antike, Universität Frankfurt.

———, ed. 2007. *Egypt in the Byzantine World, 300–700*. Cambridge: Cambridge University Press.

———, ed. 2009. *The Oxford Handbook of Papyrology*. Oxford: Oxford University Press.

Baillet, Jules. 1926. *Inscriptions grecques et latines des tombeaux des rois ou syringes*. MIFAO 42. Cairo: Institut Français d'Archéologie Orientale.

Baines, John. 1983. "Literacy and Ancient Egyptian Society." *Man*, n.s., 18 (3): 572–99.

———. 1989. "Communication and Display: The Integration of Early Egyptian Art and Writing." *Antiquity* 63:471–82.

Baines, John, and Christopher Eyre. 1983. "Four Notes on Literacy." *GM* 61:65–96.

Bandy, Kathryn E. 2010. "Hieratic." In Woods 2010a, 159–64.

Barasch, Moshe. 1992. *Icon: Studies in the History of an Idea*. New York: New York University Press.

Barclay, John M. G., trans. and commentary. 2007. *Flavius Josephus, Translation and Commentary*. Vol. 10, *Against Apion*. Leiden: Brill.

Barney, Stephen A., W. J. Lewis, J. A. Beach, and Oliver Berghof, trans. 2007. *The Etymologies of Isidore of Seville*. Cambridge: Cambridge University Press.

Barns, John. 1964. "Shenute as a Historical Source." In *Actes du Xe Congrès International des Papyrologues*, edited by Józef Wolski, 151–59. Wrocław: Polish Academy.

Basset, René, ed. (1907) 1980. *Le Synaxaire arabe jacobite (rédaction copte): Texte arabe*. Reprint, Turnhout: Brepols, 1980.

Beatrice, Pier Franco. 1995. "Pagan Wisdom and Christian Theology According to the Tübingen Theosophy." *JECS* 3:403–18.

Bedrosian, R., trans. 2008. *Eusebius' Chronicle*. Long Branch, N.J.: Sources of the Armenian Tradition. https://archive.org/details/EusebiusChroniclechronicon.

Behlmer, Heike. 1993. "Historical Evidence from Shenoute's *De extremo iudicio*." In *Sesto Congresso Internazionale di Egittologia: Atti*, edited by G. M. Zaccone and T. R. di Netro, 2 vols., 2:11–19. Turin: International Association of Egyptologists.

———. 1996. *Schenute von Atripe: De Iudicio (Turin, Museo Egizio, Cat. 63000, Cod. IV)*. Turin: Museo Egizio.

Benaissa, Amin. 2013. "Ammianus Marcellinus *Res Gestae* 17.4.17 and the Translator of the Obelisk in Rome's Circus Maximus." *ZPE* 186:114–18.

Bergman, Jan. 1968. *Ich bin Isis: Studien zum memphitischen Hintergrund der griechischen Isisaretalogien*. Acta Universitatis Upsaliensis, Historia Religionum 3. Uppsala: Almquist and Wiksell.

Besançon, Alain. 2000. *The Forbidden Image: An Intellectual History of Iconoclasm.* Translated by Jane Marie Todd. Chicago: University of Chicago Press.

Betz, Hans Dieter, ed. 1992. *The Greek Magical Papyri in Translation, Including the Demotic Spells.* 2nd ed. Chicago: University of Chicago Press.

Bleeker, Claas Jouco. 1973. *Hathor and Thoth: Two Key Figures of the Ancient Egyptian Religion.* Studies in the History of Religions (Supplements to Numen) 26. Leiden: Brill.

Blochet, E. 1913. "Études sur le Gnosticisme Musulman (continuazione e fine)." *RSO* 6 (1): 5–67.

Boardman, John. 2018. *Alexander the Great: From His Death to the Present Day.* Princeton, N.J.: Princeton University Press.

Böhlig, Alexander. 1958. "Zur Berliner achmimischen Proverbienhandschrift." *ZÄS* 83 (1): 1–4.

Bolman, Elizabeth S., Stephen J. Davis, and Gillian Pyke. 2010. "Shenoute and a Recently Discovered Tomb Chapel at the White Monastery." *JECS* 18 (3): 453–62.

Bolman, Elizabeth S., Luigi De Cesaris, Alberto Sucato, Emiliano Ricchi, Matjaz Kacicnik, Saad Mohammed Mohammed Osman, Aly Zaghloul Aly, et al. 2014. "The Tomb of St. Shenoute at the White Monastery: Final Conservation and Documentation." *Bulletin of the American Research Center in Egypt* 204:21–24.

Bowen, Anthony, and Peter Garnsey, trans. 2003. *Lactantius: Divine Institutes.* Translated Texts for Historians 40. Liverpool: Liverpool University Press.

Bowersock, Glen, Peter Brown, and Oleg Grabar, eds. 2001. *Interpreting Late Antiquity: Essays on the Postclassical World.* Cambridge, Mass.: Harvard University Press.

Bowman, Alan K. 1986. *Egypt After the Pharaohs.* Berkeley: University of California Press.

Bowman, Alan K., and Greg Woolf, eds. 1994a. *Literacy and Power in the Ancient World.* Cambridge: Cambridge University Press.

———. 1994b. "Literacy and Power in the Ancient World." In Bowman and Woolf 1994a, 1–16.

Boylan, Patrick. 1922. *Thoth, the Hermes of Egypt: A Study of Some Aspects of Theological Thought in Ancient Egypt.* Oxford: Oxford University Press.

Brakke, David. 2006. *Demons and the Making of the Monk: Spiritual Combat in Early Christianity.* Cambridge, Mass.: Harvard University Press.

———. 2008. "From Temple to Cell, from Gods to Demons: Pagan Temples in the Monastic Topography of Fourth-Century Egypt." In Hahn, Emmel, and Gotter 2008, 91–112.

Brakke, David, and Andrew Crislip. 2015. *Selected Discourses of Shenoute the Great: Community, Theology, and Social Conflict in Late Antique Egypt.* Cambridge: Cambridge University Press.

Brashear, William. 1979. "Ein Berliner Zauberpapyrus." *ZPE* 33:261–78.

Bremmer, Jan. 2015. "God against the Gods: Early Christians and the Worship of Statues." In *Römische Götterbilder der mittleren und späten Kaiserzeit*, edited by Dietrich Boschung and Alfred Schäfer, 139–58. Paderborn: Wilhelm Fink.

Bricault, Laurent, M. J. Versluys, and P. G. P. Meyboom, eds. 2007. *Nile into Tiber: Egypt in the Roman World; Proceedings of the 3rd International Conference of Isis Studies, Leiden, May 11–14, 2005.* Leiden: Brill.

Brock, Sebastian. 1984. "Some Syriac Excerpts from Greek Collections of Pagan Prophecies." *VChr* 38 (1): 77–90.

Brown, Peter. 1992. *Power and Persuasion in Late Antiquity: Towards a Christian Empire.* Madison: University of Wisconsin Press.

Brown, Virginia, ed. 2001. *Giovanni Boccaccio: Famous Women.* I Tatti Renaissance Library 1. Cambridge, Mass.: Harvard University Press.

Brunner, Hellmut. 1957. *Altägyptische Erziehung.* Wiesbaden: Harrassowitz.

Bucking, Scott. 2011. *Practice Makes Perfect:* P.Cotsen-Princeton 1 *and the Training of Scribes in Byzantine Egypt.* Los Angeles: Cotsen Occasional.

Budde, Dagmar. 2000. *Die Göttin Seschat.* Kanobos 2. Leipzig: Verlag Helmar Wodtke und Katharina Stegbauer GbR.

Budge, E. A. Wallis. 1898. *The Earliest Known Coptic Psalter: The Text, in the Dialect of Upper Egypt, Edited from the Unique Papyrus Codex Oriental 5000 in the British Museum.* London: Kegan Paul, Trench, Trübner.

———. 1915. *Coptic Texts.* Vol. 5, *Miscellaneous Coptic Texts in the Dialect of Upper Egypt.* London: British Museum.

Bull, Christian H. 2012. "The Notion of Mysteries in the Formation of Hermetic Tradition." In *Mystery and Secrecy in the Nag Hammadi Collection and Other Ancient Literatures: Ideas and Practices; Studies for Einar Thomassen at Sixty,* edited by Christian H. Bull, Liv Ingeborg Lied, and John D. Turner, 399–425. Nag Hammadi and Manichaean Studies 76. Leiden: Brill.

———. 2018. *The Tradition of Hermes Trismegistus: The Egyptian Priestly Figure as a Teacher of Hellenized Wisdom.* Religions in the Graeco-Roman World 186. Leiden: Brill.

Burgess, Richard W. 1999. *Studies in Eusebian and Post-Eusebian Chronology.* Historia Einzelschrift 135. Stuttgart: Franz Steiner Verlag.

Burgess, Richard W., and Michael Kulikowski. 2013. *Mosaics of Time: The Latin Chronicle Traditions from the First Century BC to the Sixth Century AD.* Vol. 1, *A Historical Introduction to the Chronicle Genre from Its Origins to the High Middle Ages.* Studies in the Early Middle Ages 33. Turnhout: Brepols.

Burkhard, G. 1980. "Bibliotheken im alten Ägypten: Überlegungen zur Methodik ihres Nachweises und Übersicht zum Stand der Forschung." *Bibliothek, Forschung und Praxis* 4:79–115.

Butterfield, D. J., ed. 2015. *Varro Varius: The Polymath of the Roman World.* Cambridge Classical Journal Supplementary Volume 39. Cambridge: Cambridge Philological Society.

Cameron, Alan. 1965. "Wandering Poets: A Literary Movement in Byzantine Egypt." *Historia* 14 (4): 470–509.

———. 2007. "Poets and Pagans in Byzantine Egypt." In *Egypt in the Byzantine World, 300–700,* edited by Roger S. Bagnall, 21–46. Cambridge: Cambridge University Press, 2007.

———. 2016. *Wandering Poets and Other Essays on Late Greek Literature and Philosophy.* Oxford: Oxford University Press.

Cameron, Averil. 1991. *Christianity and the Rhetoric of Empire: The Development of Christian Discourse.* Berkeley: University of California Press.

———. 2002. "The 'Long' Late Antiquity: A Late Twentieth-Century Model." In *Classics in Progress: Essays on Ancient Greece and Rome,* edited by T. P. Wiseman, 165–91. British Academy Centenary Monographs. Oxford: Published for the British Academy by Oxford University Press.

Caseau, Béatrice. 2001. "POLEMEIN LITHOIS: La désacralisation des espaces et des objets religieux païens durant l'Antiquité Tardive." In *Le sacré et son inscription dans l'espace à Byzance et en Occident,* 61–123. Série Byzantina Sorbonensia 18. Paris: Publications de la Sorbonne.

———. 2007. "Rire des dieux." In *La dérision au Moyen Age: De la pratique sociale au rituel politique,* edited by Elisabeth Crouzet-Pavan and Jacques Verger, 117–41. Paris: Presses de l'Université de Paris-Sorbonne.

Černy, Jaroslav. 1948. "Thoth as Creator of Languages." *JEA* 34:121–22.

Chadwick, Henry. 1984. "Oracles of the End in the Conflict of Paganism and Christianity in the Fourth Century." In *Memorial André-Jean Festugière: Antiquité païenne et chrétienne;*

Vingt-cinq études, edited by Enzo Lucchesi and Henri-Dominique Saffrey, 125–29. Cahiers d'orientalisme 10. Geneva: Cramer.

Champion, Timothy, and Peter Ucko. 2003. "Introduction: Egypt Ancient and Modern." In *The Wisdom of Egypt: Changing Visions Through the Ages*, edited by Peter Ucko and Timothy Champion, 1–22. Encounters with Ancient Egypt. London: UCL.

Chance, Jane. 2013. "Re-Membering Herself: Christine de Pizan's Refiguration of Isis as Io." *Modern Philology* 111 (2): 133–57.

Charles, R. H. 1913. *The Apocrypha and Pseudepigrapha of the Old Testament*. Oxford: Clarendon.

Chassinat, Émile. 1930. *Le Temple d'Edfou, tome cinquième*. MMAF 22. Cairo: Institut Français d'Archéologie Orientale.

Choat, Malcolm. 2012. "Coptic." In Riggs 2012, 581–93.

Ciampini, Emanuele M. 2015. "De origine et usu obeliscorum: Some Notes on an Eighteenth-Century Egyptological Study." In *The Forgotten Scholar: Georg Zoëga (1755–1809); At the Dawn of Egyptology and Coptic Studies*, edited by Karen Ascani, Paola Buzi, and Daniela Picchi, 185–91. Culture and History of the Ancient Near East 74. Leiden: Brill.

Clark, Elizabeth A. 1992. *The Origenist Controversy: The Cultural Construction of an Early Christian Debate*. Princeton, N.J.: Princeton University Press.

Clark, E. C. 1886. "Notes on the Roman and Early English Law of Treasure Trove." *ArchJ* 43:350–57.

Clarke, Emma C., John M. Dillon, and Jackson P. Hershbell. 2003. *Iamblichus: De Mysteriis*. Writings from the Greco-Roman World 4. Atlanta: Society of Biblical Literature.

Clarysse, Willy. 1987. "Greek Loan-Words in Demotic." In *Aspects of Demotic Lexicography*, edited by S. P. Vleeming, 9–33. Studia Demotica 1. Leuven: Peeters.

———. 2013. "Determinatives in Greek Loan-Words and Proper Names." In *Aspects of Demotic Orthography: Acts of an International Colloquium Held in Trier, 8 November 2010*, edited by S. P. Vleeming, 1–24. Studia Demotica 11. Leuven: Peeters.

Colla, Elliott. 2007. *Conflicted Antiquities: Egyptology, Egyptomania, Egyptian Modernity*. Durham, N.C.: Duke University Press.

Connerton, Paul. 1989. *How Societies Remember*. Cambridge: Cambridge University Press.

Copenhaver, Brian P. 1992. *Hermetica: The Greek Corpus Hermeticum and the Latin Asclepius in a New English Translation, with Notes and Introduction*. Cambridge: Cambridge University Press.

Coquin, René-Georges. 1994. "Discours attribué au patriarche Cyrille sur la dédicace de l'église de Raphael rapportant les propos de son oncle, le patriarche Théophile." *BSAC* 33:25–56.

———. 1997. "Discours attribué au patriarche Cyrille sur la dédicace de l'église de Raphael rapportant les propos de son oncle, le patriarche Théophile II: Version Arabe." *BSAC* 36:9–58.

Cramer, Maria. 1955. *Das altägyptische Lebenszeichen im christlichen (koptischen) Ägypten: Eine kultur- und religionsgeschichtliche Studie auf archäologischer Grundlage*. Wiesbaden: O. Harrassowitz.

Cribiore, Raffaella. 1996. *Writing, Teachers, and Students in Graeco-Roman Egypt*. ASP 36. Atlanta: Scholars.

———. 1999. "Greek and Coptic Education in Late Antique Egypt." In *Ägypten und Nubien in spätantiker und christlicher Zeit: Akten des 6. Internationalen Koptologenkongresses*, edited by Stephen Emmel, Martin Krause, Siegfried Richter, and Sofia Schaten, 2:279–86. Wiesbaden: Reichert Verlag.

———. 2009. "Education in the Papyri." In Bagnall 2009, 320–37.

Croke, Brian. 1982. "The Originality of Eusebius' Chronicle." *AJPh* 103 (2): 195–200.

———. 1983. "The Origins of the Christian World Chronicle." In Croke and Emmett 1983, 116–31.

Croke, Brian, and Alanna M. Emmett, eds. 1983. *History and Historians in Late Antiquity*. Sydney: Pergamon.

Cruz-Uribe, Eugene. 2002. "The Death of Demotic at Philae: A Study in Pilgrimage and Politics." In *A Tribute to Excellence: Studies Offered in Honor of Ernő Gaál, Ulrich Luft, and László Török*, edited by Tamás Bács, 163–84. Studia Aegyptiaca 17. Budapest: Université Eötvös Lorand de Budapest.

———. 2010. "The Death of Demotic Redux: Pilgrimage, Nubia and the Preservation of Egyptian Culture." In Knuf, Leitz, and von Recklinghausen 2010, 499–506.

Curley, Michael J., trans. 2009. *Physiologus*. Chicago: University of Chicago Press.

Curran, Brian A. 2007. *The Egyptian Renaissance: The Afterlife of Ancient Egypt in Early Modern Italy*. Chicago: University of Chicago Press.

Curran, Brian A., Anthony Grafton, Pamela O. Long, and Benjamin Weiss. 2009. *Obelisk: A History*. Cambridge, Mass.: MIT Press.

Dagron, Gilbert. 1984. *Constantinople imaginaire, étude sur le recueil des "Patria."* Paris: Presses universitaires de France.

Davidson, Ivor J. 1995. "Ambrose's *de Officiis* and the Intellectual Climate of the Late Fourth Century." *VChr* 49 (4): 313–33.

Davies, W. V. 1987. *Egyptian Hieroglyphs: Reading the Past*. London: British Museum.

Davis, Stephen J. 2004. *The Early Coptic Papacy: The Egyptian Church and Its Leadership in Late Antiquity*. Popes of Egypt 1. Cairo: American University in Cairo Press.

Dawson, David. 1992. *Allegorical Readers and Cultural Revision in Ancient Alexandria*. Berkeley: University of California Press.

Deiber, Albert. 1904. *Clément d'Alexandrie et l'Égypte*. MIFAO 10. Cairo: Institut Français d'Archéologie Orientale.

De Jonge, P. 1977. *Philological and Historical Commentary on Ammianus Marcellinus XVII*. Leiden: Brill.

Delattre, Alain. 2008. "Inscriptions grecques et coptes de la montagne thébaine relatives au culte de saint Ammônios." In *"Et maintenant ce ne sont plus que des villages . . ." Thèbes et sa région aux époques hellénistique, romaine et byzantine: Actes du colloque tenu à Bruxelles les 2 et 3 décembre 2005*, edited by Alain Delattre and Paul Heilporn, 183–88. Papyrologica Bruxellensia 34. Brussels: Association Égyptologique Reine Élisabeth.

Depauw, Mark. 2012. "Language Use, Literacy, and Bilingualism." In Riggs 2012, 493–506.

Depuydt, Leo, ed. 1993. *Encomiastica from the Pierpont Morgan Library: Five Coptic Homilies Attributed to Anastasius of Euchaita, Epiphanius of Salamis, Isaac of Antinoe, Severian of Gabala, and Theopempus of Antioch*. 2 vols. CSCO 544–45. Louvain: Peeters.

Derchain, Philippe. 1965. *Le papyrus Salt 825 (B.M. 10051), rituel pour la conservation de la vie en Egypte*. Mémoires de l'Académie royale de Belgique, Classe des lettres 58, fasc. 1a–b. Brussels: Palais des académies.

———. 1975. "Anchzeichen." *LÄ* 1:268–69.

Derchain-Urtel, Maria Theresia. 1981. *Thot: À travers ses épithètes dans les scènes d'offrandes des temples d'époque gréco-romaine*. Rites égyptiens 3. Brussels: Fondation Égyptologique Reine Elisabeth.

Desmond, Marilynn, and Pamela Sheingorn. 2003. *Myth, Montage, and Visuality in Late Medieval Manuscript Culture: Christine de Pizan's Epistre Othéa*. Ann Arbor: University of Michigan Press.

Devauchelle, Didier. 1984. "Remarques sur les méthodes d'enseignement du démotique." In *Grammata Demotika: Festschrift für Erich Lüddeckens zum 15. Juni 1983*, edited by Heinz-Josef Thissen and Karl-Theodor Zauzich, 47–59. Würzburg: Gisela Zauzich Verlag.

———. 1994. "24 Août 394–24 Août 1994: 1600 ans." *BSFE* 131:16–18.

De Vis, Henri. (1922–29) 1990. *Homélies Coptes de la Vaticane*. 2 vols. CBC 6. Reprint, Louvain: Éditions Peeters. Citations refer to the Peeters edition.

Dieckmann, Lieselotte. 1970. *Hieroglyphics: The History of a Literary Symbol*. St. Louis: Washington University Press.

Dieleman, Jacco. 2005. *Priests, Tongues, and Rites: The London-Leiden Magical Manuscripts and Translation in Egyptian Ritual (100–300 CE)*. Religions in the Graeco-Roman World 153. Leiden: Brill.

Dieleman, Jacco, and Ian S. Moyer. 2010. "Egyptian Literature." In *A Companion to Hellenistic Literature*, edited by James J. Clauss and Martine Cuypers, 429–47. Chichester, U.K.: Wiley-Blackwell.

Digeser, Elizabeth DePalma. 2000. *The Making of a Christian Empire: Lactantius and Rome*. Ithaca, N.Y.: Cornell University Press.

Dijkstra, Jitse H. F. 2008. *Philae and the End of Ancient Egyptian Religion: A Regional Study of Religious Transformation (298–642 CE)*. OLA 173. Leuven: Peeters.

———. 2011. "The Fate of the Temples in Late Antique Egypt." In Lavan and Mulryan 2011, 389–436.

———. 2012. *Syene I: The Figural and Textual Graffiti from the Temple of Isis at Aswan, with a Contribution on the Egyptian Texts by Eugene Cruz-Uribe*. Beiträge zur ägyptischen Bauforschung und Altertumskunde 18. Darmstadt: Philipp von Zabern.

———. 2013. "Monasticism on the Southern Egyptian Frontier in Late Antiquity: Towards a New Critical Edition of the Coptic *Life of Aaron*." *JCSCS* 5:31–47.

———. 2015a. "'I Wish to Offer a Sacrifice to God Today': The Discourse of Idol Destruction in the Coptic Life of Aaron." *JCSCS* 7:61–75.

———. 2015b. Review of *Shenoute of Atripe and the Uses of Poverty: Rural Patronage, Religious Conflict, and Monasticism in Late Antique Egypt*, by Ariel G. López. *VChr* 69:97–103.

———. 2016. "The Religious Background of Nonnus." In *Brill's Companion to Nonnus of Panopolis*, edited by Domenico Accorinti, 75–88. Leiden: Brill.

Dillery, John. 2015. *Clio's Other Sons: Berossus and Manetho*. Ann Arbor: University of Michigan Press.

Dillon, John. 1985. "The Magical Power of Names in Origen and Later Platonism." In *Origeniana Tertia: The Third International Colloquium for Origen Studies, University of Manchester September 7th–11th, 1981*, edited by Richard Hanson and Henri Crouzel, 203–16. Rome: Edizioni dell'Ateneo.

Dirkse, Peter A., James Brashler, and Douglas M. Parrott. 1979. "The Discourse on the Eighth and Ninth, VI, 6:52,1–63,32." In *Nag Hammadi Codices V, 2–5 and VI with Papyrus Berolinensis 8502, 1 and 4*, edited by Douglas M. Parrott. Nag Hammadi Studies 11. Leiden: Brill.

Dölger, Franz. 1929. "Der Stempel mit Pentagramm, θ und ΥΓΙΕΙΑ im Historischen Museum zu Basel, kein heidnischer oder christlicher Weihbrotstempel, sondern der Stempel eines antiken Arztes." *Antike und Christentum* 1:47–53.

———. 1932a. "Drei *Theta* als Schatzsicherung und ihre Deutung durch den Bischof Theophil von Alexandrien: Eine Szene aus dem Kampfe gegen die Heidentempel." *Antike und Christentum* 3:189–91.

———. 1932b. "Echo 41. Thetatus = 'Der im Krieg Gefallene'." *Antike und Christentum* 3:221.

Doresse, Jean. 1960. *Des hiéroglyphes à la croix: Ce que le passé pharaonique a légué au Christianisme*. Uitgaven van het Nederlands Historisch-Archaeologisch Instituut te Istanbul 7. Istanbul: Nederlands Historisch-Archaeologisch Instituut in het Nabije Oosten.

Dornseiff, Franz. 1925. *Das Alphabet in Mystik und Magie*. Leipzig: Teubner.

Doufikar-Aerts, Faustina. 2010. *Alexander Magnus Arabicus: A Survey of the Alexander Tradition Through Seven Centuries: From Pseudo-Callisthenes to Ṣūrī*. Mediaevalia Groningana, n.s., 13. Leuven: Peeters.

Dousa, T. 2002. "Imagining Isis: On Some Continuities and Discontinuities in the Image of Isis in Greek Isis Hymns and Demotic Texts." In *Acts of the Seventh International Conference of Demotic Studies, Copenhagen, 23–27 August 1999*, edited by Kim Ryholt, 149–84. Copenhagen: The Carsten Niebuhr Institute of Near Eastern Studies, University of Copenhagen.

Drake, H. A. 1976. *In Praise of Constantine: A Historical Study and New Translation of Eusebius' Tricennial Orations*. Berkeley: University of California Press.

Dreyer, Günter, Ulrich Hartung, and Frauke Pumpenmeier. 1998. *Umm el-Qaab*. Vol. 1, *Das prädynastische Königsgrab U-j und seine frühen Schriftzeugnisse*. Archäologische Veröffentlichung des Deutschen Archäologischen Instituts in Kairo 86. Mainz: Philipp von Zabern.

Droge, Arthur J. 1989. *Homer or Moses? Early Christian Interpretations of the History of Culture*. Tübingen: Mohr Siebeck.

Dulaurier, Édouard. 1833. *Examen d'un passage des Stromates de saint Clément d'Alexandrie, relatif aux écritures égyptiennes*. Paris: H. Fournier Jeune.

Dyson, R. W., trans. 1998. *The City of God Against the Pagans*. Cambridge Texts in the History of Political Thought. Cambridge: Cambridge University Press.

Eco, Umberto. 1995. *The Search for the Perfect Language*. Translated by James Fentress. Oxford: Blackwell.

Egberts, A., B. P. Muhs, and J. van der Vliet, eds. 2002. *Perspectives on Panopolis: An Egyptian Town from Alexander the Great to the Arab Conquest*. PLB 31. Leiden: Brill.

El Daly, Okasha. 2005. *Egyptology: The Missing Millennium; Ancient Egypt in Medieval Arabic Writings*. London: UCL.

Elm, Susanna. 2012. "Laughter in Christian Polemics." *StP* 54:1–8.

el-Masry, Yahia. 2001. "More Recent Excavations at Athribis in Upper Egypt." *MDAIK* 57:205–18.

el-Sayed, Rafed. 2010. "Schenute und die Tempel von Atripe: Zur Umnutzung des Triphisbezirks in der Spätantike." In Knuf, Leitz, and von Recklinghausen 2010, 519–38.

Elsner, John. 1994. "From the Pyramids to Pausanius and Piglet: Monuments, Travel, and Writing." In *Art and Text in Ancient Greek Culture*, edited by Simon Goldhill and Robin Osborne, 224–54. Cambridge: Cambridge University Press.

Emmel, Stephen. 1992. "Coptic." In *The Anchor Bible Dictionary*, edited by David Noel Freedman, 4:180–88. New York: Doubleday.

———. 2002. "From the Other Side of the Nile: Shenute and Panopolis." In Egberts, Muhs, and van der Vliet 2002, 95–113.

———. 2004. *Shenoute's Literary Corpus*. 2 vols. CSCO Subsidia 111–12. Leuven: Peeters.

———. 2008. "Shenoute of Atripe and the Christian Destruction of Temples in Egypt: Rhetoric and Reality." In Hahn, Emmel, and Gotter 2008, 161–202.

———. 2016. "Editing Shenoute, Old Problems, New Prospects: The Date of Shenoute's Death." In *Coptic Society, Literature and Religion from Late Antiquity to Modern Times: Proceedings of the Tenth International Congress of Coptic Studies, Rome, September 17th–22nd, 2012, and Plenary Reports of the Ninth International Congress of Coptic Studies, Cairo, September 15th–19th,*

2008, edited by Paola Buzi, Alberto Camplani, and Federico Contardi, 2:937–44. OLA 247. Leuven: Peeters.

Emmel, Stephen, Ulrich Gotter, and Johannes Hahn. 2008. "'From Temple to Church': Analysing a Late Antique Phenomenon of Transformation." In Hahn, Emmel, and Gotter 2008, 1–22.

Emmett, Alanna M. 1981. "Introductions and Conclusions to Digressions in Ammianus Marcellinus." *Museum Philologum Londoniense* 5:15–33.

———. 1983. "The Digressions in the Lost Books of Ammianus Marcellinus." In Croke and Emmett 1983, 42–53.

Erbse, Hartmut, ed. 1995. *Theosophorum Graecorum Fragmenta*. Bibliotheca Scriptorum Graecorum et Romanorum Teubneriana. Stuttgart: Teubner.

Erman, Adolf. (1914) 1986. "Die Obeliskenübersetzung des Hermapion." Reprinted in Erman, *Akademieschriften: 1880–1928*, 133–61. Opuscula 13. Leipzig: Zentralantiquariat der Deutschen Demokratischen Republik.

Evetts, B. T. A., ed. 1948. *History of the Patriarchs of the Coptic Church of Alexandria*. Vol. 2, *Peter I to Benjamin I (661)*. PO 1:4. Paris: Firmin-Didot.

Feldman, Louis H., trans. 2000. *Flavius Josephus: Judean Antiquities 1–4*. Leiden: Brill.

———. 2007. *Philo's Portrayal of Moses in the Context of Ancient Judaism*. Christianity and Judaism in Antiquity 15. South Bend, Ind.: University of Notre Dame Press.

Festugière, André-Jean. 1944–54. *La révélation d'Hermès Trismégiste*. 4 vols. Études Bibliques. Paris: Les Belles Lettres.

Fischer, Henry G. 1973. "Redundant Determinatives in the Old Kingdom." *MMAJ* 8:7–25.

Fluck, Cäcilia, Gisela Helmecke, and Elisabeth R. O'Connell, eds. 2015. *Egypt: Faith After the Pharaohs*. London: British Museum Press.

Fodor, A. 1970. "The Origins of the Arabic Legends of the Pyramids." *AAntHung* 23 (3): 335–63.

Fournet, Jean-Luc. 2009. "The Multilingual Environment of Late Antique Egypt: Greek, Latin, Coptic, and Persian Documentation." In Bagnall 2009, 418–51.

Fowden, Garth. 1993. *The Egyptian Hermes: A Historical Approach to the Late Pagan Mind*, 2nd ed. Princeton, N.J.: Princeton University Press.

Frankfurter, David. 1994. "The Magic of Writing and the Writing of Magic: The Power of the Word in Egyptian and Greek Traditions." *Helios* 21 (2): 189–221.

———. 1998. *Religion in Roman Egypt: Assimilation and Resistance*. Princeton, N.J.: Princeton University Press.

———. 2000a. "The Consequences of Hellenism in Late Antique Egypt." *ARG* 2 (2): 162–94.

———. 2000b. "'Things Unbefitting Christians': Violence and Christianization in Fifth-Century Panopolis." *JECS* 8 (2): 273–95.

———. 2007. "Illuminating the Cult of Kothos: The Panegyric on Macarius and Local Religion in Fifth-Century Egypt." In *The World of Early Egyptian Christianity: Language, Literature, and Social Context; Essays in Honor of David W. Johnson*, edited by James Goehring and Janet Timbie, 176–88. Washington, D.C.: Catholic University of America Press.

———. 2008a. "Iconoclasm and Christianization in Late Antique Egypt: Christian Treatment of Space and Image." In Hahn, Emmel, and Gotter 2008, 135–60.

———. 2008b. "The Vitality of Egyptian Images in Late Antiquity: Christian Memory and Response." In *The Sculptural Environment of the Roman Near East: Reflections on Culture, Ideology, and Power*, edited by Yaron Z. Eliav, Elise A. Friedland, and Sharon Herbert, 659–78. Interdisciplinary Studies in Ancient Culture and Religion 9. Leiden: Brill.

————. 2018. *Christianizing Egypt: Syncretism and Local Worlds in Late Antiquity*. Princeton, N.J.: Princeton University Press.

Gaddis, Michael. 2005. *There Is No Crime for Those Who Have Christ: Religious Violence in the Christian Roman Empire*. Transformation of the Classical Heritage 39. Berkeley: University of California Press.

Gardiner, Alan H. 1938. "The House of Life." *JEA* 24 (2): 157–79.

————. 1957. *Egyptian Grammar*. 3rd ed., rev. London: Oxford University Press.

Gascou, Jean. 1984. "Les sanctuaires dédiés aux Trois Saints Jeunes Gens en Égypte byzantine." *CdE* 59:333–37.

Gaudard, François. 2009. "Le P.Berlin 8278 et ses fragments: Un 'nouveau' texte démotique comprenant des noms de lettres." In *Verba manent: Recueil d'études dédiées à Dimitri Meeks*, edited by Isabelle Régen and Frédéric Servajean, 165–69. Cahiers de l'ENIM 2. Montpellier: Université Paul Valéry.

————. 2010. "Ptolemaic Hieroglyphs." In Woods 2010a, 173–78.

————. 2012. "Birds in the Ancient Egyptian and Coptic Alphabets." In *Between Heaven and Earth: Birds in Ancient Egypt*, edited by Rozenn Bailleul-LeSuer, 65–69. OIMP 35. Chicago: Oriental Institute.

Gero, Stephen. 1993. "The Legend of Alexander the Great in the Christian Orient." *BRL* 75:3–9.

Giehlow, Karl. 2015. *The Humanist Interpretation of Hieroglyphs in the Allegorical Studies of the Renaissance: With a Focus on the Triumphal Arch of Maximilian I*. Translated by Robin Raybould. Brill's Studies in Intellectual History 240. Leiden: Brill.

Gifford, E. H., trans. 1903. *Evangelicae Praeparationis*. Oxford: Oxford University Press.

Goldwasser, Orly. 1995. *From Icon to Metaphor: Studies in the Semiotics of the Hieroglyphs*. OBO 142. Fribourg: University Press of Fribourg; Göttingen: Vandenhoeck and Ruprecht.

————. 2002. *Prophets, Lovers and Giraffes: Wor(l)d Classification in Ancient Egypt*. Göttinger Orientforschungen 38. Wiesbaden: Harrassowitz.

Górecki, Tomasz, and Edyta Kopp. 2013. "Hieroglyphic Signs Scratched on a Sherd of an Egyptian Late Roman Transport Amphora." *Études et Travaux* 26:237–43.

Grafton, Anthony, and Megan Williams. 2006. *Christianity and the Transformation of the Book: Origen, Eusebius, and the Library of Caesarea*. Cambridge, Mass.: Belknap Press of Harvard University Press.

Green, R. P. H., ed. 1995. *Augustine: De Doctrina Christiana*. Oxford Early Christian Texts. Oxford: Clarendon.

Greenberg, Moshe. 1983. *Ezekiel 1–20: A New Translation with Introduction and Commentary*. Anchor Bible 22. New Haven, Conn.: Yale University Press.

Grégoire, Henri. 1940. "L'énigme de Tahta." *CdE* 15:119–23.

Grene, David, trans. 1987. *Herodotus: The History*. Chicago: University of Chicago Press.

Grenier, Jean-Claude. 1987. "Les inscriptions hiéroglyphiques de l'obélisque Pamphili." *MEFRA* 99:937–61.

Griffith, F. Ll. 1930. "Four Granite Stands at Philae." *BIFAO* 30:127–30.

————. 1935. *Catalogue of the Demotic Graffiti of the Dodecaschoenus*. 2 vols. Oxford: Oxford University Press.

Griffiths, J. Gwyn, ed. 1970. *Plutarch's De Iside et Osiride*. Cardiff: University of Wales Press.

————, ed. 1975. *Apuleius of Madauros: The Isis-Book (Metamorphoses, Book XI)*. Etudes préliminaires aux religions orientales dans l'Empire romain 39. Leiden: E. J. Brill.

Grossmann, Peter. 1984. "New Observations in the Church and Sanctuary of Dayr Anbā Šinūda—the So-Called White Monastery—at Suhāğ: Results of Two Surveys in October, 1981 and January, 1982." *ASAE* 70:69–73.

———. 1991. "Dayr Anbā Shinūdah: Architecture." In Atiya 1991, 3:767–69.

———. 2002. *Christliche Architektur in Ägypten*. Handbuch der Orientalistik 62. Leiden: Brill.

———. 2008a. "Modalitäten der Zerstörung und Christianisierung pharaonischer Tempelanlagen." In Hahn, Emmel, and Gotter 2008, 299–334.

———. 2008b. "Zur Stiftung und Bauzeit der großen Kirche des Schenuteklosters bei Suhag (Oberägypten)." *ByzZ* 101:35–54.

Guthrie, Kenneth. 1987. *The Pythagorean Sourcebook: An Anthology of Ancient Writings Which Relate to Pythagoras and Pythagorean Philosophy*. Grand Rapids, Mich.: Phanes.

Haarmann, Ulrich. 1996. "Medieval Muslim Perceptions of Pharaonic Egypt." In *Ancient Egyptian Literature: History and Forms*, edited by Antonio Loprieno, 605–27. PÄ 10. Leiden: E. J. Brill.

———. 2001. "Islam and Ancient Egypt." In *The Oxford Encyclopedia of Ancient Egypt*, edited by Donald Redford, 2:191–94. Oxford: Oxford University Press.

Haas, Christopher. 1997. *Alexandria in Late Antiquity: Topography and Social Conflict*. Baltimore: Johns Hopkins University Press.

Hagendahl, Harald. 1958. *Latin Fathers and the Classics: A Study on the Apologists, Jerome and Other Christian Writers*. Studia Graeca et Latina Gothoburgensia 6. Göteborg: Institute of Classical Studies, University of Göteborg.

———. 1967. *Augustine and the Latin Classics*. Vol. 1, *Testimonia: With a Contribution on Varro by Burkhart Cardauns*. Studia Graeca et Latina Gothoburgensia 20:1. Göteborg: Institute of Classical Studies, University of Göteborg.

Hahn, Johannes. 2006. "'Vetustus error extinctus est': Wann wurde das Sarapeion von Alexandria zerstört?" *Historia* 55 (3): 368–83.

———. 2008. "The Conversion of the Cult Statues: The Destruction of the Serapeum 392 A.D. and the Transformation of Alexandria into the 'Christ-Loving' City." In Hahn, Emmel, and Gotter 2008, 335–66.

Hahn, Johannes, Stephen Emmel, and Ulrich Gotter, eds. 2008. *From Temple to Church: Destruction and Renewal of Local Cultic Topography in Late Antiquity*. Religions in the Graeco-Roman World 163. Leiden: Brill.

Halbwachs, Maurice. 1992. *On Collective Memory*. Translated by Lewis A. Coser. Chicago: University of Chicago Press.

Hallo, William W., ed. 1997–2002. *The Context of Scripture: Canonical Compositions, Monumental Inscriptions and Archival Documents from the Biblical World*. 3 vols. Leiden: Brill.

Hannestad, N. 1999. "How Did Rising Christianity Cope with Pagan Sculpture?" In *East and West: Modes of Communication; Proceedings of the First Plenary Conference at Merida*, edited by E. Chrysos and I. Wood, 173–204. Leiden: Brill.

Hartung, Ulrich. 2001. *Umm el-Qaab*. Vol. 2, *Importkeramik aus dem Friedhof U in Abydos (Umm el-Qaab) und die Beziehungen Ägyptens zu Vorderasiens im 4. Jahrtausend v. Chr*. Archäologische Veröffentlichung des Deutschen Archäologischen Instituts in Kairo 92. Mainz: Philipp von Zabern.

Hebbelynck, A. 1902. *Les mystères des lettres grecques d'après un manuscrit copte-arabe de la bibliothèque Bodliénne d'Oxford*. Paris: Ernest Leroux.

Heine, Ronald E. 2004. "The Alexandrians." In F. Young, Ayres, and Louth 2004, 117–30.

Helck, Wolfgang. 1956. *Untersuchungen zu Manetho und den ägyptischen Königslisten*. Untersuchungen zur Geschichte und Altertumskunde Ägyptens 18. Berlin: Akademie-Verlag.

Hengst, D. den. 1992. "The Scientific Digressions in Ammianus' *Res Gestae*." In *Cognitio Gestorum: The Historiographic Art of Ammianus Marcellinus*, edited by J. den Boeft, D. den Hengst, and H. C. Teitler, 39–46. Amsterdam: Koniklijke Nederlandse Akademie van Wetenschappen.

Henrichs, Albert. 1970. "Pagan Ritual and the Alleged Crimes of the Early Christians." In *Kyriakon: Festschrift Johannes Quasten*, vol. 1, edited by Patrick Granfield and Josef Jungmann, 18–35. Münster: Verlag Aschendorff.

Hilhorst, Ton. 2005. "'And Moses Was Instructed in All the Wisdom of the Egyptians.'" In *The Wisdom of Egypt: Jewish, Early Christian, and Gnostic Essays in Honour of Gerard P. Luttikhuizen*, edited by Anthony Hilhorst and George H. van Kooten, 153–76. Leiden: Brill.

Hjort, Ø. 1993. "Augustus Christianus—Livia Christiana: Sphragis and Roman Portrait Sculpture." In *Aspects of Late Antiquity and Early Byzantium: Papers Read at a Colloquium Held at the Swedish Research Institute in Istanbul 31 May–5 June 1992*, edited by Lennart Rydén and Jan Olof Rosenqvist, 99–112. Transactions of the Swedish Research Institute in Istanbul 4. Stockholm: Swedish Research Institute in Istanbul.

Hoch, James E. 1997. *Middle Egyptian Grammar*. Mississauga, Ontario: Benben.

Hoffmann, Friedhelm. 2012. "Hieratic and Demotic Literature." In Riggs 2012, 543–62.

Hornung, Erik. 2001. *The Secret Lore of Egypt: Its Impact on the West*. Translated by David Lorton. Ithaca, N.Y.: Cornell University Press.

Houston, Stephen, John Baines, and Jerrold Cooper. 2003. "Last Writing: Script Obsolescence in Egypt, Mesopotamia, and Mesoamerica." *Comparative Studies in Society and History* 45 (3): 430–79.

Imhausen, Annette. 2012. "Scribes, Egypt." In *The Encyclopedia of Ancient History*, edited by Roger S. Bagnall, Kai Broderson, Craige Champion, Andrew Erskine, and Sabine R. Huebner, 11:6085–86. Malden, Mass.: Wiley-Blackwell.

Iversen, Erik. 1968. *Obelisks in Exile*. Copenhagen: Gad.

———. 1993. *The Myth of Egypt and Its Hieroglyphs in European Tradition*. Princeton, N.J.: Princeton University Press.

Jackson, Howard M. 1978. *Zosimos of Panopolis on the Letter Omega*. Texts and Translations 14 / Graeco-Roman Religion 5. Missoula, Mont.: Scholars.

Jacobsen, Thorkild. 1987. *The Harps That Once . . . : Sumerian Poetry in Translation*. New Haven, Conn.: Yale University Press.

Jaeger, Werner. 1961. *Early Christianity and Greek Paideia*. Cambridge, Mass.: Belknap Press of Harvard University Press.

Jasnow, Richard Lewis. 2011. "'Caught in the Web of Words': Remarks on the Imagery of Writing and Hieroglyphs in the Book of Thoth." *JARCE* 47:297–317.

———. 2016. "'Between Two Waters': The *Book of Thoth* and the Problem of Greco-Egyptian Interaction." In *Greco-Egyptian Interactions: Literature, Translation, and Culture, 500 BCE–300 CE*, edited by Ian Rutherford, 317–56. Oxford: Oxford University Press.

Jasnow, Richard Lewis, and Karl-Theodor Zauzich. 2005. *The Ancient Egyptian Book of Thoth: A Demotic Discourse on Knowledge and Pendant to the Classical Hermetica*. 2 vols. Wiesbaden: Harrassowitz, 2005.

———. 2014. *Conversations in the House of Life: A New Translation of the Ancient Egyptian Book of Thoth*. Wiesbaden: Harrassowitz.

Johnson, David. 1980. *A Panegyric on Macarius, Bishop of Tkôw, Attributed to Dioscorus of Alexandria*. 2 vols. Louvain: Secrétariat du CSCO.

Johnson, Janet H. 2010a. "Egyptian Demotic Script." In Woods 2010a, 165–72.

———. 2010b. "Egyptian Hieroglyphic Writing." In Woods 2010a, 149–58.

Kákosy, László. 1982. "A Christian Interpretation of the Sun-Disk." In *Studies in Egyptian Religion Dedicated to Professor Jan Zandee*, edited by H. van Voss, 70–75. Leiden: Brill.

Karig, Joachim. 1975. "Achmim." *LÄ* 1:54–55.

Keenan, James G. 2000. "Egypt." In *The Cambridge Ancient History*. Vol. 14, *Late Antiquity: Empires and Successors, A.D. 425–600*, edited by Averil Cameron, Bryan Ward-Perkins, and Michael Whitby, 612–37. Cambridge: Cambridge University Press.

Kendeffy, Gabor. 2015. "Lactantius as Christian Cicero, Cicero as Shadow-Like Instructor." In *Brill's Companion to the Reception of Cicero*, edited by William H. F. Altman, 56–92. Brill's Companions to Classical Reception 2. Leiden: Brill.

Klotz, David. 2010. "Triphis in the White Monastery: Reused Temple Blocks from Sohag." *AncSoc* 40:197–213.

———. 2012a. *Caesar in the City of Amun: Egyptian Temple Construction and Theology in Roman Thebes*. Monographies Reine Élisabeth 15. Turnhout: Brepols.

———. 2012b. "Egyptian Hieroglyphs." In Riggs 2012, 563–80.

Knuf, Hermann, Christian Leitz, and Daniel von Recklinghausen, eds. 2010. *Honi soit qui mal y pense: Studien zum pharaonischen, griechich-römischen und spätantiken Ägypten zu Ehren von Heinz-Josef Thissen*. Orientalia Lovaniensia Analecta 194. Leuven: Peeters.

Kockelmann, Holger. 2008. *Praising the Goddess: A Comparative and Annotated Re-Edition of Six Demotic Hymns and Praises Addressed to Isis*. AfP, Beiheft 15. Berlin: Walter de Gruyter.

Kofsky, Aryeh. 2000. *Eusebius of Caesarea Against Paganism*. Jewish and Christian Perspectives 3. Leiden: Brill.

Krawiec, Rebecca. 2002. *Shenoute and the Women of the White Monastery: Egyptian Monasticism in Late Antiquity*. New York: Oxford University Press.

Kristensen, Troels Myrup. 2009. "Embodied Images: Christian Response and Destruction in Late Antique Egypt." *JLA* 2 (2): 224–50.

———. 2010. "Religious Conflict in Late Antique Alexandria: Christian Responses to 'Pagan' Statues in the Fourth and Fifth Centuries AD." In *Alexandria: A Cultural and Religious Melting Pot*, edited by G. Hinge and J. Krasilnikoff, 158–76. Aarhus Studies in Mediterranean Antiquity 9. Aarhus: Aarhus University Press.

———. 2013. *Making and Breaking the Gods: Christian Responses to Pagan Sculpture in Late Antiquity*. Aarhus Studies in Mediterranean Antiquity 12. Aarhus: Aarhus University Press.

Kugler, Rob. 2005. "Hearing the Story of Moses in Ptolemaic Egypt: Artapanus Accommodates the Tradition." In *The Wisdom of Egypt: Jewish, Early Christian, and Gnostic Essays in Honour of Gerard P. Luttikhuizen*, edited by Anthony Hilhorst and George H. van Kooten, 67–80. Leiden: Brill.

Kurth, Dieter. 1983. "Die Lautwerte der Hieroglyphen in den Tempelinschriften der griechisch-römischen Zeit—zur Systematik ihrer Herleitungsprinzipien." *ASAE* 69:287–309.

———. 1986. "Thot." *LÄ* 6:497–523.

Lacau, Pierre. 1911. "Textes coptes en dialectes akhmimique et sahidique." *BIFAO* 8:43–109.

Lambrecht, Bérénice. 2001. "L'obélisque d'Hermapion (Ammien Marcellin, *Res Gestae*, XVII, 4, 17–23)." *Muséon* 114:51–95.

Lampe, G. W. H., ed. 1961. *A Patristic Greek Lexicon*. Oxford: Clarendon.

Lanzillotta, Lautaro Roig. 2007. "The Early Christians and Human Sacrifice." In *The Strange World of Human Sacrifice*, edited by Jan N. Bremmer, 81–102. Leuven: Peeters.

Lavan, Luke, and Michael Mulryan, eds. 2011. *The Archaeology of Late Antique "Paganism."* Late Antique Archaeology 7. Leiden: Brill.

Layton, Bentley. 2014. *The Canons of Our Fathers: Monastic Rules of Shenoute*. Oxford Early Christian Studies. Oxford: Oxford University Press.

Le Boulluec, Alain. 1981. *Clément d'Alexandrie. Les Stromates. Stromate V, Tome II: Commentaire, bibliographie et index*. SC 279. Paris: Les Éditions du Cerf.

Leipoldt, Johannes. 1903. *Schenute von Atripe und die Entstehung des national ägyptischen Christentums*. Leipzig: J. C. Hinrichs.

Leipoldt, Johannes, and Walter E. Crum. 1908. *Sinuthii Archimandritae Vita et Opera Omnia*. Vol. 3. Paris: e typographeo reipublicae.

———. 1913. *Sinuthii archimandritae vita et opera omnia*. Vol. 4. Paris: e typographeo reipublicae.

Leitz, Christian. 2001. "Die beiden kryptographischen Inschriften aus Esna mit den Widdern und Krokodilen." *SAK* 29:251–76.

Lepelley, Claude. 1994. "Le musée des statues divines: La volonté de sauvegarder le patrimoine artistique païen à l'époque théodosienne." *CArch* 42:5–15.

Letronne, Jean-Antoine. 1828. "Examen du texte de Clément d'Alexandrie, relatif aux divers modes d'écriture chez les Égyptiens." In *Précis du système hiéroglyphique*, 2nd ed., by Jean-François Champollion, 376–99. Paris: Imprimerie Royale.

———. 1844. *De la croix ansée égyptienne imitée par les chrétiens d'Égypte pour figurer le signe de la croix et le monogramme du Christ*. Paris: Firmin-Didot.

———. 1846. "Examen archéologique de ces deux questions: 1. La croix ansée égyptienne a-t-elle été employée par les chrétiens d'Égypte pour exprimer le monogramme du Christ? 2. Retrouve-t-on ce symbole sur les monuments antiques étrangers à l'Égypte?" *Mémoires de l'Académie des Inscriptions et Belles Lettres* 16 (2): 236–84.

Litwa, M. David. 2015. *Refutation of All Heresies, Translated with an Introduction and Notes*. Writings from the Greco-Roman World 40. Atlanta: SBL.

Lloyd, Alan B. 1976. *Herodotus, Book II: Commentary 1–98*. Leiden: Brill.

———. 1982. "Nationalist Propaganda in Ptolemaic Egypt." *Historia* 31 (1): 33–55.

———. 1988. *Herodotus, Book II: Commentary 99–182*. Leiden: Brill, 1988.

———. 2007. "Book II." In *A Commentary on Herodotus, Books I–IV*, edited by David Asheri, Alan Lloyd, and Aldo Corcella. Oxford: Oxford University Press.

López, Ariel G. 2013. *Shenoute of Atripe and the Uses of Poverty: Rural Patronage, Religious Conflict and Monasticism in Late Antique Egypt*. Transformation of the Classical Heritage 50. Berkeley: University of California Press.

Louth, Andrew. 2004. "The Cappadocians." In F. Young, Ayres, and Louth 2004, 289–301.

Lowenthal, David. 1985. *The Past Is a Foreign Country*. Cambridge: Cambridge University Press.

Lucchesi, Enzo. 1975. "À propos du mot copte 'Sphransh.'" *JEA* 61:254–56.

MacArthur, Elise. 2010. "The Conception and Development of the Egyptian Writing System." In Woods 2010a, 115–36.

MacCoull, Leslie. 2012. "Aspects of Alexander in Coptic Egypt." In *The Alexander Romance in Persia and the East*, edited by Richard Stoneman, Kyle Erickson, and Ian Richard Netton, 255–62. Groningen: Barkhuis.

Madreiter, Irene. 2013. "From Berossos to Eusebius: A Christian Apologist's Shaping of 'Pagan' Literature." In *The World of Berossos: Proceedings of the 4th International Colloquium on "The Ancient Near East Between Classical and Ancient Oriental Traditions," Hatfield College,*

Durham 7th–9th July 2010, edited by Johannes Haubold, Giovanni B. Lanfranchi, Robert Rollinger, and John Steele, 255–75. Wiesbaden: Harrassowitz Verlag.

Mahé, Jean-Pierre. 1996. "Preliminary Remarks on the Demotic 'Book of Thoth' and the Greek Hermetica." *VChr* 50 (4): 353–63.

Mango, Cyril. 1963. "Antique Statuary and the Byzantine Beholder." *DOP* 17:53–75.

———. 1994. "L'attitude byzantine à l'égard des antiquités gréco-romaines." In *Byzance et les images: Cycle de conférences organisé au musée du Louvre par le Service Culturel du 5 octobre au 7 décembre 1992*, edited by André Guillou and Jannic Durand, 95–120. Paris: La documentation française.

Marcone, Arnaldo. 2008. "A Long Late Antiquity? Considerations on a Controversial Periodization." *JLA* 1 (1): 4–19.

Marestaing, Pierre. 1911. "Le passage de Clément d'Alexandrie relatif aux écritures égyptiennes." *Recueil des travaux* 33:8–17.

———. 1913. *Les écritures égyptiennes et l'antiquité classique*. Paris: Paul Geuthner.

Marinescu, C. A. 1996. "Transformations: Classical Objects and Their Re-Use During Late Antiquity." In *Shifting Frontiers in Late Antiquity*, edited by R. W. Mathisen and H. S. Sivan, 285–98. Aldershot: Ashgate.

Markus, Robert A. 1990. *The End of Ancient Christianity*. New York: Cambridge University Press.

Maspero, Gaston. 1892. *Fragments de la version thébaine de l'ancien testament*. Mémoires publiés par les membres de la mission archéologique française au Caire 6. Paris: Ernest Leroux.

Maspero, Jean. 1914. "Horapollon et la fin du paganisme égyptien." *BIFAO* 11:164–95.

Masson, Olivier, and Jean-Luc Fournet. 1992. "À propos d'Horapollon, l'auteur des 'Hieroglyphica.'" *REG* 105 (500/501): 231–36.

Matthews, John. 1989. *The Roman Empire of Ammianus*. Baltimore: Johns Hopkins University Press.

McDowell, Andrea. 2000. "Teachers and Students at Deir El-Medina." In *Deir El-Medina in the Third Millennium AD: A Tribute to Jac J. Janssen*, edited by R. J. Demarée and A. Egberts, 217–33. Egyptologische Uitgaven 14. Leiden: Nederlands Instituut voor het Nabije Oosten.

McEvoy, James. 1993. "Platon et la sagesse de l'Égypte." *Kernos* 6:245–75.

McGowan, Andrew. 1994. "Eating People: Accusations of Cannibalism against Christians in the Second Century." *JECS* 2 (4): 413–42.

McKenzie, Judith S., Sheila Gibson, and A. T. Reyes. 2004. "Reconstructing the Serapeum in Alexandria from the Archaeological Evidence." *JRS* 94:73–121.

McLynn, Neil B. 1994. *Ambrose of Milan: Church and Court in a Christian Capital*. Berkeley: University of California Press.

Meadows, Andrew. 2012. "Ptolemaic Possessions Outside Egypt." In *The Encyclopedia of Ancient History*, edited by Roger S. Bagnall, Kai Broderson, Craige Champion, Andrew Erskine, and Sabine R. Huebner, 10:5625–29. Malden, Mass.: Wiley-Blackwell.

Merkelbach, Reinhold. 1954. *Die Quellen des griechischen Alexanderromans*. Zetemata 9. Munich: C. H. Beck.

Mingana, Alphonse. 1929. "The Vision of Theophilus; or, The Book of the Flight of the Holy Family into Egypt." *BRL* 13:383–425.

Momigliano, Arnaldo. 1963. "Pagan and Christian Historiography in the Fourth Century A.D." In *The Conflict Between Paganism and Christianity in the Fourth Century*, edited by Arnaldo Momigliano, 79–99. Oxford: Oxford University Press.

Monferrer-Sala, Juan Pedro. 2011. "Alexander the Great in the Syriac Literary Tradition." In Zuwiyya 2011, 41–72.

Morenz, Ludwig. 2001. "Neues zum *pr-'nh* – zwei Überlegungen zu einem institutionellen Zentrum der sakralen Schriftlichkeitskultur Altägyptens." *GM* 181:77–81.

Moser, Stephanie. 2006. *Wondrous Curiosities: Ancient Egypt at the British Museum*. Chicago: University of Chicago Press.

———. 2012. *Designing Antiquity: Owen Jones, Ancient Egypt and the Crystal Palace*. New Haven, Conn.: Yale University Press.

Mosshammer, Alden A. 1979. *The Chronicle of Eusebius and the Greek Chronographic Tradition*. Lewisburg, Penn.: Bucknell University Press.

———. 1984. *Georgii Syncelli Ecloga Chronographica*. Leipzig: Teubner.

Moyer, Ian S. 2002. "Herodotus and an Egyptian Mirage: The Genealogies of the Theban Priests." *JHS* 122:70–90.

———. 2003. "Thessalos of Tralles and Cultural Exchange." In *Prayer, Magic, and the Stars in the Ancient and Late Antique World*, edited by Scott Noegel, Joel Walker, and Brannon Wheeler, 39–56. Magic in History. University Park: Pennsylvania State University Press.

———. 2011. *Egypt and the Limits of Hellenism*. Cambridge: Cambridge University Press.

Mras, K. 1906. "Eine neuentdeckte Sibyllen-Theosophie." *WS* 28:43–83.

Müller, Dieter. 1961. *Ägypten und die griechischen Isis-Aretalogien*. Abhandlungen der Sächsischen Akademie der Wissenschaften zu Leipzig, Philologisch-historische Klasse 53:1. Berlin: Akademie-Verlag.

Müller, Marcus. 2015. "The Repit Temple at Athribis After the Worship of Repit." In *From the Delta to the Cataract: Studies Dedicated to Mohamed El-Bialy*, edited by Alejandro Jiménez-Serrano and Cornelius von Pilgrim, 177–88. Culture and History of the Ancient Near East 76. Leiden: Brill.

Mussies, Gerard. 1982. "The Interpretatio Judaica of Thot-Hermes." In *Studies in Egyptian Religion Dedicated to Professor Jan Zandee*, edited by M. Heerma van Voss, D. J. Hoens, G. Mussies, D. van der Plas, and H. Te Velde, 89–120. Leiden: E. J. Brill.

Nau, F. 1910. "La version syriaque de la vision de Théophile sur le séjour de la Vierge en Égypte." *ROrChr* 15:125–32.

Nicholson, Oliver. 2004. "Arnobius and Lactantius." In F. Young, Ayres, and Louth 2004, 259–65.

Nock, Arthur Darby, and André-Jean Festugière. 1974. *Corpus Hermeticum*, 3rd ed. 4 vols. Paris: Belles Lettres.

O'Connell, Elisabeth R. 2007a. "Tombs for the Living: Monastic Reuse of Monumental Funerary Architecture in Late Antique Egypt." Ph.D. thesis, University of California, Berkeley.

———. 2007b. "Transforming Monumental Landscapes in Late Antique Egypt: Monastic Dwellings in Legal Documents from Western Thebes." *JECS* 15 (2): 239–73.

O'Daly, Gerard. 2004. *Augustine's City of God: A Reader's Guide*. Oxford: Oxford University Press.

Orlandi, Tito. 1970. *Storia della chiesa di Alessandria*. Vol. 2, *Da Teofilo a Timoteo IIe*. Milan: Istituto Editoriale Cisalpino.

———. 1972. "Un encomio copto di Raffaele Arcangelo ('Relatio Theophili')." *RSO* 47:211–33.

———. 1973. "Patristica copta e patristica greca." *VChr* 10:335–37.

———. 1985. "Theophilus of Alexandria in Coptic Literature." *StP* 16:100–104.

Osborn, Eric. 2005. *Clement of Alexandria*. Cambridge: Cambridge University Press.

Otto, Eberhard. 1975. "Cheriheb." *LÄ* 1:940–43.

Papaconstantinou, Arietta. 2001. *Le culte des saints en Égypte des Byzantins aux Abbassides: L'apport des inscriptions et des papyrus grecs et coptes*. Paris: CNRS Éditions.

———. 2007. "'They Shall Speak the Arabic Language and Take Pride in It': Reconsidering the Fate of Coptic After the Arab Conquest." *Muséon* 120:273–99.

———, ed. 2010. *The Multilingual Experience in Egypt, from the Ptolemies to the Abbasids*. Burlington, Vt.: Ashgate.

———. 2012. "Why Did Coptic Fail Where Aramaic Succeeded? Linguistic Developments in Egypt and the Near East after the Arab Conquest." In *Multilingualism in the Graeco-Roman Worlds*, edited by Alex Mullen and Patrick James, 58–76. Cambridge: Cambridge University Press.

Parker, Grant. 2004. "Obelisks Still in Exile: Monuments Made to Measure?" In *Isis en Occident: Actes du IIe colloque international sur les études isiaques, Univ. Lyon III 16–17 mai 2002*, edited by Laurent Bricault, 209–22. Leiden: Brill.

Parkinson, Richard. 1999. *Cracking Codes: The Rosetta Stone and Decipherment*. Berkeley: University of California Press.

Pearce, Sarah J. K. 2007. *The Land of the Body: Studies in Philo's Representation of Egypt*. Tübingen: Mohr Siebeck.

Pendlebury, J. D. S. 1934. "Excavations at Tell El Amarna: Preliminary Report for the Season 1933–4." *JEA* 20 (3/4): 129–36.

———. 1951. *The City of Akhenaten, Part 3: The Central City and the Official Quarters, the Excavations at Tell El-Amarna During the Seasons 1926–1927 and 1931–1936*. Vol. 1, *Text*. Memoir of the Egypt Exploration Society 44. London: Egypt Exploration Society.

Petrie, W. M. Flinders. 1900. *The Royal Tombs of the First Dynasty, 1900 Part I*. Egypt Exploration Fund Memoirs 18. London: Egypt Exploration Fund.

———. 1901. *The Royal Tombs of the Earliest Dynasties, 1901 Part II*. Egypt Exploration Fund Memoirs 21. London: Egypt Exploration Fund.

———. 1908. *Athribis*. British School of Archaeology in Egypt and the Egyptian Research Account 14. London: School of Archaeology in Egypt.

Pfister, Friedrich. 1964. "Ein apokrypher Alexanderbrief: Der sogenannte Leon von Pella und die Kirchenväter." In *Mullus: Festschrift Theodor Klauser*, edited by Alfred Hermann and Alfred Stuiber, 291–97. Jahrbuch für Antike und Christentum Ergänzungsband 1. Münster.

Pharr, Clyde. 1952. *The Theodosian Code and Novels, and the Sirmondian Constitutions*. Princeton, N.J.: Princeton University Press.

Piacentini, Patrizia. 2001. "Scribes." In *The Oxford Encyclopedia of Ancient Egypt*, edited by Donald Redford, 3:187–92. Oxford: Oxford University Press.

Préaux, Claire. 1967. "De la Grèce classique à l'Égypte hellénistique: Traduire ou ne pas traduire." *CdE* 42:369–83.

Prentice, William Kelly. 1908. *Greek and Latin Inscriptions*. Publications of an American Archaeological Expedition to Syria 1899–1900, 3. New York: Century.

Quack, Joachim F. 2002. "Review of *Untersuchungen zur Überlieferungsgeschichte der Horusstelen: Ein Beitrag zur Religionsgeschichte Ägyptens im 1. Jahrtausend v. Chr.*, by Heike Sternberg el-Hotabi." *OLZ* 97:713–39.

———. 2003. "'Ich bin Isis, die Herrin der beiden Länder': Versuch zum demotischen Hintergrund der memphitischen Isisaretalogie." In *Egypt: Temple of the Whole World; Studies in Honor of Jan Assmann*, edited by Sibylle Meyer, 319–65. Leiden: Brill.

———. 2007. "Ein ägyptischer Dialog über die Schreibkunst und das arkane Wissen." *ARG* 9:259–94.

Quaegebeur, Jan. 1982. "De la préhistoire de l'écriture copte." *OLP* 13:125–36.

———. 1991a. "Pre-Coptic." In Atiya 1991, 8:188–90.

————. 1991b. "Pre-Old Coptic." In Atiya 1991, 8:190–91.

Rajak, Tessa. 1982. "Josephus and the 'Archaeology' of the Jews." *JJS* 33:485–77.

Ray, John D. 1994a. "How Demotic Is Demotic?" *EVO* 17:251–64.

————. 1994b. "Literacy and Language in Egypt in the Late and Persian Periods." In Bowman and Woolf 1994a, 51–66.

————. 2007. *The Rosetta Stone and the Rebirth of Ancient Egypt.* London: Profile.

Redford, Donald B. 1986. *Pharaonic King-Lists, Annals, and Day-Books: A Contribution to the Study of the Egyptian Sense of History.* Mississauga: Benben.

Reeves, Nicholas, and Richard H. Wilkinson. 1996. *The Complete Valley of the Kings: Tombs and Treasures of Egypt's Greatest Pharaohs.* New York: Thames and Hudson.

Regulski, Ilona. 2008a. "The Origin of Writing in Relation to the Emergence of the Egyptian State." In *Egypt at Its Origins 2: Proceedings of the International Conference "Origin of the State: Predynastic and Early Dynastic Egypt," Toulouse (France) 5th–8th September 2005,* edited by B. Midant-Reynes, Y. Tristant, J. Rowland, and S. Hendrickx, 983–1008. OLA 172. Leuven: Peeters.

————.2008b. "Scribes in Early Dynastic Egypt." In *Zeichen aus dem Sand: Streiflichter aus Ägyptens Geschichte zu Ehren von Günter Dreyer,* edited by Eva-Maria Engel, Vera Müller, and Ulrich Hartung, 581–612. MENES 5. Wiesbaden: Harrassowitz.

————. 2009. "The Beginning of Hieratic Writing in Egypt." *SAK* 38:258–74.

————. 2016. "The Origins and Early Development of Writing in Egypt." *Oxford Handbooks Online.* https://doi.org/10.1093/oxfordhb/9780199935413.013.61.

Reid, Donald M. 2002. *Whose Pharaohs? Archaeology, Museums, and Egyptian National Identity from Napoleon to World War I.* Berkeley: University of California Press.

————. 2015. *Contesting Antiquity in Egypt: Archaeologies, Museums, and the Struggle for Identities from World War I to Nasser.* Cairo: American University in Cairo Press.

Reinink, G. J. 1975. "Das Land Seiris (Šir) und das Volk der Serer in jüdischen und christlichen Traditionen." *JSJ* 6:72–85.

Rémondon, Roger. 1952. "Egypte et la suprème résistance au christianisme." *BIFAO* 51:63–78.

Remus, Harold. 2004. "The End of 'Paganism'?" *Studies in Religion/Sciences Religieuses* 33 (2): 191–208.

Richter, Tonio Sebastian. 2009. "Greek, Coptic and the 'Language of the Hijra': The Rise and Decline of the Coptic Language in Late Antique and Medieval Egypt." In *From Hellenism to Islam: Cultural and Linguistic Change in the Roman Near East,* edited by Hannah Cotton, Robert Hoyland, Jonathan Price, and David Wasserstein, 401–46. Cambridge: Cambridge University Press.

Riggs, Christina., ed. 2012. *The Oxford Handbook of Roman Egypt.* Oxford: Oxford University Press.

Ritner, Robert K. 1989. "Horus on the Crocodiles: A Juncture of Religion and Magic in Late Dynastic Egypt." In *Religion and Philosophy in Ancient Egypt,* edited by William Kelly Simpson, 103–16. YES 3. New Haven, Conn.: Yale University Press.

————. 1997. *The Mechanics of Ancient Egyptian Magical Practice.* SAOC 54. Chicago: Oriental Institute.

————. 1998a. "Egypt Under Roman Rule: The Legacy of Ancient Egypt." In *The Cambridge History of Egypt.* Vol. 1, *Islamic Egypt, 640–1517,* edited by Carl F. Petry, 1–33. Cambridge: Cambridge University Press.

————. 1998b. "The Wives of Horus and the Philinna Papyrus (PGM XX)." In *Egyptian Religion: The Last Thousand Years: Studies Dedicated to the Memory of Jan Quaegebeur, Part II,* edited by Willy Clarysse, Antoon Schoors, and Harco Willems, 1027–41. OLA 85. Leuven: Peeters.

Rochette, Bruno. 1994. "Traducteurs et traductions dans l'Égypte gréco-romaine." *CdE* 69:313–22.

Rohrbacher, David. 2007. "Ammianus' Roman Digressions and the Audience of the Res Gestae." In *A Companion to Greek and Roman Historiography*, edited by John Marincola, 468–73. Malden, Mass.: Wiley-Blackwell.

Rojas, Felipe, and Valeria Sergueenkova. 2014. "Traces of Tarhuntas: Greek, Roman, and Byzantine Interaction with Hittite Monuments." *JMA* 27 (2): 135–60.

Romer, F. E. 1998. *Pomponius Mela's Description of the World*. Ann Arbor: University of Michigan Press.

Rossi, Francesco. 1893. "Un nuovo codice copto del Museo Egizio di Torino contenente la vita di s. Epifanio ed i martiti di s. Pantoleone, di Ascla, di Apollonio, di Filemone, di Ariano e di Dios con versetti di vari capitoli del 'Libro di Giobbe.'" *RAL* 1:3–136.

Rossini, Carlo Conti. 1912. "Il discorso su Monte Coscam attribuito a Teofilo d'Alessandria nella versione etiopica." *RAL* 21:395–471.

Rubenson, Samuel. 1995. *The Letters of St. Antony: Monasticism and the Making of a Saint*. Minneapolis: Fortress.

Runia, D. T. 1993. *Philo in Early Christian Literature: A Survey*. Jewish Traditions in Early Christian Literature 3. Minneapolis: Fortress.

Rusten, J. S. 1980. "Pellaeus Leo." *AJPh* 101 (2): 197–201.

Ryholt, Kim. 2005. "On the Contents and Nature of the Tebtynis Temple Library." In *Tebtynis und Soknopaiu Nesos: Leben im römerzeitlichen Faijum; Akten des Internationalen Symposions vom 11. bis 13. Dezember 2003 im Sommerhausen bei Würzburg*, edited by Sandra Lippert and Maren Schentuleit, 141–70. Wiesbaden: Harrassowitz.

Saradi, Helen. 2008. "The Christianization of Pagan Temples in the Greek Hagiographical Texts." In Hahn, Emmel, and Gotter 2008, 113–34.

Saradi-Mendelovici, Helen. 1990. "Christian Attitudes Toward Pagan Monuments in Late Antiquity and Their Legacy in Later Byzantine Centuries." *DOP* 44:47–61.

Sauer, Eberhard. 2003. *The Archaeology of Religious Hatred in the Roman and Early Medieval World*. Charleston, S.C.: Tempus.

Sauneron, Serge. 1962. "Les conditions d'accès à la fonction sacerdotale à l'époque gréco-romaine." *BIFAO* 61:55–57.

———. 1971. "Villes et légendes d'Égypte § XXXII. Le Chaudron de Sohag: Comment naît une légende." *BIFAO* 69:53–58.

———. 1982. *L'écriture figurative dans les textes d'Esna*. Esna 8. Cairo: Institut Français d'Archéologie Orientale.

———. 2000. *The Priests of Ancient Egypt*. New ed. Translated by David Lorton. Ithaca, N.Y.: Cornell University Press.

Schorn, Stefan. 2014. "Pythagoras in the Historical Tradition: From Herodotus to Diodorus Siculus." In *A History of Pythagoreanism*, edited by Carl A. Huffman, 296–314. Cambridge: Cambridge University Press.

Schott, Siegfried. 1963. "Die Opferliste als Schrift des Thot." *ZÄS* 90:103–10.

———. 1972. "Thoth als Verfasser heiliger Schriften." *ZÄS* 99:20–25.

Schroeder, Caroline T. 2007. *Monastic Bodies: Discipline and Salvation in Shenoute of Atripe*. Philadelphia: University of Pennsylvania Press.

Schwartz, Jacques. 1966. "La Fin du Serapeum d'Alexandrie." *ASP* 1:97–111.

Selden, Daniel L. 2011a. "The Coptic Alexander Romance." In Zuwiyya 2011, 133–56.

———. 2011b. "Guardians of Chaos." *JCoptStud* 13:117–55.

Severin, Hans-Georg. 1991. "Dayr Anbā Shinūdah: Architectural Sculpture." In Atiya 1991, 3:769–70.

Shisha-Halevy, Ariel. 1975a. "Two New Shenoute-Texts from the British Library." *Orientalia* 44 (2): 149–85.

———. 1975b. "Two New Shenoute-Texts from the British Library II (Commentary)." *Orientalia* 44 (4): 469–84.

Shorrock, Robert. 2011. *The Myth of Paganism: Nonnus, Dionysus and the World of Late Antiquity*. Classical Literature and Society. London: Bristol Classical.

Sidarus, Adel. 2011. "Alexandre le Grand dans la tradition syriaque." *OC* 95:1–15.

———. 2012. "Nouvelles recherches sur la légende d'Alexandre le Grand dans les littératures arabe chrétienne et connexes." *POr* 37:137–76.

———. 2013. "Alexandre le Grand chez les Coptes (recherches récentes et perspectives nouvelles)." In *Orientalia Christiana: Festschrift für Hubert Kaufhold zum 70. Geburtstag*, edited by Peter Bruns and Heinz Otto Luthe, 477–95. Wiesbaden: Harrassowitz Verlag.

Simpson, William Kelly, ed. 2003. *The Literature of Ancient Egypt: An Anthology of Stories, Instructions, Stelae, Autobiographies, and Poetry*. 3rd ed. New Haven, Conn.: Yale University Press.

Smelik, Klaas A. D., and Emily A. Hemelrijk. 1984. "'Who Knows Not What Monsters Demented Egypt Worships?' Opinions on Egyptian Animal Worship in Antiquity as Part of the Ancient Conception of Egypt." *ANRW* II.17.4:1852–2000.

Smith, Harry S., and William John Tait. 1983. *Saqqâra Demotic Papyri I*. London: Egypt Exploration Society.

Smith, Mark. 2002. "Aspects of the Preservation and Transmission of Indigenous Religious Traditions in Akhmim and Its Environs During the Graeco-Roman Period." In Egberts, Muhs, and van der Vliet 2002, 233–47.

———. 2009. *Traversing Eternity: Texts for the Afterlife from Ptolemaic and Roman Egypt*. Oxford: Oxford University Press.

Smith, Morton. 1978. *Jesus the Magician*. San Francisco: Harper and Row.

Stadler, Martin Andreas. 2008. "On the Demise of Egyptian Writing: Working with a Problematic Source Basis." In *The Disappearance of Writing Systems: Perspectives on Literacy and Communication*, edited by John Baines, John Bennet, and Stephen Houston, 157–81. London: Equinox.

———. 2009. *Weiser und Wesir: Studien zu Vorkommen, Rolle und Wesen des Gottes Thot im ägyptischen Totenbuch*. Orientalische Religionen in der Antike 1. Tübingen: Mohr Siebeck.

———. 2012. "Thoth." In *UCLA Encyclopedia of Egyptology*, edited by Jacco Dieleman and Willeke Wendrich. Los Angeles. Retrieved from https://escholarship.org/uc/item/2xj8c3qg.

———. 2017. *Théologie et culte au temple de Soknopaios: Études sur la religion d'un village égyptien pendant l'époque romaine*. Paris: Éditions Cybele.

Stauder, Andréas. 2010. "The Earliest Egyptian Writing." In Woods 2010a, 137–47.

Steiner, Deborah T. 1994. *The Tyrant's Writ: Myths and Images of Writing in Ancient Greece*. Princeton, N.J.: Princeton University Press.

Sternberg el-Hotabi, Heike. 1994. "Der Untergang der Hieroglyphenschrift: Schriftverfall und Schrifttod im Ägypten der griechisch-römischen Zeit." *CdE* 69:218–45.

———. 1999. *Untersuchungen zur Überlieferungsgeschichte der Horusstelen: Ein Beitrag zur Religionsgeschichte Ägyptens im 1. Jahrtausend v. Chr.* 2 vols. Ägyptologische Abhandlungen 62. Wiesbaden: Harrassowitz.

Stewart, Peter. 1999. "The Destruction of Statues in Late Antiquity." In *Constructing Identities in Late Antiquity*, edited by Richard Miles, 159–89. London: Routledge.

Stoneman, Richard. 2008. *Alexander the Great: A Life in Legend*. New Haven, Conn.: Yale University Press.

Suciu, Alin. 2013. "'Me, This Wretched Sinner': A Coptic Fragment from the Vision of Theophilus Concerning the Flight of the Holy Family to Egypt." *VChr* 67 (4): 436–50.

Swetnam-Burland, Molly. 2015. "Egyptian-Style Monuments." In *The Oxford Handbook of Roman Sculpture*, edited by Elise A. Friedland, Melanie Grunow Sobocinski, and Elaine K. Gazda, 307–22. Oxford: Oxford University Press.

Tait, W. J. 1994. "Some Notes on Demotic Scribal Training in the Roman Period." In *Proceedings of the 20th International Congress of Papyrologists, Copenhagen, Denmark, 21–29 August 1992*, edited by Adam Bülow-Jacobsen, 188–92. Copenhagen: Museum Tusculanum Press.

———. 1997. "Aspects of Demotic Education." In *Akten des 21. Internationalen Papyrologenkongresses*, 2:931–38. AfP, Beiheft 3. Stuttgart: Teubner.

Tallet, Pierre. 2014. "Des papyrus du temps de Chéops au ouadi el-Jarf (golfe de Suez)." *BSFE* 188:25–49.

Tassier, Emmanuel. 1992. "Greek and Demotic School-Exercises." In *Life in a Multi-Cultural Society: Egypt from Cambyses to Constantine and Beyond*, edited by Janet H. Johnson, 311–15. SAOC 51. Chicago: Oriental Institute.

Tattam, Henricus. 1852. *Prophetae majores in dialecto linguae Aegyptiacae memphitica seu Coptica*. 2 vols. Oxford: Oxford University Press.

Te Velde, H. 1986. "Scribes and Literacy in Ancient Egypt." In *Scripta Signa Vocis: Studies about Scripts, Scriptures, Scribes and Languages in the Near East, Presented to J. H. Hospers by His Pupils, Colleagues and Friends*, edited by H. L. J. Vanstiphout, K. Jongeling, F. Leemhuis, and G. J. Reinink, 253–64. Groningen: Egbert Forsten.

Thelamon, Françoise. 1981. *Païens et chrétiens au IVe siècle: L'apport de l'Histoire Ecclésiastique de Rufin d'Aquilée*. Paris: Études Augustiniennes.

Thissen, Heinz-Josef. 1998. *Vom Bild zum Buchstaben—vom Buchstaben zum Bild: Von der Arbeit an Horapollons Hieroglyphika*. Stuttgart: Franz Steiner Verlag.

———, ed. 2001. *Des Niloten Horapollon Hieroglyphenbuch, Band I: Text und Übersetzung*. Archiv für Papyrusforschung und verwandte Gebiete, Beiheft 6. München: K. G. Saur.

Thomas, J. David. 1977. "Avoidance of *Theta* in Dating by Regnal Years." *ZPE* 24:241–43.

Thompson, Herbert. 1932. *The Coptic Version of the Acts of the Apostles and the Pauline Epistles in the Sahidic Dialect*. Cambridge: Cambridge University Press.

Timbie, Janet. 2014. "Review of *Shenoute of Atripe and the Uses of Poverty: Rural Patronage, Religious Conflict, and Monasticism in Late Antique Egypt*, by Ariel G. López." *JECS* 22 (1): 160–61.

Timm, S. 1984–2007. *Das christlich-koptische Ägypten in arabischer Zeit*. 7 vols. Wiesbaden: Dr. Ludwig Reichert.

Totti, Maria. 1985. *Ausgewählte Texte der Isis- und Serapis-Religion*. Subsidia Epigraphica 12. Hildesheim: Georg Olms Verlag.

Tovar, Sofía Torallas. 2010. "Linguistic Identity in Graeco-Roman Egypt." In Papaconstantinou 2010, 17–43.

Trombley, Frank. 1993. *Hellenic Religion and Christianization, c. 370–529*. 2 vols. Leiden: Brill.

van den Broek, Roelof. 1978. "Four Coptic Fragments of a Greek Theosophy." *VChr* 32 (2): 118–42.

————. 2000a. "Hermes and Christ: 'Pagan' Witnesses to the Truth of Christianity." In van den Broek and van Heertum 2000, 116–44.

————. 2000b. "The Hermetic Apocalypse and Other Greek Predictions of the End of Religion." In van den Broek and van Heertum 2000, 98–113.

van den Broek, Roelof, and Cis van Heertum, eds. 2000. *From Poimandres to Jacob Böhme: Gnosis, Hermetism and the Christian Tradition*. Pimander: Texts and Studies Published by the Bibliotheca Philosophica Hermetica 4. Amsterdam: Bibliotheca Philosophica Hermetica.

van den Hoek, Annewies. 1988. *Clement of Alexandria and His Use of Philo in the Stromateis*. Leiden: E. J. Brill.

van der Horst, Pieter Willem. 1982a. "The Secret Hieroglyphs in Classical Literature." In *Actus: Studies in Honour of H. L. W. Nelson*, edited by J. den Boeft and A. H. M. Kessels, 115–23. Utrecht: Instituut voor Klassieke Talen.

————. 1982b. "The Way of Life of the Egyptian Priests According to Chaeremon." In *Studies in Egyptian Religion Dedicated to Professor Jan Zandee*, edited by M. Heerma van Voss, D. J. Hoens, G. Mussies, D. van der Plas, and H. Te Velde, 61–71. Leiden: E. J. Brill.

————. 1984. *Chaeremon: Egyptian Priest and Stoic Philosopher. The Fragments Collected and Translated with Explanatory Notes*. Études préliminaires aux religions orientales dans l'Empire romain. Leiden: E. J. Brill.

van der Vliet, Jacques. 1993. "Spätantikes Heidentum in Ägypten im Spiegel der koptischen Literatur." In *Begegnung von Heidentum und Christentum im spätantiken Ägypten*, 99–130. Riggisberger Berichte 1. Riggisberg: Abbeg-Stiftung.

van de Walle, Baudoin, and J. Vergote. 1943a. "Traduction des *Hieroglyphica* d'Horapollon." *CdE* 18 (35): 39–89.

————. 1943b. "Traduction des *Hieroglyphica* d'Horapollon (2e partie)." *CdE* 18 (36): 199–239.

van Hoof, Lieve, and Peter van Nuffelen, eds. 2015. *Literature and Society in the Fourth Century AD: Performing Paideia, Constructing the Present, Presenting the Self*. Mnemosyne Supplements 373. Leiden: Brill.

van Minnen, Peter. 2002. "The Letter (and Other Papers) of Ammon: Panopolis in the Fourth Century A.D." In Egberts, Muhs, and van der Vliet 2002, 177–99.

van Nuffelen, Peter. 2004. *Un héritage de paix et de piété: Étude sur les histoires ecclésiastiques de Socrate et de Sozomène*. OLA 142. Leuven: Peeters.

————. 2010. "Theology Versus Genre? The Universalism of Christian Historiography in Late Antiquity." In *Historiae Mundi: Studies in Universal History*, edited by Peter Liddel and Andrew Frear, 162–75. London: Duckworth.

————. 2011. "Eusebius of Caesarea and the Concept of Paganism." In Lavan and Mulryan 2011, 89–109.

Vasunia, Phiroze. 2001. *The Gift of the Nile: Hellenizing Egypt from Aeschylus to Alexander*. Classics and Contemporary Thought 8. Berkeley: University of California Press.

Verbrugghe, Gerald P., and John M. Wickersham. 2001. *Berossos and Manetho, Introduced and Translated: Native Traditions in Ancient Mesopotamia and Egypt*. Ann Arbor: University of Michigan Press.

Vergote, Jozef. 1939. "Clément d'Alexandrie et l'écriture égyptienne." *Muséon* 52:199–221.

————. 1941. "Clément d'Alexandrie et l'écriture égyptienne." *CdE* 31:21–38.

Vernus, Pascal. 1990. "Les espaces de l'écrit dans l'Égypte pharaonique." *BSFE* 119:35–56.

Volokhine, Youri. 2004. "Le dieu Thot et la parole." *RHR* 221 (2): 131–56.

von Lemm, Oscar. 1903. *Der Alexanderroman bei den Kopten: Ein Beitrag zur Geschichte der Alexandersage im Orient*. St. Petersburg: Académie Royale des Sciences.

von Lieven, Alexandra. 2009. "Script and Pseudo Scripts in Graeco-Roman Egypt." In *Non-Textual Marking Systems, Writing and Pseudo Script from Prehistory to Modern Times*, edited by Petra Andrássy, Julia Budka, and Frank Kammerzell, 101–11. Lingua Aegyptia Studia Monographica 8. Göttingen: Seminar für Ägyptologie und Koptologie.

Warburton, William. (1738–65) 1978. *The Divine Legation of Moses Demonstrated*. Reprint in 4 vols., New York: Garland.

Wasserstein, Abraham, and David Wasserstein. 2006. *The Legend of the Septuagint: From Classical Antiquity to Today*. Cambridge: Cambridge University Press.

Watts, Edward Jay. 2010. *Riot in Alexandria: Tradition and Group Dynamics in Late Antique Pagan and Christian Communities*. Transformation of the Classical Heritage 46. Berkeley: University of California Press.

Weber, Manfred. 1981. "Lebenshaus I." *LÄ* 3:954–57.

Weingärtner, Dieter Georg. 1969. *Die Ägyptenreise des Germanicus*. Papyrologische Texte und Abhandlungen 11. Bonn: Habelt.

Weinreich, Otto. (1929) 1968. "Türöffnung im Wunder-, Prodigien- und Zauberglauben der Antike, des Judentums und Christentums." Reprinted in Weinreich, *Religionsgeschichtliche Studien*, 200–429. Darmstadt: Wissenschaftliche Buchgesellschaft.

Wendel, Carl. 1940. "Zum Hieroglyphen-Buch Chairemons." *Hermes* 75 (2): 227–29.

Wente, Edward. 1995. "The Scribes of Ancient Egypt." In *Civilizations of the Ancient Near East*, edited by Jack Sasson, 4:2211–21. New York: Charles Scribner's Sons.

Werner, Daniel S. 2012. *Myth and Philosophy in Plato's Phaedrus*. New York: Cambridge University Press.

West, Stephanie. 1985. "Herodotus' Epigraphical Interests." *CQ* 35 (2): 278–305.

Westerfeld, Jennifer T. 2012. "Saints in the Caesareum: Remembering Temple-Conversion in Late Antique Hermopolis." In *Memory and Urban Religion in the Ancient World*, edited by Martin Bommas, Juliette Harrisson, and Phoebe Roy, 59–86. Cultural Memory and History in Antiquity. London: Bloomsbury Academic.

Whitmarsh, Tim. 2013. "Addressing Power: Fictional Letters Between Alexander and Darius." In *Epistolary Narratives in Ancient Greek Literature*, edited by Owen Hodkinson, Patricia A. Rosenmeyer, and Evelien Bracke. Mnemosyne Supplements 359. Leiden: Brill.

Widmer, Ghislaine. 2014. "Sésostris, figure de légende dans la littérature greque et démotique." In *Sésostris III, pharaon de légende*, edited by Fleur Morfoisse and Guillemette Andreu-Lanoë, 232–35. Ghent: Snoeck.

Wilken, Robert. 1984. *The Christians as the Romans Saw Them*. New Haven, Conn.: Yale University Press.

Williams, Malayna Evans. 2011. "Signs of Creation: Sex, Gender, Categories, Religion and the Body in Ancient Egypt." Ph.D. thesis, University of Chicago.

Williams, Ronald. 1972. "Scribal Training in Ancient Egypt." *JAOS* 92 (2): 214–21.

Wilson, Penelope. 2004. *Hieroglyphs: A Very Short Introduction*. Oxford: Oxford University Press, 2004.

———. 2005. "Naming Names and Shifting Identities in Ancient Egyptian Iconoclasm." In *Negating the Image: Case Studies in Iconoclasm*, edited by Anne L. McClanan and Jeffrey Johnson, 113–33. Burlington, Vt.: Ashgate.

Winand, Jean. 2014. *Décoder les hiéroglyphes, de l'antiquité tardive à l'expédition de l'Égypte*. L'Académie en poche. Brussels: Académie royale de Belgique.

Winiarczyk, Marek. 2002. *Euhemeros von Messene: Leben, Werk und Nachwirkung*. Beiträge zur Altertumskunde 157. Munich: K. G. Saur.

Winkler, John J. 1985. *Auctor and Actor: A Narratological Reading of Apuleius' Golden Ass*. Berkeley: University of California Press.

Winlock, Herbert E., and Walter E. Crum. 1926. *The Monastery of Epiphanius at Thebes, Part 1: The Archaeological Material; The Literary Material*. New York: Metropolitan Museum of Art.

Wipszycka, Ewa. 1992. "Le nationalisme a-t-il existé dans l'Egypte byzantine?" *JJP* 22:83–128.

———. 2005. "Le nombre des moines dans les communautés monastiques d'Égypte." *JJP* 35:265–309.

Wisse, Frederik. 1991. "The Naples Fragments of Shenoute's De certamine contra diabolum." *OC* 75:123–40.

Witt, R. E. 1966. "The Importance of Isis for the Fathers." *StP* 8 (2): 135–45.

Woods, Christopher, ed. 2010a. *Visible Language: Inventions of Writing in the Ancient Middle East and Beyond*. OIMP 32. Chicago: Oriental Institute.

———. 2010b. "Visible Language: The Earliest Writing Systems." In Woods 2010a, 15–25.

Young, Dwight. 1981. "A Monastic Invective Against Egyptian Hieroglyphs." In *Studies Presented to Hans Jakob Polotsky*, edited by Dwight Young, 348–60. East Gloucester, Mass.: Pirtle and Polson.

Young, Frances, Lewis Ayres, and Andrew Louth, eds. 2004. *The Cambridge History of Early Christian Literature*. Cambridge: Cambridge University Press.

Youtie, Herbert. 1978. "Avoidance of *Theta* in Dating by Regnal Years: Superstition or Scribal Caution?" *ZPE* 28:269–70.

Žabkar, Louis V. 1988. *Hymns to Isis in Her Temple at Philae*. Hanover, N.H.: University Press of New England for Brandeis University Press.

Zauzich, Karl-Theodor. 1992. *Hieroglyphs Without Mystery: An Introduction to Ancient Egyptian Writing*. Translated by Ann Macy Roth. Austin: University of Texas Press.

———. 2000. "Die Namen der koptischen Zusatzbuchstaben und die erste ägyptische Alphabetübung." *Enchoria* 26:151–57.

Zinn, Katharina. 2011. "Temples, Palaces and Libraries: A Search for an Alliance Between Archaeological and Textual Evidence." In *Palace and Temple: Architecture—Decoration—Ritual, 5th Symposium on Egyptian Royal Ideology*, edited by Rolf Gundlach and Kate Spence, 181–202. Wiesbaden: Harrassowitz Verlag.

Zoega, Georg. 1797. *De origine et usu obeliscorum*. Rome.

———. (1810) 1903. *Catalogus codicum copticorum manuscriptorum*. Reprint, Leipzig: J. C. Hinrichs'sche Buchhandlung.

Zuwiyya, Z. David, ed. 2011. *A Companion to Alexander Literature in the Middle Ages*. Brill's Companions to the Christian Tradition 29. Leiden: Brill.

Index Locorum

Subject Index

Acknowledgments

Many of the central questions animating this project first took shape while I was at the University of Chicago, and I owe a great debt of gratitude to my mentors there—to Janet Johnson, for her guidance, generosity, and unwavering support; to Robert Ritner, my first teacher of Coptic, in whose classes I began to grapple with many of the texts discussed in these pages, and to David Martinez, who encouraged me to look beyond the literary sources as often as possible. I would never have become an Egyptologist without the support of Peter Dorman, who taught my very first classes in Middle Egyptian and somehow saw potential in my work despite my utter inability early on to tell one form of sḏm=f from another. I feel fortunate that my experience at Chicago was one of great collegiality, and my work benefited from endless discussions with friends and classmates, among them Solange Ashby, Ari Bryen, Ginger Emery, Malayna Evans and Jackie Jay of the writing support group and supper club, Bryan Kraemer, Foy Scalf, and Phil Venticinque.

The History Department at the University of Louisville is now my academic home, and I am especially grateful to Ann Allen, Blake Beattie, Brad Bowman, Chris Ehrick, Daniel Krebs, and Tom Mackey for welcoming me as a colleague. Outside the History Department, Pamela Beattie, John Fischer, Linda Gigante, and Susan Jarosi both made me welcome and pushed me to sharpen my thinking on many issues. The members of the Medieval and Renaissance Research Group and the Kentucky Society of the Archaeological Institute of America have surely heard more about hieroglyphs in the past few years than they ever anticipated, and I appreciate their patience. I am also extremely grateful to the staff of the Interlibrary Loan Department at Ekstrom Library, without whose tireless efforts this book would never have seen the light of day. I'll return all my overdue books soon, I promise.

I have presented material from this book at a number of conferences and colloquia over the past several years, including the Annual Meeting of the American Research Center in Egypt and the International Congresses of

Egyptology and Coptic Studies, and the thoughtful questions and comments of participants in those meetings have added much to this project.

At the University of Pennsylvania Press, Deborah Blake has been a marvelous guide through the publishing process, and I am grateful both for her patience and for her periodic nudges as she tried to keep me on some kind of reasonable schedule. Sincere thanks also go to the anonymous reviewers for the Press, whose careful reading of the manuscript and thoughtful feedback was enormously helpful. It goes without saying that any remaining errors of fact or infelicities of interpretation are mine alone. Thanks are also due to managing editor Noreen O'Connor-Abel and copyeditor Kathleen Kageff for their work in shepherding the manuscript through the production process.

I have incurred many debts to academic friends and colleagues in the process of writing this book, and only a few can be singled out here. Thanks to Blake and Pam Beattie, Brad Bowman, and Jackie Jay, who all read drafts of various chapters-in-progress; to John Fischer, who performed heroic feats of proofreading and fed me when I was too busy to cook; and to Peter Dorman, Foy Scalf, and Steve Vinson, who dug into their photographic archives on my behalf. Eugene Cruz-Uribe sadly did not live to see the project into print, but his exhortations to "finish the book already" spurred me ever onward.

Thanks to the friends outside the world of Egyptology who have helped me keep not only a sense of purpose, but also a sense of humor, through this long process: Cheryl Farney, Uma Gunasekaran, Cami and Damon Huber, Lee Keeling, Jason Smith, Mike Suh, Mary Upton, and Lorraine van Meter-Cline.

My most heartfelt love and thanks go to my family: to my sister, Kate McCurdy, who has cheered me on from the start, and to my parents, Bill and Cathy Westerfeld, to whom this book is dedicated. They have supported me wholeheartedly from the day I first called home and said, "Guess what? I'm going to be an Egyptologist!" and I owe them more than I can say. A final dedication must also be made in memory of my mother, Jeanne Westerfeld, who spent the summer of 1984 teaching an unwilling and fidgety kindergartener how to read and, in so doing, made all things possible.